UNDERSTANDING COLLEGE STUDENTS' SPIRITUAL IDENTITIES

Different Faiths, Varied Worldviews

Discourse and Social Processes
Lesley A. Rex, series editor

Educating Toddlers to Teachers: Learning to See and Influence
the School and Peer Cultures of Classrooms
David E. Fernie, Samara Madrid, & Rebecca Kantor (eds.)

The Rhetoric of Teaching: Understanding the Dynamics of Holocaust
Narratives in an English Classroom
Mary M. Juzwik

Sites of Possibility: Critical Dialogue Across Educational Settings
*Louise B. Jennings, Pamela C. Jewett, Tasha Tropp Laman,
Mariana Souto-Manning, & Jennifer L. Wilson* (eds.)

Sociocultural Positioning in Literacy: Exploring Culture, Discourse,
Narrative and Power in Diverse Educational Contexts
Mary B. McVee, Cynthia H. Brock, & Jocelyn A. Glazier

Discourse of Opportunity: How Talk in Learning Situations
Creates and Constrains Interactional Ethnographic Studies
in Teaching and Learning
Lesley A. Rex (ed.)

Narrative Analysis for Literacy Teacher Education: Sociolinguistic
Tools for Understanding Teacher and Learning Interactions/
Dialogues/Classroom Talk
Lesley A. Rex & Mary M. Juzwik (eds.)

Classroom Discourse Analysis: A Tool for Critical Reflection
Betsy Rymes

Place Stories: Time, Space and Literacy in Two Classrooms
Margaret Sheehy

Understanding College Students' Spiritual Identities: Different Faiths,
Varied Worldviews
Jenny L. Small

Action, Reflection and Social Justice: Integrating Moral Reasoning
into Professional Development
Edward P. St. John

UNDERSTANDING COLLEGE STUDENTS' SPIRITUAL IDENTITIES

Different Faiths, Varied Worldviews

Jenny L. Small

HAMPTON PRESS, INC.
NEW YORK, NEW YORK

Printed in the United States of America

Library of Congress Cataloging-in-Publication Data

Small, Jenny L.
    Understanding college students' spiritual identities : different faiths, varied worldviews / Jenny L. Small
        p. cm. -- (Discourse and social processes)
    Includes bibliographical references and index.
    ISBN 978-1-61289-048-7 (hardbound) -- ISBN 978-1-61289-049-4 (paperbound)
    1. College students--Religious life--United States. 2. Cultural pluralism--United States. I. Title.

    BL625.9.C64.S63 2011
    204'.408420973--dc23
                                                2011033748

Hampton Press, Inc.
307 Seventh Avenue
New York, NY 10001

Dedicated to
Josh, Sophie, and Nathan

Contents

Foreword, *Edward P. St. John*   ix

Acknowledgments   xiii

Prologue   xv

1   *The Purpose of This Book*   1
   Introduction to the Current Book   2
   The Questions that Guide Me   5
   Definitions of Core Terms   9
   Religion, Spirituality, and Faith in the Higher Education Context   12
   The Purpose and Organization of this Work   17
   My Perspective   19

2   *The Distinctive Faith Frames of Four Groups of Students*   23
   Christian Faith Frame   28
   Jewish Faith Frame   38
   Muslim Faith Frame   47
   Atheist/Agnostic Faith Frame   56
   Faith Frames Compared   67
   Conclusion   69

3   *The Relationship Between Faith Frames and Discourse in*
     Intra- and Interfaith Dialogue   71
   Dialogue and the Christian Faith Frame   74
   Dialogue and the Jewish Faith Frame   81
   Dialogue and the Muslim Faith Frame   87
   Dialogue and the Atheist/Agnostic Faith Frame   94
   Exceptional Discourse Moves: Post-Hoc Positioning
     and Post-Hoc Face Saving   100
   Summary of Relationship between Faith Frames
     and Discourse   105
   Conclusion   106

4   *The Relationship Between Faith Frames and Students'*
    Awareness of Religious Privilege and Marginalization   109
    Three-Tiered Structure of Religious Privilege in
      American Society   112
    Religious Marginalization Awareness and the Christian
      Faith Frame   116
    Religious Marginalization Awareness and the Jewish
      Faith Frame   119
    Religious Marginalization Awareness and the Muslim
      Faith Frame   121
    Religious Marginalization Awareness and the
      Atheist/Agnostic Faith Frame   124
    Religious Marginalization Awareness Scale   126
    Benefits from a Closer Examination of Religious Diversity
      and its Relationship to Privilege   128
    Conclusion   130

5   *The Impact of the College Environment on Students'*
    Diverse Faith Identities   131
    Catalysts for Positive Growth in Faith   132
    Catalysts for Stifling Growth in Faith   137
    Conclusion   140

6   *Implications for Educators Working With Students of*
    Diverse Faiths   143
    Utilization of Faith Frames as an Educational Tool
      with Individual Students and in Intrafaith Settings   144
    Utilization of Faith Frames as an Educational Tool
      with Multiple Students and in Interfaith Settings   149
    Additional Implications for Morality and Equity in
      Practice and Research   154
    Conclusion   159

    Appendix   161
    References   169
    Author Index   179
    Subject Index   183

Foreword

Although secular colleges and universities seem to be opening up once again to a discourse on spirituality, the more complicated question of how faculty and student service personnel can communicate with students of different faiths in and outside the classroom has gone largely unaddressed. Contemporary notions of spirituality are broad enough to include all faiths and nonbelievers, at least in a general way, but the specific values held by different groups across and within faiths are often in conflict, sometimes limiting the exchange of ideas to superficial matters. There are also stark differences across faith traditions with respect to core commandments and prophetic voices thought to be truths to live by, as well as arguments about whose values are true and authentic and whose are not. There are deeply dividing value differences within faith traditions. For example, fundamentalists of the major monotheistic faith traditions—Islamic, Christian, and Jewish—hold more limited views on the role of women than do the more liberal sects within them. Based on faith, some Catholics supported President Obama's health care legislation whereas others did not. These differences are too easily oversimplified when values are generalized into universal constructs of spirituality. To create open, inclusive discursive space in classrooms and student living communities, it is often necessary to explore values in deeper ways than can be postulated within a generalized concept of spirituality. In *Understanding College Students' Spiritual Identities: Different Faiths, Varied Worldviews*, Jenny L. Small provides a way through this puzzle for educators. Small started her journey toward this book with the insight that the standard faith-based construct of moral development postulated originally by James Fowler was Christian-centric. She came to understand this as a Jewish woman who worked in student affairs and explored related questions in graduate school. Eventually she hypothesized faith-centered concepts of moral development consonant with the faith-based literature on moral development in Christianity, Judaism, Islam, and nonbeliever spirituality. These distinctions are important because the concept of spirituality is generally thought to be broad enough to include the nonbelievers who hold to spiritual values with people of faith, but such broad notions do not go very deep. By making these distinctions clear, exploring their meaning in focus groups that were faith-centered and mixed-faith, and reconstructing notions of moral development in ways compatible with the major faith traditions, Jenny Small has given us a way to talk about differences in values and faith while maintaining the connectivity of underlying shared values.

This is important because it provides educators with a way of keeping questions of values at a general level so as not to preclude exploration of differences and nuances of values. Breaking through the superficial barriers requires intergroup dialogue about faith.

Some readers might ask: Why is the general notion of spirituality a problem? One answer lies in the history of higher education and American society. Deism, an 18th-century construct of generalized faith similar to modern spirituality, was central in creating consensus among leaders from the American colonies with different Christian traditions. The general belief in God, commonly held, made it possible for the leaders representing different traditions to organize the American Revolution and construct the U.S. Constitution. Yet over time, matters of faith have been reinterpreted in ways that too often prohibit conversations about faith in secular classrooms, especially in public schools and college. History teaches us that generalized concepts of values—be they centered in the Enlightenment or in postmodern concepts of spirituality—are not sufficient to hold a consensus in rapidly changing societies. We need alternative ways of going about the exploration and discussion of differences in values as a means of building shared understandings of the strengths gained from accepting differences within communities.

The overemphasis on generalized concepts of spirituality runs the risk of glossing over differences, providing no means of addressing issues that led to and sustain terrorism in the 21st century. Radical fundamentalists of Christian, Jewish, Islamic, and Hindu origins threaten the stability of modern governments. If we cannot talk about the underlying values that cause these differences as part of education in college classrooms and living communities, then where can they be openly discussed in contemporary society? It is overly simplistic for any one group to persecute another merely as a matter of faith, yet the world has many examples of just this.

Jenny Small's book is important because it illuminates a way through the serious problem of failure to communicate about differences in values and matters of faith. I encourage faculty and administrators to read this book, to explore alternative ways of thinking about the problems they face in working with students who hold different core values, and to experiment with new approaches to opening conversations to be inclusive of faith differences. This may be our best path toward peace in our time.

Edward P. St. John
University of Michigan

Acknowledgments

I have many people to thank for helping to bring this book to fruition. It has been many years in the making, and along the way, various kind souls have supported me, prodded me, and given me necessary criticism that has made my writing stronger.

First, I would like to thank Dr. Lesley Rex, my wonderful editor, who has been with me since before I even started crafting my dissertation at the University of Michigan and taught me everything I know about discourse analysis. Throughout the dissertation process, Lesley gave me the confidence I needed to embrace my identity as a qualitative researcher. She also read innumerable versions of this text, constantly helping me to improve my writing and my ability to make incisive points, and facilitating my goal of having a completed book in which I hold so much pride.

I would also like to thank the other fantastic members of my dissertation committee: Dr. Edward St. John, who chaired the committee and gave me the freedom to select the research agenda of my dreams, and who also contributed the powerful Foreword for this book; Dr. John Burkhardt, who taught me that it is legitimate to be an academic with heart, and who has been my strongest advocate for so many years; and Dr. David Schoem, who bolstered my instinct that religion, spirituality, and faith are important topics in the academy. As well, I offer a hearty thank you to Dr. L. Lee Knefelkamp, of Teachers College, Columbia University, who was the very first faculty member who encouraged me to challenge the status quo through my research, even though I was merely a young master's student.

Thank you also to Dr. Danielle Molina and Dr. Staci Shultz, both of whom read drafts of this work, gave me much needed feedback, and were enthusiastic cheerleaders. Thank you to Heather Jefferson, who improved my writing with her copyedits, and to Laura Held, for additional copyediting support. Thank you to Barbara Bernstein, my publisher and guide at Hampton Press. As well, I am grateful to two anonymous reviewers, who pushed me to make this book more accessible to readers and to contribute material of substance to the literature base of our field.

A much deserved thank you also goes out to the 21 college students who shared their lives with me and with each other, who openly spoke about their faith identities, and without whom there would be no subject matter for this text.

Finally, thank you to my entire family, including my family of friends, for supporting me throughout my research and writing, all of these years. This is especially true for Josh, who never let me give up. I could not have completed the hard work without all of you.

Prologue

Religion, religious diversity, conflicts between and within religions, and dialogue among them—these are some of the most critical topics of discourse in the United States today. Demographics begin to tell the story. According to Diana L. Eck (2001), a professor at Harvard University, "the United States has become the most religiously diverse nation on earth" (p. 4). Data gathered by the Pew Forum on Religion & Public Life also suggest that the face of religion has changed greatly. Today, only 56% of Americans report belonging to the same faith of their childhoods (Pew Forum on Religion & Public Life, 2009, p. 1). In addition, there has been a movement toward greater secularization in the country, "although this trend has been partly masked by massive immigration of people with relatively traditional worldviews, and high fertility rates, from Hispanic countries" (Swanbrow, 2004). Although there is some scholarly disagreement about the level and impact of this religious diversity (T. W. Smith, 2002), there is also evidence to suggest that "a religious hegemony does exist, and, at a minimum, it works to erode, marginalize, and support the persecution of religious groups who fall outside the mainstream" (Beaman, 2003, p. 314). The "lovely sentiment" that all religions are means to the same end is "untrue, disrespectful, and dangerous" (Prothero, 2010).

Alongside this growing religious diversity exists continued religious conflicts. Anger against Pope Benedict XVI and the Roman Catholic Church surged in the days surrounding Easter 2010 due to alleged inactions toward stopping the sexual molestation of children by priests (Wakin, 2010). That same month, the Episcopal Church confirmed Mary Douglas Glasspool as the first openly lesbian bishop, an act that has led to "parishes and a handful of dioceses [breaking] away from the Episcopal church in protest" (Gilgoff, 2010). In 2007, when Keith Ellison became the first Muslim to be elected to the U.S. Congress, conservatives became extremely upset by his utilization of the Koran while taking his oath of office (Patel, 2008). A new funeral prayer book published by the Reform movement of Judaism is considered controversial due to the efforts included within to comfort atheists (BBC, 2010). Although some of us might shake our heads at these and other incidents, ranging from incendiary to outlandish, the fact that clashes, both within and between religions, remain hot topics in the news is truly no surprise.

Despite the continued presence of religious conflicts, there is a critical movement that aims to engage the interfaith in dialogue with one another. Catherine Cornille (2008), a leader in the field of dialogue, states in her timely book, *The Im-possibility of Interreligious Dialogue*, that "recent times have witnessed the emergence of numerous organizations dedicated to the promotion of dialogue, from international movements to local ones, and from interfaith organizations to confessional ones" (p. 1). This movement, existing on both the micro- and macroscales, seeks to progress from diversity to actual pluralism:

> Diversity simply refers to people of different cultural, ethnic, racial, and religious backgrounds living in close quarters. Pluralism, however, is the active engagement of those diverse groups, with the intention of building familiarity, understanding, cooperation—and a common society. (Patel, 2008, p. 20)

Examples from the field of interfaith dialogue demonstrate the type of work being done. Some American Muslims have responded to the terrorist attacks of September 11, 2001, with a push to engage in a "process of the indigenization of American Islam [that] is intertwined with the construction of a distinctly American Islamic civic identity" (Takim, 2004, p. 344). These efforts have included holding dialogues with members of other, non-Muslim religious groups. The Council of Centers on Jewish-Christian Relations reports 27 member organizations, typically units at higher education institutions within the United States and Canada (Council of Centers on Jewish-Christian Relations, 2009), all working to enhance understanding between Christians and Jews. Humanists, too, have been implored to enter into dialogue with the religious "because we live in a world . . . where we can no longer afford to misunderstand one another or to be ignorant about what makes each other tick" (Epstein, 2009, p. xviii).

This book is situated within the religious and social climate just described, one that features increasing religious diversity and the inherent progressions and complications arising from that diversity. It is also aimed as a contribution to the efforts toward moving from simple religious diversity to true religious pluralism.

1

THE PURPOSE OF THIS BOOK

—

Just as in the macrocosm of U.S., so too is religion a complex and contested topic in the institutions of American higher education. The most recent statistics available on the religious affiliations of American college students depict an extremely religiously diverse college population, although one that leans heavily toward Christianity. The most prevalent religious preference among 4-year college students is Roman Catholic (26.9%), followed next by no religious affiliation (21.9%). Protestant Christian denominations hold the next six slots, in terms of prevalence, while "other religion"—specific religious minorities such as Judaism, Islam, and Buddhism—and minor Christian denominations all claim less than 3% each of the student population (*This year's freshmen at 4-year colleges: Highlights of a survey,* 2010).

Intriguing new developments have given rise to more opportunities for students to experience spiritual life during the college years. For example, service to humanist students is increasing. Individual campuses, such as Harvard and Rutgers, have made news for hiring humanist chaplains specifically to serve the religious nonbelievers among their students, and at Tufts, the student Freethought Society has requested the same from the administration (Kolowich, 2009). These groups join the Secular Student Alliance, which has linked together and supported nontheistic students around the country since 2000 (Secular Student Alliance, 2006).

Dialogue among students has also become a facet of college life, with curricula such as the Program on Intergroup Relations at the University of Michigan engaging students in dialogue along multiple streams of identity and also training students on how to facilitate dialogues themselves (*The program on intergroup relations*, 2009). At a broader level, the Interfaith Youth Core (n.d.) brings together young people from a variety of religious backgrounds around "[building] relationships on the values that [they] share, such as hospitality and caring for the Earth, and how [they] can live out those values together to contribute to the betterment of [their] community."

INTRODUCTION TO THE CURRENT BOOK

This book takes the broad social situation described in the prologue, brings it down to the institutional level of one university campus, and then examines all of its implications through the close study of students' language. Language is a window into identity. Through their words and the ways they deploy them in conversation, college students declare themselves, connect with their peers, and distance themselves from controversy. They also reveal the social positions of their faith groups and how religious privilege and religious marginalization impact their lives. Finally, they give educators clues as to how they may react and make choices during certain situations in college. In this book, you will meet a number of these students. Some of them are struggling with relating across faith boundaries, as represented below by Kristin and Meghan, or with relating with peers similar to themselves, like Jasmine. Others, like Sam and Yusuf, are finding common ground they never before knew existed. This book examines many such student experiences, as well as informs how to recognize and constructively capitalize on students' explorations and growth in faith on our college and university campuses to construct more moral and equitable learning environments.

We will start with Meghan, a 21-year-old unaffiliated, atheist woman, and Kristin, a 20-year-old Methodist Christian woman, reflecting on the ways they interacted in an interfaith conversation.[1] Meghan and Kristin show us how challenging it can be for students to abandon their natural impulses toward self-preservation and open themselves to challenging new ideas:

---

[1]All names of students are pseudonyms. Faith labels were those self-assigned by the students unless otherwise noted.

"It is also frustrating to try and express my passion for Christ without coming off as insulting to others; I felt that perhaps I insulted [Meghan] when I asked her about her goals and if she actually finds fulfillment in life—I wasn't trying to be rude or pretentious, but rather honestly wanted to know. As much as I don't like offending people, though, I do prefer to offer up my ideas, however unpopular or unpleasant they may seem."
—Kristin

"I didn't like it when I was asked to be specific about anything ... because the other people were so driven by their own religions and very judgmental. I didn't like when one of the girls [Kristin] asked me about how I am goal driven. I really didn't like the ... [interfaith discussion] group."
—Meghan

Jasmine, a 21-year-old Jewish woman from the Reconstructionist denomination,[2] expresses concern that she will be judged and not accepted by other Jewish students. Unlike Meghan and Kristin, her primary concern is with people who are most like herself:

"I think there is such a need, for myself and within Judaism, of ... Jews wanting to prove themselves as more authentically Jewish—or ... maybe not authentically Jewish but ... who's more of a Jew than another person."
—Jasmine

Sam, an 18-year-old Conservative Jewish man, and Yusuf, a 19-year-old Muslim man, connect through their definitions of the terms *religion* and *spirituality*. They reach out to one another and find an area where their beliefs converge:

"I had some major issues ... differentiating between religion and spirituality, and I feel like from this discussion I may have gotten it. Religion seems to be more of the means ... that you can find to get to—and spirituality is more of the ends, spirituality is more of the being at peace with yourself, and being at peace with what's going on, appreciating the beauty in things regardless of what you attribute that beauty to—whether it's God, whether it's nature, whether it's whatever—whether it's the good in people, whatever you want to attribute that beauty to ... I feel like, again, religion gives you that thing to attribute it to, and spirituality is kind of the end that we all seem to share, kind of those shared morals and shared ethics and shared appreciation for ... things that are beautiful."
—Sam

---

[2]"Reconstructionist Judaism is a progressive, contemporary approach to Jewish life which integrates a deep respect for traditional Judaism with the insights and ideas of contemporary social, intellectual and spiritual life" (Jewish Reconstructionist Federation, 2007).

"I never heard that put to words, but I think that's exactly it…. We all share the same goal of … spirituality and what that does for us, and we all just have a different way of looking at it. And that's why we're … able to connect so well, I think, because we all realize that, and then we just think about the small differences."
—Yusuf

In this book, I call on fellow higher education professionals and academics in the United States to more effectively and completely consider the impact of faith diversity on college campuses. We have just begun to consider minority religious voices, opening the door to consideration of a critical social justice issue. Some of us have begun to realize that much of the related American higher education literature base is predicated on the assumption that all spirituality and faith development mirror that of mainstream Christians. We know that has become problematic in light of the religious diversity of college campuses. Religious diversity must be one element of treating all students in a just manner, one that honors their individual needs as learners and community members. *Understanding College Students' Spiritual Identities: Different Faiths, Varied Worldviews* moves such literature forward by arguing that religious privilege and marginalization relate to students' faith, and that they should be considered in higher education settings. It is an invitation to those educators who have not yet considered this situation to begin conversing on the topic with those of us who are already convinced of the need.

This volume reflects the new knowledge that students' faith identities are influenced by their religious affiliation, and it breaks with the general pattern of previous works, much of which lumped students of all religious groups into a categorical definition aligned with mainstream Christianity. It considers the marginalizing impact of this unexamined religious privileging and provides an alternate way of understanding faith and spirituality, with the potential to influence both research and practice in higher education, in the United States and in other countries, as well as the lives of religious minority college students.

Within current fields of higher education research and practice, only a small number of scholars are making the unusual claim that students' faith identities, and indeed the ways they make meaning of the world, differ in relation to their religious ideals (or lack thereof). My work, however, is based squarely on this assertion. In my research, I have observed students negotiating their relationships with each other in dialogue to make sense for themselves of conflicting, overlapping, or mutually exclusive faith perspectives. Atheist, agnostic, and other nonbelieving college students particularly understand themselves in a distinct manner, one distinguished by more than solely a disbelief or doubt in the existence of

God. But they are not unique in this; students from alternative world-views, such as Islam and Judaism, have important identity differences from Christians. These distinctions, in the case that they remain unacknowledged, contribute to some students being rendered invisible or powerless on college campuses and to the unintentional dominance of certain others. By adding my voice to those bringing this situation to light, I aim to promote change in these conditions.

The topic of this book is both important and timely. The American College Personnel Association, a major national association of professional student affairs administrators, has called for practitioners on college campuses to rise above "simple tolerance, respect, and celebration of religious difference" (American College Personnel Association, 2006, p. 2). Rooted in the Judeo-Christian origins of higher education in this country, tolerance and respect have understandably held sway as the ethical barometer guiding campus procedures. However, the religious diversity on today's college campuses calls for a reexamination of this barometer. Treating students of all worldviews as if they are the same as Christians is no longer a moral or equitable stance. Making that shift in understanding requires that all educators—not just the early adopters of these ideas—become aware of the distinct differences between religious affiliations and faith identities and how these impact students' lives.

THE QUESTIONS THAT GUIDE ME

Throughout *Understanding College Students' Spiritual Identities*, I examine several key questions about the faith identities of Christian, Jewish, Muslim, and atheist/agnostic college students in the United States. These four groups were chosen because they are the ones currently dominating the discourse on religion and spirituality during the college years. First, I consider how students' talk and their usage of language with each other demonstrate the uniqueness of their faith identities. Second, I look at the relationships between these students' expressions of their faith identities and their interactions with each other by using a methodological tool called *discourse analysis*. Third, I take a closer look at the relationships between students' awareness of religious marginalization, their faith identities, and justice/morality on American college campuses. I follow this presentation with a discussion of how the college environment can influence growth in faith and also how certain situations can actually stifle growth. At the end of the book, I leave fellow educators with thoughts on how we can continue to improve research and practice to serve all of our students. I situate this in an argument for improving the morality and equity in our practices surrounding faith diversity.

To address these topics, I present important new understandings of college student faith and spirituality and the ways higher education institutions can contribute to identity growth. This information represents the next step in higher education research—moving beyond the knowledge that students' religious lives matter in their college outcomes to demonstrate that the details of those lives, and what they believe, also have an impact. To do so, I use as supporting material students' voices from a study designed to bring together students of a variety of religious backgrounds to create discourse around their faith identities. By listening to these young adults speak with one another about the ways they make meaning, about their beliefs, insecurities, and spiritual searches, I learned a great deal about the interconnectedness of identity, dialogue, privilege, and marginalization, and I came to understand how those of us in higher education can engage in more just practice.

The students in the study were all enrolled at a large, public research university in the Midwestern United States. Holding my conversations at a public institution allowed me access to students from a wide variety of religious backgrounds and, potentially, a more varied mix in their levels of sophistication regarding faith (some having very little knowledge, and some having vast knowledge). In this way, they were similar to the students on campuses around the country, some with deeply held and well-considered beliefs and others with less self-awareness about their own faith identities.

Figure 1.1 depicts the aggregated religious preferences for students who entered the university from 2002 to 2005,[3] the time period in which

---

[3]In 2005, this university enrolled 25,467 undergraduate students and 14,526 graduate students (Campus Information Centers, 2006). Data on the religious backgrounds of all entering students at the university is collected annually through the CIRP and analyzed by the Division of Student Affairs. Roughly, this is the equivalent of the total students enrolled in the university during the 2005–2006 academic year, as first-year students in 2002–2003 would be in their fourth year in 2005–2006. Although this is not an entirely accurate accounting of these students, due to transfers in and out of the institution, it is the only representation available. The university does not collect religious background information for students other than during their entering year. In the figure, the category "Catholic" is comprised of Roman Catholic and Eastern Orthodox. The category "Protestant" is comprised of Baptist, Church of Christ, Episcopal, Lutheran, Methodist, Presbyterian, Unitarian, United Church of Christ, and other Christian. The category "Other" is comprised of Buddhist, Hindu, LDS (Mormon), Quaker, and other religion. Notably, the university has fewer Catholic (1.1%) and many fewer Protestants (15.8%) than institutions nationally, although more Jews (9.8%), Muslims (0.4%), other religion (1.0%), and no religion (4.7%). Because of the greater prevalence of minority faiths at the institution than nationally, this institution faces more interfaith complexities than most.

the students in my study enrolled in the institution. The figure also contains religious background information for students nationally during the 2005–2006 academic year ("This year's freshmen at 4-year colleges: A statistical profile," 2006) as a frame for comparison. The 2005–2006 academic year was chosen for this comparison because it corresponds to one of the years in which the students in the study enrolled. (This accounts for any differences from the demographics presented at the beginning of this chapter.)

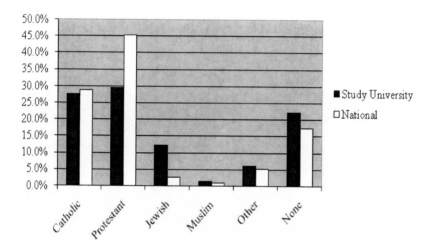

Figure 1.1. Study university and national student religious backgrounds[4]

I recruited 21 American students from four faith groups—Protestant Christian, Jewish, Muslim, and atheist/agnostic—to participate in the study. I present demographic information about them in Table 1.1. The worldview, race, and major information that is included is as submitted by the participants themselves, and their ages were at the time of the study. The names listed are pseudonyms chosen to be culturally appropriate.

All of the students participated in two sets of focus group conversations I convened to shed light on the variety of faiths of Christians, Jews, Muslims, and atheists/agnostics. The focus groups offered me the oppor-

---

[4]Data Source: Cooperative Institutional Research Program.

Table 1.1. Final Participant List.

Name	Sex	Age	Worldview	Race	Major
Brooke	F	19	Christian: Agnostic	African American	Anthropology & Arabic Studies
Carl	M	23	No affiliation	White	Biopsychology & Philosophy
David	M	18	Christian:Lord of Light Lutheran	White	History, German
Inaara	F	18	Muslim:Sunni	Persian (from Afghanistan)	Sociology & Psychology
Jada	F	23	Christian:Nondenominational	African American/Native American	Dance
Jasmine	F	21	Jewish:Reconstructionist	White	Comparative Literature, Arabic & Islamic Studies
Jesse	M	18	Jewish	White	Undecided, pre-law
Joanna	F	20	Jewish:Cultural/Atheist Jew, raised Reform	White	Atmospheric Science
Judy	F	18	Jewish:Conservative	White	Undecided, possibly Psychology
Karen	F	19	Christian:Methodist	White	Undecided
Kristin	F	20	Christian:Methodist	White	Undecided, pre-med
Meghan	F	21	No affiliation	Mexican/Chinese	English
Melanie	F	20	Unitarian Universalist[5]	White	Cello Performance, Anthropology, & Classical Archeology
Misty	F	21	Agnostic/No religious affiliation	African American and White	Industrial Operations Engineering and General Studies
Rick	T	20	Druid, Unitarian Universalist, Secular Humanist, Zen	White	Sociology & Center for Afroamerican and African Studies
Sabur	M	19	Muslim	Asian/Pacific Islander	Pre-law & Biology
Sam	M	18	Jewish:Conservative	White	Aerospace Engineering
Shashi	F	18	Muslim	Asian/Pacific Islander	Political Science & Middle Eastern Studies
Suha	F	19	Muslim	Asian/Pacific Islander	Economics & South Asian Studies
Will	M	26	Christian:Episcopalian	Asian/Pacific Islander	Master's of Public Health
Yusuf	M	19	Muslim	White	Undecided

[5] According to the association governing Unitarian Universalist congregations, "Unitarian Universalism is a caring, open-minded religion that encourages seekers to find their own spiritual path. Our faith draws on many religious sources, welcoming people with different beliefs. We are united by shared values, not by creed or dogma" (Unitarian Universalist Association of Congregations, 2010).

tunity to hear potential commonalities within these students' experiences, as well as the distinct differences brought about by mainstream or marginalized status.

In the first group, the students talked with those from similar faith backgrounds. I started this way so that the students could begin thinking about their faith identities in the relatively safe space of a group with which they affiliated religiously or otherwise. Nevertheless, I also suspected that students from different subgroups within a religion (such as Evangelical and non-Evangelical Christians) would perceive themselves as having quite dissimilar values and perspectives. To bolster my ability to gather rich data from students from faiths other than my own (Jewish), I included a co-facilitator in each of the three other homogenous focus groups, Christian, Muslim, and atheist/agnostic. The co-facilitators affiliated with the faith at hand, as well as had familiarity with research protocols and focus group leadership. I empowered these additional researchers to ask students follow-up questions or to focus the conversation on a particular topic. As well, they acted as symbols of my sensitivity to other religious and nonreligious ideas, which was necessary due to my self-disclosure as a Jew.

During the second round of focus groups, the students were intermixed by their faiths. I held these groups to provide students with the slightly more challenging experience of speaking about their faith identities among people with varied worldviews. Because this was their second time as participants, I believed they were prepared for this type of challenge. In addition, the students could hear each other's comments in direct reaction to one another.

Following the focus groups, I requested the students submit written reflections to elicit their reactions to the study and to provide them with some personal assessment of their experiences. Finally, I individually interviewed eight students, a male and a female from each faith group. I utilized discourse analysis techniques to analyze all the spoken and written data, which made it possible to document the way identity was co-constructed (or constructed through the process of people talking together) during group interaction.[6]

DEFINITIONS OF CORE TERMS

Before presenting what I learned, I offer definitions of my core terms. In my explorations of this topic, I have come to discover that scholars dis-

---

[6]See the Appendix for further information on methods, including the types of questions asked in the focus groups and discussions of trustworthiness and interpretive lens.

cussing faith development and spirituality are not in consensus about the meanings of the topics of their research. In addition, Love and Talbot (1999) point out that there are no accepted definitions of *faith* and *spirituality* in higher education. Some scholars suggest that the terms are synonymous, some equate one or the other to *religion*, and still others label each term as mutually exclusive. In this book, I follow the lead of Peter C. Hill et al. (2000), who maintain that historically the understandings of religion and spirituality have been too strongly separated. Therefore, *spirituality* will refer to core beliefs about the sacred, whereas *religion* will mean the actions surrounding that core, typically occurring within an institutional body.

These two terms, however, are not as inclusive as I would like them to be. My learning about how atheist, agnostic, and other nonbelieving students define themselves helped me to understand that labeling beliefs as *religious* is an inadequate way of describing the development of all young adults. These students pushed back against the societal privilege of the religiously affiliated, including the terminology that goes along with it. To be a conscientious researcher, I am responding here to their insistence on inclusion.

Therefore, throughout this text, rather than saying that what distinguishes people from each other is religious and nonreligious beliefs, or spiritual identities, terms often inadequate to describe the full life experiences of atheists, I suggest that it is diversity of faith that matters. I define *faith* as "one's way of understanding the world through religion, spirituality, and/or other forms of meaning-making." This language affirms the fact that while all humans hold belief systems that guide their views of the world and their development over time, not everyone subscribes to a religious or spiritual belief system. It also allows for augmentation of the terms *atheist* and *nonbeliever*, which imply an absence of something, so that the terms can invoke a presence of what they do have: complex and complete ways of framing the world through faith. In addition, the students from the three worldviews with whom I spoke also offered definitional nuances, which I will indicate throughout as well.

In addition to this modification of language surrounding diversity of faith, I also have carefully selected the terms I use to describe the students with whom I worked. For the three groups of religiously affiliated students, I remained with the simplest possible labels: Christian college students, Jewish college students, and Muslim college students. I did so because the students were brought together through their shared identification with each of these religions. However, I do not claim that the five to six participants in each faith group are typical or representative of all things Christian, Jewish, or Muslim. The number of participants necessary to make such a sample claim would be prohibitive, if indeed a sample could represent the entirety of a religion's belief systems. (Such a condition would not even be possible with a large-scale quantitative survey.) Because I did not engage in a sampling procedure to ensure representative participation, but rather aimed for purposeful and theoretically productive samples, the general traditional labels to which participants responded seemed adequate and functional.

Choosing a label for the final group of students, the atheist, agnostic, and otherwise non-God-believing students, entailed a bit more work. To prepare for a study in which I would include those whose faiths do not take God into account, I relied on existing literature to inform me of what other researchers have learned about these students' faith identities. I started with the definition of *atheism*. Contrary to what might be the popular understanding of the term, atheism is *not* defined as a disbelief in God, but as a *lack of belief* in God (Campbell, 1998; Scobie, 1994). In fact, *"atheism, in its basic form, is not a belief: it is the absence of belief.* An atheist is not primarily a person who *believes* that a god does *not* exist; rather, he does *not* believe in the existence of a god" (G. H. Smith, 1979, p. 7; italics original).

Because of this broad definition, however, atheism is quite difficult to characterize. Nash (2003) describes seven varieties of student atheism that he has encountered in his years of conducting seminars on religious pluralism. They include social justice atheists and *apatheists*, a term he created "to describe students who have no feeling whatever for religion, spirituality, immortality, metaphysics, or the supernatural" (p. 12). According to Christian Smith and Patricia Snell (2009), these emerging adults may be termed "Religiously Indifferent," "Religiously Disconnected," or "Irreligious" (p. 168) depending on their level of remove from religious institutions. Dalton, Eberhardt, Bracken, and Echols (2006) identify two distinct types of "secular seekers ... who are engaged in spiritual search outside the context of religion" (p. 7). According to Ray Billington (2002), there are several forms of nontheistic religious expression, including reverence of the arts, communing with nature, being in community, and even experiencing sexual relations. One particular form of atheism is *secular humanism*, which is defined as "a comprehensive nonreligious life stance that incorporates a naturalistic philosophy, a cosmic outlook rooted in science, and a consequentialist ethical system" (Flynn, 2002, p. 42).

Atheists explain their adoption of a nonreligious worldview in one of four ways: "(1) metacognitive considerations, (2) problems of theodicy, (3) self-liberation, and (4) negative experience with religious education" (Oser, Reich, & Bucher, 1994, p. 52). When believers become nonbelievers, their religious belief systems may be replaced with totally self-serving ideologies or ones that are society-serving.

Choosing an appropriate term to use as a label for the atheist and agnostic students is especially complicated given their wide variety of ideologies, as well as the specific beliefs to which they find themselves in opposition. Nash (2003) suggests utilizing the term preferred by Stein (1985) to describe the nature of this group: "unbelief,... because it's the closest synonym to 'heterodoxy,' which means 'not holding orthodox or traditional opinions on religious matters'" (p. 20). This would make these students *unbelievers*, a term that becomes somewhat inaccurate when considering all of their carefully weighed faith perspectives. Although certain of Nash's labels for subgroups of atheists do apply to students with whom I spoke, I feel that labeling them in such an individual manner would only lead to confusion within the purposes of this book.

Therefore, for simplicity's sake, I have settled on the somewhat inadequate label of *atheist/agnostic* students. I will also sometimes refer to them as nonbelievers, when the topic at hand is religion and/or God. In addition, I will continue to use the terms *heterodox* or *religiously unaffiliated* to reflect these students' occasionally reactionary stances against and lack of commitment to religious institutions.

Finally, I offer a definition for Christian privilege. Christian privilege is "the conscious and subconscious advantages often afforded the Christian faith in America's colleges and universities" (Seifert, 2007, p. 11), which remains problematic in higher education (Watt, Fairchild, & Goodman, 2009). Although Christian students may be unaware of their privileges (Schlosser, 2003),[7] religious minority students may be acutely aware of their marginalization. This distinction is one of the core topics I will discuss in this book.

RELIGION, SPIRITUALITY, AND FAITH IN THE HIGHER EDUCATION CONTEXT

I situate this text within a history of study and practice in the field of higher education. Religion and spirituality have long been considered an integral part of college student identity by student affairs practitioners—higher education professionals who have declared an interest in the "whole student" (Braskamp, 2007; Rodgers, 1990). In the foundational documents of the field of student affairs administration, the American Council on Education stated the importance of religious growth for col-

---

[7]Also see Schlosser (2003) for a "beginning list of Christian privileges" (p. 48) and C. Smith and Snell (2009) on how "liberal Protestantism's core values—individualism, pluralism, emancipation, tolerance, free critical inquiry, and the authority of human experience—have come to so permeate broader American culture" (p. 288).

lege students (1937/2004a) and then reaffirmed its own role in supporting that growth (1949/2004b).[8]

The research on individual faith development and spirituality within
the U.S. higher education setting began nearly 30 years ago. James Fowler
fashioned a model for the full lifespan, and Sharon Daloz Parks focused
on young adulthood. The theories proposed by these two scholars have
been highly influential, but they were not adequately designed to include
people from religious minority backgrounds. Fowler's (1981) original
study consisted of a sample that was a combined 85% Protestant and
Catholic, and that was 98% White. Parks (1980) used a similarly uniform
sample. She (2000) discussed qualitative differences in how religious congregations support their young adults. She did not, however, consider
how varied religious contents may affect them.

In his first major work on the subject, *Stages of Faith: The Psychology of
Human Development and the Quest for Meaning,* Fowler (1981) defines *faith*
as being held by all people, even doubters and disbelievers, not just those
who have a religious affiliation. This is because he sees faith as "the most
fundamental category in the human quest for relation to transcendence"
(p. 14). For Fowler, human faith development begins at birth with the
Undifferentiated Stage of infancy and proceeds throughout the lifespan
through as many as six additional stages.

Fowler's Stages 1 and 2 are the faiths of younger and older children,
respectively. Stages 3 and 4 tend to be the faith stages where traditional-
aged college students are located. Stage 3, Synthetic-Conventional faith,
is marked by a strongly held but tacit belief system, a direct association
between symbols and the meanings behind them, and a conventional
relationship to authority figures, including, for believers, a perceived personal relationship with God. At this stage, God is understood anthropo-
morphically.

---

[8]According to the American Council on Education (1937/2004a):

Assisting the student to reach his maximum effectiveness through clarification of his purposes, improvement of study methods, speech habits, personal appearance, manners, etc., and through progression in religious, emotional, social development, and other non-academic personal and group
relationships. (p. 7)

The student discovers ethical and spiritual meaning in life. ... The religious
counselor and the religious-activities program with a broad social reference
may assist the student in developing an understanding of proper concepts
of behavior, ethical standards, and spiritual values consistent with his
broadened horizons resulting from newly acquired scientific and technical
knowledge. (American Council on Education, 1949/2004b, p. 18; italics
original)

The transition to Stage 4, Individuative-Reflective faith, occurs when a young adult is forced to begin critically examining his or her beliefs or congruence with an authority figure. This stage is marked by an acceptance of one's internal authority over commitments, beliefs, and values, and a breaking down of the previously tacit assumptions. "The two essential features of the emergence of Stage 4, then, are the critical distancing from one's previous assumptive value system and the emergence of an executive ego" (p. 179). Stage 4 individuals also tend to deconstruct symbols, seeing them rationally as separate from their meanings.

For adults who progress from Stage 4 to Stages 5 and 6, there is a widening of concern for all humans, an ability to hold conflicting beliefs in dynamic tension with one another, and a renewed understanding of the power of symbols. Fowler considers Stage 6 to be extremely rare. People at Stage 6 can be said to live a "transcendent moral and religious actuality" (p. 200). These people are often experienced as being subversive of existing religious structures; however, Fowler believes that to reach these stages, one has to embrace a God concept, claiming that faith at these stages "will take essentially religious forms" (pp. 292–293).

Many researchers have criticized the overwhelming dominance of Christians and Catholics in Fowler's original sample and/or the insistence that the theory is universally applicable to all worldviews. Harold V. Hartley (2004) critiques the monotheistic nature of the samples in most studies of student spirituality. C. Ellis Nelson (1982) asserts that Fowler has "a vague Judeo-Christian slant," and his theory is based on a "generalized Judeo-Christian myth" (p. 170). A key signal to potential Western bias is Fowler's (1981) embracing of "radical monotheism" (p. 22), which he privileges over "pantheism, dualism, or polytheism" (Hoehn, 1983, p. 78). Streib (2003) concludes that "the research is not yet sufficient to provide empirical evidence of Fowler's universality claim, a claim that Fowler has not revoked but also has not repeated lately" (p. 28).

Parks (2000) is a theologian and developmental theorist, and a prominent supporter of Fowler's work. She has embraced much of Fowler's design. Beginning with her dissertation, Parks (1980) has sought to expand the middle stages of Fowler's theory to speak more thoroughly to the faith development of young adults. She describes the shifting of the locus of authority during the phases of young adulthood as beginning outside the self, during adolescence, to shifting to a "validating internal authority" (p. 135) as various authority figures come into conflict. Although there emerges an element of choice, the young adult still searches for an authority to rely on. At this point, "the emerging self is yet fragile, there may yet be a dependence on and a straining after the security of choosing/knowing that one side of the tension is 'right' or 'better'" (p. 140). Parks (2000) also explains that "the most profound marker of the threshold of young adulthood is the capacity to take self-aware responsibility for choosing the shape and path of one's own fidelity" (p. 64).

Following her initial exploration, Parks expanded her theory in two more books (Parks, 1986, 2000), evolving its applications. In *The Critical Years*, Parks focused on higher education, "the institution of preference for the formation of young adults in our culture" (p. 133), as the main type of mentoring community, communities that foster young adult growth in faith. In *Big Questions, Worthy Dreams*, she discussed the roles of other groups and organizations, including the workplace, travel, nature, family, and religion. Particularly relevant to this discussion are religious communities, which she describes as "a shared way of making meaning" (p. 197). In describing these communities, her Christian framework is revealed to the reader: "Religious faith communities that serve as a home for the formation of faith in the young adult years are most effective if they are themselves open to possibilities for ongoing transformation at the hand of Spirit" (p. 198).

Parks' theory is susceptible to many of the same critiques as Fowler's, as her work is situated within his framework. This situatedness is evidenced by her evoking the same religious language, such as "Kingdom or Commonwealth of God" (Parks, 1986, p. 97). An obvious limitation of Parks' work stems from her samples. Her original sample consisted of 10 male and 10 female undergraduates, 18 of whom were White and at a private Protestant, residential, liberal arts institution. It is unclear in future explications of her theory whether or not she has expanded her sample.

Despite the influence of Fowler and Parks on subsequent researchers and in the practice of student affairs professionals, not until recently has there been a chorus of voices from educators calling for a concentrated focus on spirituality in higher education.[9] Many of us have followed the lead of scholars involved with the Spirituality in Higher Education Project at the University of California, Los Angeles, which has amassed a large database for use in understanding "the spiritual growth of students during their undergraduate college years" (Higher Education Research Institution, n.d.). Studies have shown current students to be highly inter-

---

[9]Scholars who have joined the call in recent years include Cawthon and Jones (2004); Cherry, DeBerg, and Porterfield (2001); Chickering, Dalton, and Stamm (2005); Claerbaut (2004); Dalton et al. (2006); Higher Education Research Institution (2005); Hoppe and Speck (2005); Jablonski (2001); Kazanjian and Lawrence (2000); Love (2002); Love and Talbot (1999); Mayrl (2007); Mayrl and Oeur (2009); Miller and Ryan (2001); Nash (2001, 2007); Nash, Bradley, and Chickering (2008); Newman and Smith (2004); Riley (2005); Rogers and Love (2007); Seifert (2007); Social Science Research Council (n.d.); and Tisdell (2003).

ested in these issues and strongly influenced by their families, their peers, and the campus environment, particularly including faculty members.[10] In Robert J. Nash's (2007) opinion, the "real pluralism on college campuses today is religious, and this phenomenon presents all of us with an educational opportunity that is unique" (p. 4). As we look to the future of higher education, it is time to "introduce students to issues of diversity other than those based just on race or ethnicity" (Pascarella, 2006, p. 511), including faith diversity.

Still, despite this upsurge and interest, "research on students representing non-majority religious perspectives lags far behind" (Bryant, 2006, p. 2). Recent research on faith development theory and college student spiritual development taking place in the United States has focused primarily on the historically dominant religious group, "mainline" Christians (McCullough, Weaver, Larson, & Aay, 2000; Stamm, 2005) and has rarely distinguished between the experiences of religious minorities (Hartley, 2004). These studies do not sufficiently address the diverse situation on college campuses today. Around 9% of students at 4-year colleges are affiliated with a non-Christian religion, and 21.9% state that they have no religion (*This year's freshmen at 4-year colleges: Highlights of a survey*, 2010).[11] Even excellent resources such as the texts compiled by Christian Smith and his colleagues, featuring both longitudinal quantitative and qualitative data, lack a detailed breaking down of their findings to describe the varied lives of religious minorities (C. Smith, with Denton, 2005; C. Smith, with Snell, 2009). It is time to build on our findings and current knowledge to truly determine the differential effects of affiliating with minority religions:

> The privileging of the Christian faith in the United States has worked to establish a pseudonormalcy of one faith. This myth of normalcy associated with Christian privilege must be debunked in order to

---

[10]Recent studies that demonstrate these results include Bowman and Small (2010, in press); Cherry, DeBerg, and Porterfield (2001); Clydesdale (2007); Dalton et al. (2006); Gunnoe and Moore (2002); Hartley (2004); Higher Education Research Institution (2005); Hodges (1999); Holmes, Roedder, and Flowers (2004); J. Lee (2000); J. J. Lee (2002); Pascarella and Terenzini (2005); Regnerus and Uecker (2007); Small (2007); Small and Bowman (2011), Uecker, Regnerus, and Vaaler (2007); and Wuthnow (2007).

[11]There are 400,000 Jews and 75,000 Muslims enrolled in college today (Schmalzbauer, 2007). There are "251 affiliated Hillel Centers, Foundations, and Jewish Student Organizations in North America" (p. 3), and "the Muslim Student Association has 600 chapters in the United States and Canada" (p. 4). Even less mainstream, "Unitarian Universalist campus groups are active at 108 schools" (p. 5), and "the 'freethinkers, skeptics, secularists and humanists' ... network has expanded to include over 130 collegiate chapters" (p. 5).

move beyond the marginalization of significant populations of students, with the goal of providing existential development for all students. (Fairchild, 2009, p. 10)

Student affairs practitioners and other higher education administrators already make use of developmental theory in their work, and "student affairs practice without a theoretical base is not effective or efficient" (Evans, Forney, & Guido-DiBrito, 1998, p. 19). By further developing our understandings of students' faith identities and related growth during the college years, we have the timely opportunity to serve them with even greater success. Issues related to religion and spirituality do arise on campus, and professionals versed in the unique perspectives of individuals within faith groups will be able to respond appropriately. When more campus administrators and associations for student affairs professionals become better educated on the varied needs of students of diverse faiths, campuses can be made into more welcoming places that serve their needs.

This book aims to address two interactive demographics: the nearly 30% of students on American college campuses who do not identify as Christians, as well as students of diverse faith backgrounds. The material presented here capitalizes immediately on the knowledge that religious backgrounds correspond with spiritual understandings of the world and embraces the knowledge that faith is highly relevant and influential. It explores the contextual and situational, underscored with the understanding that the way one presents one's identity may likely change in relation to one's audience.

The research study used as background for this text, although conducted in the United States, would be applicable to other countries, as issues of difference in faith and religious privilege have parallels in other locations. A framework around faith rather than around religion makes inter- and intracultural translation possible. All public colleges and universities can benefit by considering the topics of students' faith identities, spiritual diversity, and religious privilege.

THE PURPOSE AND ORGANIZATION OF THIS WORK

Because these varied students are on our campuses, seeking avenues for spiritual and faith exploration, and because many of us in turn are seeking tools to address their myriad questions and points of entry into the conversation, I address this book mainly to higher education practitioners, in such areas as student affairs, residential life, judicial affairs, ministry, and community service. These professionals act as mentors to students as they seek out their purposes during the college years, as well as aid and advise them in their day-to-day life choices. I aim for the material to speak to those other educators, such as faculty and academic advisors, who assist students in choosing their academic directions and vocations, as well as interact with them in the classroom environment. My intention is to promote insight among practitioners and teachers who strive to make college campuses equitable spaces for students of all backgrounds, including from all faith groups. This is especially important for public institutions, which house so much of higher education's faith diversity. To do so, I will discuss four major phenomena involving discourse and faith that lead to new understandings of student identity, the American college environment, and resultant social justice imperatives. Each section of the book will utilize passages from the students' own voices and conversations to illustrate my points.

The first phenomenon I will discuss is *the relationship between discourse and faith identity* among traditional-age American college students. The students with whom I talked exhibited strong discourse evidence of seeing the world with perspectives corresponding to their religious affiliation or nonaffiliation, perspectives I have labeled "faith frames." These frames, as I am describing them, are used to make meaning, and they allow room for growth over time. Each is made up of common understandings, points of disagreement, and faith-specific issues that arose in dialogue among the four faith groups. The idea of a frame of worldview, in itself, is consistent with previous literature:

> Faith traditions provide all-encompassing frameworks of belief for the people who adopt them. They shape the ways their members see and interpret events and give a sense of direction and purpose to the ways in which believers engage in the world as their lives unfold. (Fried, 2007, p. 1)

Within this section, I will introduce the frames, how these students view religion, spirituality, and God, and how their worldviews impact intra- and interfaith dialogues. My descriptions are illustrated with quotations directly from the students.

The second major phenomenon to be discussed in the book is *the ways students from specific faith groups use language to negotiate their relationships with each other*. Throughout their interactions, my students exhibited evidence of utilizing certain discourse techniques to achieve their goals. These goals further illuminated their faith frames, such as the feelings of anxiety or guilt inherent within them. I was able to observe this during the students' interactions, and I have included transcripts so that readers can see for themselves how all of this transpired. In addition, some students admitted later on that they had deliberately omitted facts or softened their opinions for their within-group peers. These actions illustrated that these students were more comfortable positioning themselves outside of each other's presences. As well, they saved face for themselves and others by not raising conflicting points directly. Examples of these techniques will be used to further illustrate the faith frames.

The third major phenomenon I will discuss is *the linkage among faith diversity, awareness of religious privilege, and social justice imperatives on college campuses.* A critical element of the four faith frames is the way students become aware, over time, over religious marginalization, and how that element in society impacts them on at their individual levels. As well, students perceive a three-tiered structure of religious privilege in American society, one that impacts their day-to-day experiences on the college campus. This structure leads to feelings of disempowerment among some of the marginalized, as well as attempts by others to dismantle privilege. In discussing this phenomenon, I will highlight how all students, including Christians, can benefit from a closer examination of faith diversity and its relationship to privilege.

Finally, the fourth major phenomenon of the book is *the impact of the college environment on students' faith.* Students described critical situations in their lives that both catalyzed growth in faith and stifled it. Their stories demonstrate for practitioners moments in which support and intervention can be utilized both to promote positive change and to help students constructively engage in, and not avoid, challenging situations.

After closely examining each of these four important phenomena, I converge the discussions of all four faith groups to offer implications for research and practice to make college campuses more moral and equitable. I discuss how educators can work both with students and on their own to deconstruct privilege, making college campuses stronger learning environments for students of all faiths. I also discuss how the knowledge of this book (about the faith frames, discourse techniques, religious marginalization awareness, and the influence of the college environment) can be applied during inter- and intrafaith dialogue sessions. In addition, I describe several scenarios in which the faith frames can be utilized to foster individual growth among students—in situations involving residence life, the classroom, and still more common higher education settings. I base my suggestions on the distinctive identities and needs of the particular groups of students involved in my work.

MY PERSPECTIVE

I come to this project as both an academic/professional and as someone with a personal stake in the material. I was raised as a Reform Jew, and for 4 years as a young adult I worked for the umbrella organization for

Reform synagogues in North America, the Union of American Hebrew Congregations (now called the Union for Reform Judaism). For 2 of those years, I was also enrolled as a master's student in the field of student personnel administration. Faculty in my program introduced me to the theories of Fowler and Parks, which I was disappointed to find did not fully speak to the spiritual lives of the Jewish college students with whom I worked professionally. This initial, gut-level reaction that existing theories of faith development were incomplete set me on the path that I have followed for nearly a decade since.

My personal mission and beliefs led me to continue exploring and working in these topical areas. As a doctoral student and an administrator in the field of higher education, I continued to believe that the lack of consideration of alternative religious voices was a critical social justice issue that was being overlooked by many (although certainly not all) scholars. Treating all students in a just manner, one that honors their individual needs as learners and community members, has been a focus of many researchers and practitioners in higher education. Yet the call by previous advocates to specifically consider the impact of religious diversity on campus has not been satisfactorily addressed. Hearing that call, I felt compelled to answer and contribute in some small way to the work that was beginning in this area.

On an academic level, I had seen that faith development theories were rife with the opportunity to expand and include a comprehensive understanding of other (non-Christian) ways of being in the world. By entering the research arena, I could contribute to a new area of scholarship, hopefully leading to more complete practices on campus. I first conducted a small study on students' talk about spiritual transformation (Small, 2007). I gained additional insights into the varied ways faith identities and affiliations influence students' perspectives on the world and their interactions with each other through my discussions with the 21 religiously diverse American college students who participated in the larger research study that informed this book. Finally, after that in-depth qualitative study, I worked with a colleague to bolster our understandings of religious minority students through quantitative work utilizing the data from the Spirituality in Higher Education project at UCLA (Bowman & Small, 2010, in press; Small & Bowman, 2011).

Although the time I have spent on my path has yielded these publication successes, the work has not always been easy. I have often felt like an outsider speaking in the field of higher education about religion, spirituality, and faith, while race and ethnicity have carried more weight as the focuses of diversity concern. As a researcher, I have also experienced sticky moments, such as when Joanna, a student in the study discussed in this book, stated in her interfaith discussion that "Reform [Judaism], which is the lowest level of Judaism,... still isn't atheism," an assertion that offended me as a committed Reform Jew. Still, I remain fully dedicated to this line of inquiry. (I also allowed Joanna's comment to stand in the conversation without correction, which would have violated my role as researcher in the study.) Fortunately, as well, I have been supported by many colleagues and peers in the field, several of whom have been influential throughout the shaping of this book.

The perspective I take in this text begins with the influences of key developmental theorists, such as Fowler and Parks, and their predecessors, such as Lawrence Kohlberg. Kohlberg is the pioneer of Moral Development Theory. He posited a cognitive-structural developmental theory of moral judgment, which was based on a sequence of distinct stages culminating in a "structured whole.... [The] stages form an order of increasingly differentiated and integrated structures to fulfill a common function" (Kohlberg, 1984, p. 14). However, I also embrace the contributions of less frequently cited scholars, those who have taken up the call to specifically address the faith perspectives of non-Christian college students and adults. These include:

- Michael J. Shire (1987), a Jewish educator who integrated Fowler's theory into a Jewish context. Shire does this seemingly reluctantly saying that, "the normative design of the stage sequence, which posits a more individuative faith with each succeeding stage, has little parallel in a Jewish understanding of spirituality" (p. 24). Despite his concern that "a universalist and syncretistic approach blurs the significant differences between religious traditions and often assumes a Western Rationalist position" (Shire, 1997, p. 53), Shire does not offer an alternative theory. Instead, he maps Jewish ritual observance throughout the lifespan onto Fowler's schema (Shire, 1987). He describes Stage 3 as being highly conformist toward the expectations of the synagogue and the rabbi, Stage 4 as being focused on internal meaning and prayer rather than prescripted behavior, Stage 5 as the re-embracing of the power of rituals, and Stage 6 as a holy union with God.
- Lori Peek (2005), who identified a three-stage process of religious development among young adult Muslims. Peek, who interviewed 127 highly religious Muslim college students in New York and Colorado, labeled these stages "Religion as Ascribed Identity," "Religion as Chosen Identity," and "Religion as Declared Identity" (p. 223). Unfortunately, she does not reference Fowler or Parks, so it is unknown whether she feels her stages correspond with theirs.

- Markus Achermann (1981; as cited in Oser, Reich, & Bucher, 1994, p. 47), who examined atheist faith development in Germany. Achermann offered a developmental framework of faith for atheists. Oser, Reich, and Bucher point out that in Achermann's model, "other human beings (in particular an interactive social network) take the place occupied by God in the eyes of believers" (p. 49). They also report from their studies in Germany on how children and young adults develop as nonbelievers. They found four different types of atheism: transitional atheism, which occurs at a particularly critical stage of spiritual development; "worked-through" atheism, which states that God and religion can be replaced with other ideologies; unchurched atheism, which merely identifies those who do not express their religious belief in a formal worship setting; and atheism due to religious indifference.

By blending these lesser known, but no less critical, theories with the dominant ones in the field, I aim to bolster educators' skills in working with students of all faith backgrounds in the professional field that I identify as my own. Each is discussed in the context of broader literature in the next chapter.

2

THE DISTINCTIVE FAITH FRAMES OF FOUR GROUPS OF STUDENTS

College students see the world in varied ways based on the multiple elements of their identities. As student affairs practitioners, we may be accustomed to viewing students based on some of these elements, such as their gender, race, and sexual identity. Religious affiliation, however, is likely less understood by some practitioners, although it is no less salient to students. In fact, for some students, faith may take precedence in their self-concept. Muslim students, for example, are more likely to think of themselves within the rubrics of religion and nationality than within a racial category. Atheist students are quite used to (although not necessarily pleased with) their heterodoxy being used as a way of labeling them in society.

The critical nature of a student's religious affiliation and faith identity may be raised when student affairs professionals are least expecting it. It seems obvious that faith would be at the forefront during an overtly religious experience, such as when attending worship services, or even during a controversial situation, as when a blessing is offered by a clergy member before a school-wide event such as a commencement ceremony.

But consider a less obvious situation, such as that of a junior who has come to the office hours of an academic advisor purportedly to discuss the completion of requirements for a politics major, only to reveal that he is no longer certain that he wants to go on to law school. He is facing a vocational crisis, realizing that he prefers to enter a field where he can help people in need more directly. The reasons for this, he explains, come from his own experience as a religious minority in this country and his understanding that this type of status can lend a certain social instability to people's lives. Although this attitude may be prevalent among the current population of college students, those reared on compulsory volunteerism during the high school years, it may in this case come from a more spiritual place within.

The traditional-age American college students with whom I worked in my study demonstrated through their spoken (and unspoken) words a link between their worldviews and their faith identities. Some examples demonstrate this link. Misty attributes the definition of her spirituality specifically to her lack of belief in sacred texts. She looks within herself, rather than to an external authority, to guide her behavior:

> *"I identify as agnostic, and my personal definition is that I don't know there's a God, I can't disprove or prove it, and regardless, it really wouldn't change the way that I behave or my actions. And especially with my definition of spirituality being just very self-reflective and taking whatever experience sets that off ... I don't need to read a particularly religious text to shape the way I should be behaving."*
> —Misty, 21-year-old unaffiliated, agnostic student

Inaara's deeply held Islamic beliefs guide her to follow the model of the prophet Mohammed, whom she holds up as the ultimate example of living with God consciousness. Her definitions of spirituality closely align with Islam's definitions:

> *"I guess I would not define myself as religious or spiritual, but rather, just God conscious.... Just ... this constant remembrance of God and that ... sometimes we let that go when we get caught up in so many other things, but ... at the end of the day, you come back to that. Or ... during the five daily prayers. I remember, 'Oh wait a minute, hold on, rewind ... let's just get back to me and God and that whole relationship real quick.' And I guess ... when I think of religious I think of the example of the prophet Mohammed, and you know kind of epitomizing the Koran. And I obviously don't even come close to epitomizing that at all. And it's ... this constant struggle, so I wouldn't necessarily say that I'm religious, but at least that I attempt to try to always be in remembrance of God and that ... I have all these inner struggles and everything in overcoming that is you know going to take a long while. But ... religious, I don't—I wouldn't really use that label.... It's kind of ... a dangerous term to just shove onto someone."*
> —Inaara, 18-year-old Sunni Muslim student

While Karen defines herself as being "around the middle" of the range of spiritual commitedness, the range in itself is based on Christian teachings. Her spirituality is not separated from the Christian religious behaviors she values, which include going to church, reading the Bible, and believing in God and Jesus:

> "I'm not as religious as some in the aspect of going to church on every single week. I go quite often with my family, but I don't go as much as I probably 'should' and I don't read the Bible every night. I hardly read it at all actually, which is another thing that you're 'supposed' to do.... But, in my own sense, I do believe in God, and I do have faith in God, so in my mind I am ... probably about as religious or spiritual as I'm going to be, in a way, 'cause I've kind of hit the point where, yes, I do believe in God. I believe in Jesus, and I have my beliefs and how I feel about everything. And ... I will continue to go to church, not every single Sunday for the rest of my life. But I'm not going to, probably, change my entire life routine to read the Bible more often.... I'm kind of at a mid-point. I'm not as outgoing with it as some people are, but I definitely have my views set about how I feel about everything, ... for the most part, at least, and I feel that that's kind of my spirituality, but there are others that are still questioning it and don't know where they stand with things. So I'd say I'm kind of around the middle somewhere that it all."
> —Karen, 19-year-old Methodist Christian student

Jesse describes religious commitment as being subjectively determined, although he is similar to Karen in basing the scale on the valued behaviors of his religion, Judaism. Although he questions the ability of others to pass judgment, he supposes they would be doing so on the basis of Judaism's guidelines:

> "You can consider yourself religious and someone else might not consider you religious or vice versa, whatever, but I think basically it's following the rules of you religion I guess to a higher extent... I guess for Judaism it would be ... the more mitzvot you follow, the more religious you are, one could say, or you could just feel very religious and just, I could say, even though you follow more mitzvot then I do, I'm still more religious 'cause I feel that way. So that's why it's kind of subjective.... Spiritual I think ... can be with a group, but also it can be very individual like, I guess your connection with God or the higher power, just ... basically ... feeling a connection, knowing that there's something there is enough to be spiritual."
> —Jesse, 18-year-old Jewish student

Each of these four selections from focus groups and students' interviews illuminates a particular perspective on the nature of religion and spirituality. The students, while suggesting that they determine their beliefs independently, all are shaped somewhat by the tenets of their faiths. In addition to speaking to the mindset of an individual, they help to demonstrate the very different outlooks on the world held by Christians, Jews, Muslims, and atheists/agnostics in the United States. These four students, despite attending the same prestigious university and being in the same age bracket, had different perceptions of these elements of their identities. The perceptions are both unique from each other and tied in with their faiths.

I call these student perspectives, corresponding with their religious affiliations or lack thereof, "faith frames." These frames, as I am describing them, are used to make meaning of the world. This means that when a student considers a major or postgraduation employment, decides whom he or she is going to befriend or date, and chooses where to spend free time, his or her faith circumscribes that thinking process. This is not necessarily a conscious process. A student may not pause to overtly consider how participating in a particular co-curricular activity coincides with her ideologies. Nonetheless, the influence of faith exists.

I developed the specifics of these components through a systemic approach using discourse analysis (detailed in Chapter 3) and qualitative coding of the entire body of discussion groups, interviews, and questionnaires provided by the students. Examining closely the entire data corpus, I determined that each faith frame can be productively viewed as comprised of three primary components: common understandings between members of the same group, points of disagreement between them, and faith-specific issues that arise in dialogue.

The common understandings within a faith frame stem from the foundational concepts in the students' shared religious backgrounds, the spiritual paths, beliefs, and values influenced by years of involvement with a complex religious organization. This component is manifested in part through the students' core topics of concern and interest, what they choose to focus on when speaking with each other. Students are familiar with these concepts, and they easily utilize them as references in conversation; agreement is often assumed.

The points of disagreement between students of similar affiliations come from those topics that are contested within religions; they tend to be those that are debated between different denominations and what may even fundamentally divide those subgroups. They evoke passion in students because they are contested by valued others, members of their own community. Finally, the issues that arise in dialogues specific to each faith are the higher order areas of concern, those that are brought to mind as the students work together through their common understandings and points of disagreement. They may relate to the religious group's place in society, its reflections on itself, or its relationship to other worldviews and ways of being. (Religious marginalization awareness, a key factor in the frames, is discussed fully in Chapter 4 of this book.)

The frames go beyond students' perspectives on religion and spirituality. They also include perspectives on other religious groups and their ideologies, ways of relating to similar and diverse peers, and other related topics that concern them. The frames are not prescriptive, however; they allow room for growth over time and for students to change their minds, even about core beliefs, because they are attached to student learning and so develop too. For example, where a Muslim student is likely to have concern about the balance of sacred and secular behaviors in her life, her position on where to strike that balance can evolve. What will stay with her is the connection to this debate as part of her identity.

One benefit of focusing in on frames, as opposed to a stage model of development, is that frames can avoid the criticisms that have been levied against such models.[12] Frames do not list a series of tasks that individuals must pass through and do not imply that those at earlier stages of development are inferior to those who are at later ones. They take into account multiple, situated influences on identity, although certain fundamentals are likely to remain consistent over time. In addition, acknowledging that students' ideologies and values impact their ways of viewing the world leads to the consideration of multiple faith frames, allowing for still greater inclusion. Lumping all people together into a supposedly universal system does a disservice to each person. A unified system even detracts from the Christian perspective, as it brands it as neutral or baseline, stripping it of its true meaning. Allowing for a Christian frame honors Christian students as having a specific viewpoint of their own, rather than labeling their beliefs as generic ones that should be the same as all non-Christians.

Identities are constructed within groups, and individuals necessarily diverge in some respects from others in their groups of membership. People will also be changed through interactions with others. Therefore, as with all models, even faith frames by the nature of categorization will also in some ways essentialize, oversimplify, or fix people's identities. That, however, is not my intention in illustrating them. Instead, in representing the frames, I have taken care to include a wide diversity of examples of each one. In this way, I intend to demonstrate how the frames can provide a window into identity and ways of being in the world. As such they are meant to be a tool for understanding and not a classification system. To that end, the following are descriptions of the four faith frames as I came to understand them through my direct conversations with students.

---

[12]For examples of such criticisms, see Evans, Forney, and Guido-DiBrito (1998); Kuh, Whitt, and Shedd (1987); Stamm (2006); and Winkle-Wagner (2007).

CHRISTIAN FAITH FRAME

Christian students are probably the best known (in terms of their religious beliefs and practices) by campus educators and researchers on religion, spirituality, and faith. They have been the focus of abundant literature and are often treated as a sort of default definition of who college students are. Not surprisingly, Christian college students, however, are more than what is visible through a generic model. They hold a faith perspective related directly to their religious beliefs and social position.

Quotations from some of the Christian students with whom I spoke illustrate that there was a certain Christian specificity that guided their worldviews. For Kristin, Christianity had become synonymous with living a correct life:

> *"And that was when I finally understood, … 'Ok, it's not just about coming to church and … milling myself into this building with other people. It's about the community that we share together. It's about serving other people.' Just as I started to realize that being a Christian applies to every aspect of your life, and it's not an aspect of your life. You know, that was my moment, I guess, when I got it all."*
> —Kristin, 20-year-old Methodist Christian student

Brooke was specifically reacting to the Christianity of her family and her childhood church:

> *"My mom makes me go to church, but I don't like it…. If anything, it just fosters more resentment…. I mean, in my family at least, … you're not a Christian if you're not going to church, or going to church somehow defines who you are…. I feel like it's a standard that people set that's unrealistic for a lot of people, and that going to church isn't what makes someone a Christian, or what defines someone's religious experience. Some people, but not all people."*
> —Brooke, 19-year-old agnostic Christian student

David had concerns about the perception of Christianity as an aggressively and inappropriately missionary religion:

> *"I think that … when you talk to someone about your faith, … you often get the connotation that you're being religious, … you're forcing … your faith down … someone else's throat. You get that kind of a conflict."*
> —David, 18-year-old Lord of Light Lutheran Christian student

These are but three brief demonstrations of the inextricable link among these students' affiliation with Christian denominations, their understandings of faith, and their social positions. Despite these important links, which will be discussed in detail, the individual landscapes of these students' beliefs did vary. Several of these students defined themselves as being both religious and spiritual, but some did not. For some, diverging from the dominant perspective within Christianity was permissible, but for others it was not. There were many topics about which they cared to engage with each other and also difficulties inherent in such conversations.

Christianity and religion/spirituality/faith/belief in other literature. There is much in the way of previous literature that can help create a picture of Christian college students. The most influential theoretical works on faith development, which relegate Christianity to being the default worldview, are those of Fowler and Parks. In a review of the work done on faith development in the 30 years since he started his research, Fowler (2004) discovered that liberal and moderate religious groups, including United Methodists, liberal Baptists, Episcopalians, and Disciples of Christ, had found his model to be useful.

This is not to say that Fowler's theory has been warmly welcomed by all Christians, particularly when it comes to theology (Downs, 1995). Lutherans have been among the groups least receptive (Fernhout, 1986) because they believe that "if faith is a gift, the human attempt to develop one's faith is inappropriate" (Avery, 1990, p. 75). Varied reactions toward this view of faith from different denominations are explained as "while the more conservative traditions do not find the theory specific enough in theological content, some from less conservative traditions find it overly specific" (Steele, 1990, p. 93).

Moving away from the theoretical, other research has attempted to specifically describe Christians during their college years. Ma (2003) conducted a study on 59 Christian campuses. When students were asked what they perceive the influence of college experiences to be on their spiritual formation, "the five most influential items were peer relationships, working through crises while at college, personal spiritual disciplines, praise and worship sessions, and Bible or theology classes" (p. 330). Females tended to rate nonacademic experiences higher than males did.

Gender differences have been found by other researchers. Hammersla, Andrews-Qualls, and Frease (1986) conducted a study with a sample of 542 undergraduates at a Christian evangelical institution. They found a difference between the male and female participants: "Among women, God appears more salient, respected, and awesome than among men, and less punitive, indicating a greater sense of God's deistic qualities (all-wise, eternal, holy) among women and a greater unwillingness to attribute negative terms to God" (p. 430).

Bussema (1999), in a study of 127 students at a Reformed, Christian liberal arts college, also found differences between the faiths of the male and female participants, saying that "the men interviewed reported having more discussions and theological debates about religious and church issues, while the women talked more about discussions about faith life" (p. 25).

Three of the mainline Protestant denominations were singled out in the Higher Education Research Institution's (2005) Spirituality in Higher Education Study. Episcopalian students show "slightly above average scores on Charitable Involvement and Ecumenical Worldview, and relatively low scores on Religious Commitment and Religious/Social Conservativism" (p. 21). Presbyterians and members of the United Church of Christ tend to resemble students in general, meaning that they exhibit few, if any, extremities in belief. Presbyterians "earn slightly above average scores on Religious Engagement and Charitable Involvement, and relatively low scores on Religious Skepticism." Members of the United Church of Christ "score slightly below average on Religious/Social Conservativism and Religious Skepticism" (p. 22).

Notably, two other Christian denominations covered by the Higher Education Research Institution (2005), Baptists and "other Christians," are similar to each other, scoring high on the measures of Religious Commitment, Religious Engagement, Religious/Social Conservatism, Spirituality, and Equanimity, and low on Religious Skepticism. The differences between these students and the mainline denominations act as a reminder that evangelical Christian students do not necessarily inhabit the mainstream in higher education. In a 2005 study, Bryant found that "the evangelical religious organization was accepted to a point ... but it also encountered elements of disdain from some segments on campus ... and experienced intermittent collaboration and competition with the plethora of other Christian ministries on campus" (p. 23). These students may be engaged in efforts "to reveal their identity as evangelical Christians but also [attempt] to authenticate that dimension of identity" (Moran, 2007, p. 428). This may be a different priority from mainline Protestant students.

I will add to this knowledge of Christian college students by describing the particular viewpoints on religion, spirituality, God, and other elements of faith held to by six Christian students in my study. I present their perspectives using examples from the students' interactions about these topics. I assume this medium of illustration will be useful to higher education practitioners, in that seeing what these six students said can help practitioners recognize how their own students talk about their faith frames.

Getting to know six Protestant Christian college students. Before I begin, I offer more detailed description of the six Christian students who informed me of their understandings, at the time of my study, of religion and spirituality. These students affiliated with a variety of denominational backgrounds that contributed important distinctions to their individual faith perspectives. I also provide information on their views of religious privilege in society, particularly as it relates to each of them being members of the dominant group.

- David, age 18, was a White man who affiliated with the Lord of Light Lutheran denomination of Christianity. His faith was highly personalized, and he described himself as being both religious and spiritual. David was open to religious diversity but remained disconcerted by internal Christian disagreements on truth. He did not recognize the dominance of Christianity in American society, instead seeing Christians as being under attack.
- Brooke, age 19, was an African-American woman who described herself as an agnostic Christian. She had made a firm break with her family's religion and her home church. Brooke retained a lot of anger against what she perceived to be the constraints of religion, and her beliefs still existed very much in opposition to those of others. She was aware of, and disliked, Christian privilege in this country.
- Karen, age 19, was a White, Methodist Christian woman. She considered herself to be both religious and spiritual. Karen was flexible and was willing to learn. She harbored a feeling of personal connection to God. She was aware of Christian privilege in the United States but did not reflect on it very often.
- Kristin, age 20, was also a White, Methodist Christian woman. As with some of the others, she also considered herself to be both religious and spiritual. She had an awakening in her faith at the end of high school and had spent time in college finding a community to support her deepened interest in religion. She was beginning to turn away from her "own needs and selfish desires" in favor of a life dedicated to Christian values. She was somewhat inflexible and certain that her own ideas were correct. She did not discuss the possibility of Christian privilege.
- Jada, age 23, was a biracial African American/Native American and a nondenominational Christian. Of the Christian students I spoke with, she was the closest to being

a fundamentalist. She had a lifetime of exploring different churches, trying to find one that was sufficiently "operating in Spirit." Her faith was highly personalized. She did not discuss the possibility of Christian privilege; like David, she felt that Christians were on the receiving end of bias.

- Will, age 26, was an Asian-American man who affiliated with the Episcopalian denomination of Christianity. Will considered himself to be both religious and spiritual. He had a strong sense of what his key values were but was open to interpretation on smaller issues. He opposed the dominance of Christianity and was taking steps to dismantle it in America.

Of the six students, David, Karen, Kristin, and Will occupied a sort of middle ground of Christian belief. On opposite sides of the four stood Jada and Brooke, who during the dialogues were miles apart with regard to ideas. Jada took Christian teachings more literally than any of the others, whereas Brooke was ready to discard the Bible as an "absurd book of absurd fairytales." Brooke eschewed any notion of herself as religious but also had difficulty owning a self-definition as spiritual. She stated that being spiritual was "implicit," and that "it doesn't even need to be affirmed" because of its obviousness. However, with the amount of negativity Brooke expressed toward established religious belief systems, the implicitness of her spirituality was not likely to have been obvious to her fellow Christians.

Jada also tried to distance herself from classification as religious, which she defined as the "fleshly part of [herself]" that struggled to wake up on Sunday mornings for church. Instead, she worked toward the "challenging" goal of becoming "completely spiritual" in nature. To Jada, being spiritual was anything but implicit because it was a state that requires constant "will power."

The divergences between these women illustrated just one part of the multiplicity of Christian identities within this group. The students' denominational backgrounds gave them varied perspectives on diversity between religions and even within Christianity itself. Some embraced using the labels religious and spiritual as self-descriptors, whereas others rejected them based on certain subtexts to the words. The students also demonstrated different comfort levels with their own identities, which were somewhat related to their ages. Despite these obvious divergences, the students' Christian faith perspective did share sufficient commonalities that can be represented as a faith frame.

Faith frame. With all four of the faith frames being discussed in this chapter, I will delineate the three main components that comprise them: the common understandings, the points of disagreements, and the faith specific issues that arose in dialogues on these topics. The first element of the Christian faith frame was a common understanding of the meanings of the words religion and spirituality and their interpretations of the concept of God. The Christian students tended to describe religion in terms of its institutional nature, which sometimes had a negative implication. They were concerned with religion's imparting of duties and obligations, including its manifestation as church attendance:

> *"Well, 'religious' has ... implications of tradition and something ... somewhat stagnant, it seems like to me... And ... almost drone-like,... something you just do out of some sort of obligation."*
> —Jada, 23-year-old nondenominational Christian student

The Christian students most frequently described spirituality as a connection to something greater than themselves, a concept that included both specific mentions of God and more vague senses of connectedness. In addition, they viewed spirituality as personal and discrete from religion, possibly even from Christianity itself:

> *"I picture that, where spiritual—I think of more different varieties of religion, and I think of more personal and individual experiences and relationships with any sort of higher being or non-higher being, whatever the actual religion is."*
> —Karen, 19-year-old Methodist Christian student

The Christian students with whom I spoke utilized a wide variety of descriptors for their images of God. Most commonly, they described their personal relationships with God, a God in whom they believed, on whom they depended, and who was good, loving, and understanding. A very interesting element of the Christian students' images of and associations with God was the use of uniformly positive descriptors. Some other students offered statements of what God is *not* (i.e., Jewish student Joanna questioning, "One of my housemates,... she'll be like, 'I have a test, I'm worried about it, but it's in God's hands.' What does that mean? That means you don't study for it?") The Christian students did not provide this type of negative definition even once during all of their combined dialogue.

What could the possible reasons be for the Christian students to be so uniformly affirmative in their understandings of God? One potential answer is that because Christianity is the typical religion in this country, their definition of the nature of God was also conventional. No alternative understanding of God's nature was available in their repertoire, and therefore nothing required negation. Although there was recognition of other belief systems, there was an inclination toward assimilating them into the Christian worldview:

> *"God is love and because God is love, He understands the fact that there are different people in this world who … have interpreted … who He is differently. And because of that, He is more than willing to accept all those who love Him."*
> —David, 18-year-old Lord of Light Lutheran Christian student

These core definitions and beliefs were but one aspect of the common understandings inherent within the Christian faith frame. From my students, I learned that those who viewed the world through the Christian frame shared understandings of the core tenets of Christian ideology, within which they focused on Jesus Christ, the Bible, and heaven and the afterlife. These theological topics also demonstrated the speech habits of the Christian students, and how a religious understanding of the world permeated their talk. Christian ideas, which have theological bases and prominence, were spoken about freely and with the implicit understanding that listeners would be in basic agreement with them. For example, this excerpt of speech from Jada shows that she found the traits of Jesus to be so obvious to her peers that they did not even require elucidation:

> *"… and you want to delve into the Word, to get more wisdom and to change and to … be more Christ-like, which is, you know, all those great, wonderful … traits that everyone wants."*
> —Jada, 23-year-old nondenominational Christian student

The ease with which the Christian students used their own group's language in the all-Christian setting demonstrated that there was some level of common agreement and community being built between them, despite the fact that they made general protestations that they were more comfortable in the mixed settings. In the interfaith conversation, Christian students did not have to compete with students from other denominations for providing the most appropriate interpretation of Christian ideology.

Although some of them did not enjoy, per se, their experiences of talking with their fellow Christians, they were able to relate to each other in a much more familiar manner. In the interfaith dialogue, however, they found themselves having to use much more explanatory language to get their points across. For example, Kristin felt that she had the responsibility for representing all of Christianity for the students of other worldviews. A high usage of theological ideas when speaking to other Christians, contrasted with a diminished usage of similar ideas when speaking with students of other faiths, indicated that they were able to build a community among themselves (even if temporary) on the strength of these shared values. The balance between intrafaith competition and community had yet another component.

A recognition of the inherent discrepancies in beliefs and practices among each of them and among Christians of other denominational affiliations (what Karen called "different ... versions almost of Christianity") was another one of the common understandings that comprised this Christian faith frame. Will, Jada, and Brooke had all either changed their denominational affiliation or searched around for a specific church that would match their denominational commitments. Acknowledging the breadth of beliefs within Christianity, the students inquired of each other why they had made their choices.

Finally, these students shared a common understanding of the critical relationship between Christianity and other world religions. They demonstrated a range of comprehension of Christianity's place as the dominant religion in the United States, some feeling pained for the effect on other religions, some suggesting it was perhaps a myth that actually harmed Christians themselves. Either way, they knew it was considered an important component of their social standing. Will, the oldest of the Christian students with whom I talked, painstakingly described his opinion on the relationship between Christianity and other world religions:

> "I'm not going to mince words. Missionary work is fraught with problems of colonialism.... Too many Christians have conflated Western culture with Christianity. That's bad.... But ... if you go and live the Gospel,... I think people will come to ... an understanding of Christ ... that comes from their culture and is genuine."
> —Will, 26-year-old Episcopalian Christian student

Several of the points of disagreement within the Christian faith frame directly resulted from the students' common understandings. For example, while the Christian students recognized that there were inherent denominational differences in ideology, they had trouble reconciling those discrepancies with what they considered the overall truth of Christianity. These types of reactions led directly to additional competition between certain of the students to demonstrate that their chosen denominational specifics were the most legitimate. They challenged each other about the frequency of church attendance and whether it was appropriate to question one's beliefs and the teachings of one's church.

These disagreements also occurred because some students were more confident in their own internalized beliefs and were therefore more comfortable in taking Christian teachings less literally and in allowing for discrepancies among the Christian movements. In addition, tolerance of others' faith related strongly to self-confidence and self-awareness. Because others did not view their faith identities with the same assuredness, clashes arose over degrees of orthodoxy in beliefs. This was most challenging for Jada, who tended more toward fundamentalism than the others, and for David, who was relatively young and taken aback by more radical interpretations of Christianity.

In these conversations with fellow Christians, the students employed language laden with value judgments, high risk of conflict, judgment, and hurt feelings. This risk was most often averted through self-censorship but, when approached directly, often resulted in antagonism between students. Quotations from two women highlighted some of the conflicts that occurred when Christian students talked together. These excerpts came from Jada and Brooke, who again represented the extremes in diversity within the Christian conversation:

> "I felt like in our group, there were ... people who were very religious, and then people who weren't so religious, and also I feel like ... some of them assumed that because we were in the same group ... there was ... a basic understanding. But I felt like I didn't have the same basic understanding as a lot of people in the group ... and I also feel like when they were talking about things, instead of [in the interfaith group] people say, 'I believe this' and 'I think,' ... someone in front of me kept saying, 'This is how it is' and you know, 'This is what God wants.' ... I don't know, it was just really, really frustrating and ... I just felt like, 'Stop assuming ... what I think or that we agree. Or stop, you know, forcing your beliefs on me.' ... I don't know, it was really intense. Well, one particular person in the group [Jada] was just really intense."
> —Brooke, 19-year-old agnostic Christian student

> "The girl who said she'd done all she needed to do [Brooke] was right in one sense, but she on the other hand is missing out on developing a stronger relationship with God. She's missing out on the Peace because she doesn't depend on Christ hardly ever, she is missing out on all of those things mentioned above in question one. She is choosing to stay a 'baby' Christian in that she is choosing not to exercise her faith, choosing to stay weak in her faith. Which is her choice, and of course she will still go to heaven if she truly believed with her heart and only she and God will know if she truly believed into Him or not.... The only thing that was challenging for me was the feeling of heaviness afterward in my heart for the girl who was so angry and so

*gnarled up in bitterness toward her experience of humans twisting the faith.
I will pray for her."*
—Jada, 23-year-old nondenominational Christian student

There are some final notes to add about the Christian frame. It also was comprised of certain issues specific to the faith that arose in the students' dialogue, these being the legitimacy of non-Christian belief systems and a less-than-full sincerity in terms of open-mindedness toward others. The former issue was consonant with the points of disagreement just discussed because some students could make allowances in their belief systems for other religions, whereas others could not. Within the Christian students' faith frame was the implicit understanding of Christianity's societal dominance, a dominance with which they were not necessarily comfortable. This dominance was somewhat tempered by the apprehension of trampling other religions. Christian students, with their varied levels of understanding of their religion's societal privilege, may have felt some hesitance about this status and the implications for the non-Christians around them.

As for the latter, there are several possible interpretations, including a lack of full disclosure in order to protect one's vulnerable outlook, as well as a willingness to stifle one's harsher opinions to foster ecumenism. Other students chose instead to conceal their true opinions to avoid conflict during interfaith dialogues. They had different motivations for this, to either conform to the norms around them or facilitate more fluid conversation by presenting themselves in a diplomatic manner. This behavior was not specific to only the Christian students because many others self-censored for one reason or another. (The discourse strategies students employed will be discussed in depth in Chapter 3.)

Summary. The Christian students with whom I spoke were a multifaceted group whose shared faith frame extended beyond that which existing literature has said about their beliefs. These students found religion to be institutional in nature, perhaps negatively so, with spirituality as separate and more personal. They described God positively, even Brooke, who considered herself to be an agnostic. They spoke frequently of core topics of religious concern: Jesus, the Bible, church attendance, tolerance of other faith groups, and whether they should question their own beliefs.

Extrapolating beyond these specific students, the Christian faith frame appears to be fluid and changeable. The common understandings that were listed above remain foundational throughout this evolution. At the center of this frame are Christian interpretations of the world and a community of like-minded believers that have an impact on how these interpretations are developed. The changing nature of the frame leads to areas of disagreement between students, including literalism of beliefs, denominational distinctions, and how those distinctions impact the truth of Christianity. These disagreements occur because some students are more confident in their own beliefs; they are more comfortable taking Christian teachings less literally and allowing for discrepancies between the Christian movements. Because others do not view their faith identities with the same assuredness, clashes can arise over degrees of orthodoxy in beliefs.

This faith frame is unique due to Christianity's relationship with religious privilege. As we examine the other three frames, it will become clear that privilege and marginalization impact all of them, yet in critically different ways. The full impact of privilege and marginalization will be examined in depth in Chapter 4.

JEWISH FAITH FRAME

Jewish college students have not been the focus of research in higher education nearly as much as their Christian peers. Much can be learned about this population, and discussing their faith frame can contribute to this knowledge. A few quotations from Jewish college students introduce the elements of the frame. Judy's political commitments centered on the Jewish homeland of Israel:

> "I'm just ... not a very political person.... I know nothing about American politics or anything, but the only things that I kind of do know about is Israeli politics and that's what I find to be most important for me to know about.... I guess all of my politics have to do with being Jewish because I really don't know much about, and I'm not interested in knowing that much about American politics."
> —Judy, 18-year-old Conservative Jewish student

Joanna felt a deep connection to the Jewish people and the horrors they have suffered historically—despite her lack of religious observance:

> "You see it in talking about World War II. The countries practically disowned Jews until the Nazis came after the country people too, and we had nowhere to go, we didn't have a country until Israel. And I can empathize with ... these parts of Judaism, this is all the cultural stuff. You don't have to bring any religion into it to feel this connection with Jews.... I can still feel that six million of my people were murdered in the Holocaust. I can make that connection. The connection I can't make is ... why are we kosher? It doesn't make sense to me. I'm not observant, pretty much at all."
> —Joanna, 20-year-old atheist/cultural Jewish student

Jesse selected the elements of Judaism that resonated with him to incorporate into his personal observances:

> *"A guy with a black hat and a beard is most definitely not ... my ideal as a Jew or a person or anything. I see a lot wrong with that style of Judaism, that's just my personal belief.... I incorporate Judaism through my life, I think Judaism plays a big part in my life, it could play a bigger role, it could play a smaller role. But I kind of pick and choose what's right for me, what I think is being a good person. I see that kind of as the most important thing.... I guess ... the ideal is just being a good person and ... also ... be a good Jew but on your own terms, rather than on someone else's terms."*
> —Jesse, 18-year-old Jewish student

As these excerpts show, these students' Jewish religion weighed heavily in their life choices and how they viewed the world, historically, politically, and morally. Their talk, especially among each other, was heavily laden with references to Jewish obligations and ritual practice. The Jewish faith frame surrounded them, yielding shared understandings, such as the traditional boundaries of Jewish beliefs and practices and the minority position of their religious group in U.S. society. There were also specific points of disagreement, such as the acceptability of breaking with normative Jewish behavior, which demonstrated that the students also interacted with the faith frame in an individualized manner.

Judaism and religion/spirituality/faith/belief in other literature. There is some literature on Jewish college students that provides a foundation for the new understandings being presenting here. One theorist, Michael J. Shire (1987), has presented a model of Jewish faith development that is based on Fowler's work. His theory was presented briefly in Chapter 1.

Empirical work has filled in more details about Jewish college students. In a study of young adult British Jews, Sinclair and Milner (2005) found a relationship between age and security in participants' Jewish identities. Older participants were "more concerned than their younger counterparts to identify sources of spiritual meaning and value in their lives . . . and, specifically, what made Jewish observance worthwhile" (p. 110). For all participants, new situations were triggers to reexamining identity issues; for the younger adults, this happened upon entry to college, and for those in their later 20s, it was the start of a new job.

In 2002, Hillel: The Foundation for Jewish Campus Life commissioned researchers at Higher Education Research Institution (HERI) to use national data to compare Jewish students to the general student population, both in the 1999 cohort and in trends since 1971 (Sax, 2002). Briefly summarized, they found that Jewish freshmen have higher "intent to participate in volunteer or community service while in college" (p. 6), "less frequent attendance at religious services, fewer hours per week devoted to praying/meditating, and lower levels of 'spirituality' " (p. 6), and they are more committed to "keeping up to date with political affairs, developing a meaningful philosophy of life, and helping to promote racial understanding" (p. 50).

Bryant (2006) had the following findings for her sample of 2,100 Jewish college students in the College Students' Beliefs and Values Pilot Survey (Higher Education Research Institution, 2003): 75% of Jewish students self-rate as the most compassionate religious group (Bryant, 2006, p. 7). Eighty percent have the same religion as their parents, but most are not very inclined to say that they have a spiritual guide in their lives. Relatively few self-identify as religious (19%), report praying (45%), or believe in God (60%).

Also according to the recent Higher Education Research Institution (2005) data on spirituality:

> Jewish students earn above average scores on Ecumenical World-view, Ethic of Caring, and especially Religious Skepticism, and below average scores on Religious Commitment, Religious Engagement, and Religious/Social Conservativism.... [Their] scores on Spirituality tend to be considerably below average.... Jewish students obtain only average scores on Spiritual Quest and Charitable Involvement. (p. 21)

Other studies have shown Jewish college students to differ from Christian college students. According to Mayhew (2004), Jewish students are likely to frame their spiritual experiences in terms of their families, whereas Christian students are likely to frame them in terms of God. The Jewish students in Zabriskie's (2005) study differed significantly from the Christian students, with only 41.2% defining themselves as both spiritual and religious, compared with 65.5% of Catholics, 69.1% of non-Evangelical Protestants, and 71.1% of Evangelicals.

I will add to this existing literature base on Jewish college students by describing the particular perspectives on religion, spirituality, God, and other elements of their faith of five Jewish students. Their perspectives help define an otherwise understudied population with a long-standing, important presence on American campuses.

Getting to know five Jewish college students. Five Jewish students informed me of their understandings of religion, spirituality, and faith based on their Jewish perspectives on the world. They also shared their viewpoints on religious privilege. These students were:

- Sam, age 18, was a White, Conservative Jewish man. He considered the terms religious and spiritual to be equivalent, identifying himself as both. He had made very few changes in his beliefs since coming to college. His participation in the discussion groups, however, introduced him to some new ideas that caused some reconsideration. Sam's position on privilege was that Jews are victimized abroad, but he had little to say about how this may operate in the United States.

- Judy, age 18, was a White, Conservative Jewish woman. She explained that there were both spiritual and religious aspects to her Jewish activities. She came to college with the realization that she had to better embrace her religious identity so that others would recognize it. She chose a Jewish peer group to support her growth. Judy felt a vague negative social status impact because of her Jewishness.

- Jesse, age 18, was a White man who defined himself as Jewish without a specific denomination. He described his religion as being through Judaism and his spirituality as being "more common." He had conducted personal exploration of Judaism to determine what he believes. He was not fully settled on all his values and expressed some doubts. Jesse did not note any social status disadvantages having to do with being Jewish, but he saw some opportunities for empowerment.

- Joanna, age 20, was a White woman who described herself as a cultural/atheist Jew and was previously affiliated with the Reform denomination. She did not consider herself to be either religious or spiritual. Joanna grew up in a household where religion was not discussed much, and she was facing new confrontations over religion. She resisted any modifications in her own ideas, and she was often reactionary to the practices of others. She felt a certain amount of anger toward the religious and was caught between her two forms of identity. Joanna felt herself to be negatively influenced by Jewish social status, believing that it provided her with no benefits.

- Jasmine, age 21, was a Reconstructionist Jewish White woman. She defined herself as religious through Judaism but found her spirituality to be more universal in nature, a feeling of connection that was "something meaningful but not Jewish." Jasmine was dealing with the experience of having minority beliefs within her own religious group. Although she was confident in her beliefs and has thought them through, she was still influenced by the judgments of those around her. Jasmine believed it was a mixed blessing that Jews had been easily able to assimilate into American culture.

These students were not a uniform group of Jewish young adults. They held a range of comfort levels with their own faith identities, some questioning portions of Jewish doctrine and others accepting Jewish teachings in a less critically examined way. Their attitudes toward Judaism itself also varied, with some embracing it wholeheartedly and others feeling more ambivalent.

In addition, three of the students, Judy, Sam, and Jesse, represented the broad middle of the road of American Judaism. The former two identified with Conservative Judaism (33% of the American Jews who are synagogue members, as opposed to only 2% who are Reconstructionists[13] like Jasmine); Jesse, while not declaring a denomination, fit with them ideologically. In addition, they all told stories of Jewish private schools, camps, fraternity/sorority houses, and/or the campus Hillel Foundation and admitted that most of their friends are Jewish. This contrasted with Jasmine and Joanna, who did not embrace this type of Judaism-permeated lifestyle and harbored beliefs that were strongly opposed to the Jewish mainstream.

Faith frame. Just as with the others, the Jewish faith frame is divided into three main components (the common understandings, points of disagreements, and the faith-specific issues that arose in their dialogues on these topics). The first elements were their common understandings of the meanings of the words religion and spirituality and their interpretations of the concept of God.

The Jewish students with whom I spoke were unique from the other three groups of students, in that they were more aligned within their group in the definitions of religion and spirituality they offered. They tended to describe religion as being related to one's ritual or observance level, which made sense given the practice focus of Judaism:

> *"To me … religion is more—I feel most Jewish when I'm praying or doing something."*
> —Judy, 18-year-old Conservative Jewish student

As with their Christian peers, the Jewish students most frequently described spirituality as a connection to something greater than themselves. Interestingly, two other definitions demonstrated an internal difference in thought within this group, as some students felt that spiritual-

---

[13]According to the United Jewish Communities (2003).

ity was discrete from religion, whereas others felt that spirituality was the same or tightly linked with religion. This pairing was particularly noteworthy due to their complete mutual exclusivity. Two student quotations highlighted this difference:

> *"I have two definitions of spiritual. One,... that kind of not really fitting into any religion sort of one-with-nature spiritual sort of sense and then also spiritual does seems to imply a connection with God regardless of religion."*
> —Joanna, 20-year-old atheist/cultural Jewish student

> *"Whenever I have an experience that could be considered religious or spiritual, I automatically classify it in the religious category, just 'cause ... I'm pretty sure every experience that can be considered spiritual has something to do with religious, and I just kind of let them both ... kind of mesh, at least for me, just because,... my spirituality comes from my religion. It comes from the fact that I consider myself religious, and comes from ... going to services, comes from ... kind of acting Jewish-ly, and ... having kind of a Jewish mind.... So my spirituality comes from my religiousness, so it's very hard to separate the two."*
> —Sam, 18-year-old Conservative Jewish student

The Jewish students were very different from the Christian students in the ways they described God. They generally viewed God as being a source of tests, and that their lives were a matter of God's will. This also encapsulated the idea that God creates challenges and barriers for humans to overcome, the reasons for some of which are beyond our ability to comprehend. In addition, the Jews conceived of God as being all-powerful and/or all-knowing.

The Jewish students also provided definitions of what God is not. They were not convinced of having a personal relationship with God (a common belief among the Christians) or of being dependent on God (a common belief among the Muslims). According to Jesse, God is not the obstacle of free will ("God can't make it that everyone's good. Because then ... there wouldn't be free will because everyone just would do good"). Joanna did not believe in leaving important matters "in God's hands" and was not "afraid of what God is going to do to" her because she did not think there was a God taking such an active role in human affairs. Jasmine wasn't even sure that the name God means the same thing to all people ("God isn't actually one thing").

They may have provided these negations as a way of compensating for the dominant Christian image of the divine in American society. Jasmine simply did not understand the mindset of having a personal and direct connection with God:

*"I don't really ... talk to God really; specifically ... I can't imagine saying
like, 'Please God save me' or something. I don't have that kind of relationship.... Like, I would never pray to God."*
—Jasmine, 21-year-old Reconstructionist Jewish woman

It is also important to note that two Jewish students, the women who
did not fall in the mainstream of Judaism, had some doubts and even
strong disbelief in God. Jasmine described a period of time during middle and high school when she did not believe in God. During this time,
she did not abandon her religious community, and at the time of the
study she maintained ties with her home synagogue even as her beliefs
had returned in a more complex form. As Joanna explained in the mixed
group, Judaism is a multifaceted faith that incorporates religion and ethnicity; doubt and disbelief do not result in immediate exclusion from the
community. She, therefore, could define herself as an atheist/cultural Jew
and have that label make some sense.

Even as Joanna and Jasmine doubted and questioned, they did so
within a Jewish framework. These core definitions and beliefs were but
one part of the common understandings inherent within the Jewish faith
frame. I learned from my students that those who viewed the world
through the Jewish faith frame were focused on religious rituals and the
choices people make to practice them or not, as well as Judaism's place in
the world in comparison to other religions. The rituals they needed to
make choices about included keeping kosher, studying Torah, observing
holidays, and even participating in the campus Hillel chapter. As Jewish
students discussed these areas of concern, they also addressed whether to
accept the divergent beliefs of other religious groups, their family members' religious practices, and the relationship between Jewish religion and
Jewish culture.

Much like the Christian students, the Jewish students talked easily
about their beliefs and practices when they were in their intrafaith discussion group. For example, the vast majority of their uses of Hebrew took
place in that session or in the one-on-one interviews with me (who, again,
they knew is Jewish). The frequency of this dropped dramatically in the
mixed sessions. Like the Christian students, this evidenced some form of
community having been established in the session despite some of the
students' later declarations that they felt uncomfortable there.

Aside from these common understandings, however, contentions did
arise during dialogue among these Jewish college students. The areas of
disagreement that became apparent were the acceptability of breaking
with normative Jewish behavior and the place of certain beliefs in the
core of Jewish ideology. An excerpt from one student demonstrated this
idea of normative beliefs:

"As far as political view points are concerned, my Judaism makes me very, very Zionistic.... I feel like it's an obligation,... almost even ... a religious obligation ... to be supportive of Israel and to be supportive of the Jewish homeland."
—Sam, 18-year-old Conservative Jewish student

These two points of disagreement were tightly linked, as a student who was more tolerant of breaks in normative behavior was also more accepting of breaks in normative beliefs. This in turn was likely linked with individual students' comfort levels with their own Jewish faith identities. Those who harbored their beliefs uncritically, or who were reactionary toward others, may not have felt comfortable with someone who had a faith identity that was individualized and therefore not wholly consistent with literal religious teachings. In addition, this focus on what was normative, or *normal,* indicated a certain concern with uniformity, as if any form of dissension weakened the group as a whole.

One particular break with normative Jewish behavior and beliefs deserves more detailed attention. Although not a ritual per se, the topic of Israel was particularly delicate for many Jewish students. For some, an emotional connection to the country went hand in hand with their religious beliefs. Some individuals also connected with the place spiritually but rejected aligning their political views with that connection. For those students, voicing this dissenting opinion could have been a risky move, particularly within a small or closely knit Jewish campus community. To speak out against Israel's policies could have been to risk being ostracized by Jewish peers. To not speak out, however, could have been to risk emotional or cognitive dissonance surrounding a critical belief. In the following quotation, Jasmine expressed concern that she would be judged by other Jewish students for admitting that political support of Israel was not a part of her identity. Her primary concern in this moment was the acceptance of other Jewish students:

"In a conversation, those are not always things I think I would say to a group of Jews just because ... I always feel judged or ... not as Jewish or like I have to ... make up for it in some way ... I'll feel myself ... talking about ... studying the Torah or something because I want to show that I still have a connection.... When I think about it rationally, it's not important to me, I don't feel like I have to be proven in somebody's eyes that I am Jewish. If I think I'm Jewish, I'm Jewish."
—Jasmine, 21-year-old Reconstructionist Jewish student

As the topic of Israel demonstrated, it was their Jewish conversation partners who would call them out for straying too far from the condoned

path or make them feel as if they did not belong in their own community. For good or for bad, the Jewish students felt a connection to each other
that did not necessarily automatically exist with students from other
faiths:

> *"I do tend to connect more with other Jews then I would with Christians or
> Muslims, I mean, not that I can't be friends with them. But there is a con-
> nection because I know you're Jewish. I know you have this similar back-
> ground,... maybe at a different level but you know, you're gonna know what
> I'm talking about when I go 'oy vey.' You know, it's just that connection."*
> —Joanna, 20-year-old atheist/cultural Jewish student

I would add a final note about the Jewish frame, that one important
component was the issues specific to the faith that arose in the students'
dialogue. In particular, the concern for the places of oneself and others
within the Jewish community may have been important to those who
were still unsure of their places in a new college environment. Such students were negotiating their positions relationally, and relational work is
potentially conflict-ridden. The same can be said for those concerned
with establishing the place of Judaism in a Christian-dominant society,
especially at a time when Jewish students were learning that being part
of a minority group compelled one to stand up for the rights of one's
group. Again, these issues reflected a certain amount of anxiety that permeated the Jewish faith frame, an uneasiness with the place of Jews in the
microcosm of college campuses and the macrocosm of broader society.

Summary. The concept of a Jewish faith frame provides more information than was already known about these students from previous
research and theory. The Jewish students were similar to the others in
more frequently describing religion as ritualistic. Like the other religious
students, they considered spirituality to be a connection to something
greater, although they differed within their group as to whether spirituality and religion were discrete. They were also unique, however, in
terms of their descriptions of God, spending nearly as much time talking
about what God is *not* as about what God *is*. Their conversations, both in
this type of intrafaith discussion and in Jewish home bases such as Hillel
and fraternity/sorority houses, reinforced their focus on core beliefs and
practices. They cared to talk about topics important to their faith: Israel,
Jewish culture, the religious practices of their family members, tolerance
of other faiths, and whether their needs could be met by campus religious
groups.

Expanding beyond these five students, this faith frame is distinct
from the Christian frame, in part due to Judaism's status in between the

privilege of the religious over the nonreligious in this country and the marginalization consequent of the dominance of the Christian religion in particular over minority religions. The reason for this in-between status for Jewish college students likely relates to the fine line generally being walked by Jews in this country between assimilation into broader American culture and maintaining a distinctly Jewish identity (Amyot, 1996; Cohen, 1988). Jewish students must straddle two social positions, and it is clear that the tenuousness of this is related to a certain level of anxiety among them. This anxiety propels them to question each other and their behavioral decisions, and to feel concern when others are not toeing the line of what they believe to be acceptable. As we next examine the Muslim faith frames, it will continue to become clear that privilege and marginalization yields a sort of complicated bridging situation for students of both of these minority religions.

MUSLIM FAITH FRAME

Just as with Jewish college students, their Muslim peers have not been the focus of much research in the field of higher education. Knowledge of a faith frame specific to their worldview will go a long way toward improving this situation. Several quotations from the Muslim students with whom I spoke introduce elements of their identities. Yusuf embraced the prophet Mohammed as a model for his moral behavior:

> *"We haven't been acting right,... our community hasn't, and I guess maybe in selfish ways ... so ... it makes me feel like we have to ... change ourselves first. We have to ... start acting right, start having ... love for each other and thinking about each other... One saying that I feel ... is missing is ... that the prophet Mohammed [said] ... 'One does not believe until he loves for his brother what he loves for himself.' Which means, ... one is not ... truly Muslim until he is unselfish basically. And that's missing a lot as we can see ... in the Arab world."*
> —Yusuf, 19-year-old Muslim student

Sabur questioned his faith in God but from the Muslim perspective:

> *"So the questions are like, why would it benefit me to believe in God? What is God to me if I can't touch God? ... I love science, and that's probably what I'm going to major in. So a huge thing in science is ... concrete belief, but ... how? And I don't believe there's ... really concrete proof of God, other than if you believe that God created the earth and that would be a concrete proof. But that still takes a leap and bounds for beliefs,... that's still blind faith, and ... I've always questioned,... why have blind faith? And ... I find it easier*

and more relaxing to believe in something greater than you, and not believe that you are the greatest thing, because I follow the belief that there's always something better than you out there."
—Sabur, 19-year-old Muslim student

Shashi utilized the cultural elements of being a Muslim in America to help define her political beliefs and personal actions:

"Being a Muslim with ... all the news coverage on Muslims across the world, ... you kind of wield this power by being, ... 'that Muslim girl' or ... just a Muslim in general... I think, to some extent I like to play the analogy that ... Muslims today are ... the angry, raging teenager that doesn't really know where they stand on issues but we're trying to figure it out... As a Muslim,... I feel ... I use my religion as kind of a political ... sword more so than ... defining my life and ... my individual actions."
—Shashi, 18-year-old Muslim student

These excerpts demonstrated that the Muslim students with whom I spoke had many questions about determining the religious elements of their identity with the secular world around them. They did not, however, question the existence of God or their obligation to consider God throughout their daily actions. They also bore a heavy social burden for Islam itself, feeling themselves to be obligatory representatives of their people to the non-Muslims around them. This responsibility contrasted with the fact that not all of the students sought religious and spiritual outlets for their own personal satisfaction.

Islam and religion/spirituality/faith/belief in other literature. Some literature exists on Muslim college students, although not nearly enough in this diverse, post-September 11th world wherein Islam and Muslims are frequently scrutinized. Although "Muslim students are increasingly visible on college and university campuses across the country" (Leonard, 2003, p. 111), Islam has only minimally been integrated into the higher education and developmental theory literature bodies. The important religious identity development model created by Lori Peek (2005) was presented in Chapter 1.

Other literature helps create a picture of Muslim college students. Bryant (2006) found the 826 Muslim college students who were in her sample to be highly religiously active, more so than any of the other minority religious groups she examined. She describes them in the following way:

> Muslim students are the most religiously devout in both belief and behavior compared to other religious minority groups. This trend is apparent in how they perceive themselves religiously and spiritually relative to peers, their fervent belief in God, their commitment to prayer and religious service attendance, and the evident link between faith and the central aspects of their identity and life purpose. Coinciding with their high levels of religiousness, Muslim students' faith is rooted in strong familial bonds. Nearly all Muslim students share the same religious preference as their parents and are more inclined than other groups to "frequently" discuss religion and spirituality in the context of family conversations. Although many do not feel disillusioned with their religious upbringing, close to one-third feel obligated "to a great extent" to follow their parents' religion. (Bryant, 2006, p. 21)

Despite this family connection, Muslim undergraduates are often interested in expressing their religious beliefs more publicly than their parents ever did (Mubarak, 2007). This is not easy. Two Muslim women writing about their own experiences (Nasir & Al-Amin, 2006) described experiencing "negative stereotyping, difficulty practicing their religion, and discrimination" (p. 22) on college campuses. In addition, Mayhew (2004) states that Muslim students have a close relationship with God and remain heavily connected to parents and other role models.

Finally, in a small qualitative study focused on Muslim women, Cole and Ahmadi (2003) found that the primary reasons that young Muslim women began veiling were "parental expectations, peer pressure and religious obligation," all of which added up to "establishing a 'good Muslim' identity" (p. 54). Women who eventually chose to stop veiling usually did so when negative reactions from non-Muslims caused them to reevaluate their belief in the practice. Those who continued to veil despite obstacles expressed that the criticism helped to build up their resolve.

I plan to add to this existing knowledge base about Muslim college students by presenting their faith frame, and in particular discussing their viewpoints on religion, spirituality, and God. There is much we can learn about these students to better serve them and their specific needs during their college years.

Getting to know five Muslim college students. I would next like to introduce the five Muslim students who informed me of their understandings of religion, spirituality, and faith, and helped me to build knowledge of the Muslim faith frame. I also include their perspectives on religious privilege and marginalization, which are especially critical in this post-September 11th world.

- Inaara, age 18, described herself as a Sunni Muslim, Persian woman. She refused to use the labels religious and spiritual, favoring instead her own label, *God conscious*. She was the Muslim student who gave priority to her religion in the most publicly visible way, given that she wore the *hijab*. She had found a way to shape her life to keep both the secular and religious elements of it progressing. She did not display a complex understanding of Muslims as a minority within the United States. However, she did express concern that the Muslim political focus was confined to world issues such as Iraq and tended to overlook "America's third world."
- Shashi, age 18, was a Muslim, Asian-American woman. She had let her religious life recede in college. Without a community around her, she did not give it as much attention or thought. Shashi resisted any form of self-labeling, memorably conceding herself to be "selectively spiritual." She was aware of Muslims' place in society, seeing them as negatively marginalized. She felt a vague sense of empowerment due to this but did not necessarily act on it.
- Sabur, age 19, was a Muslim, Asian-American man. He had given religion less priority since being in college and was concerned about this. Sabur did not address a spiritual side of his identity and refuted the idea of being a religious Muslim. He had not been able to find a way to successfully express his religion. Although he had many interpretations of the meaning of his religion, he did not tend to act on them. Sabur's awareness of Muslim marginalization had some complexity to it, as he also considered the role played by race.
- Yusuf, age 19, identified as a Middle Eastern, Muslim man. He perceived his development to be gradual because he still lived at home with his parents. He had made individual determinations about religion and tended to use religion to both serve his life and live out his responsibilities. He resisted using any common term similar to religious or spiritual to label himself. Yusuf was aware of the negative elements of Muslims' social status and used them to motivate himself toward positive action.
- Suha, age 19, was a Muslim, Asian-American woman. In describing her self-understanding, she used the word faith in addition to spirituality, but she did not employ the word religious in any way. She had developed a complex faith identity that was informed academically and through experiences with family and peers. She considered herself a pluralist and was

open to rethinking her ideas and continuing to grow. She was comfortable with living her Islamic life in a secular world. She expressed concern for the denominational divisions and violence within Islam, seeing the social position of Muslims as internally complex.

Despite their closeness in age, the faith identities of these five young adult Muslims varied greatly. Not all were completely sure of their beliefs or that the university they attended offered them the outlets they desired for religious expression. The basic terms religious and spiritual were even contested. Interestingly, one commonality between them was that they all had a heightened awareness of Islam's marginalized status in the United States, although their responses to that fell along a spectrum.

Faith frame. I once again begin elucidating the Muslim faith frame with their shared definitions of the terms religion and spirituality, as well as their conceptualizations of God. The Muslim students most commonly discussed religion as relating heavily to duties and obligations, as well as to rituals and one's level of religious observance:

> *"I guess the structures that are in my religion, like the example that was set by the prophet Mohammed—you know,... how you eat ... with your right hand—all those ... small things, like ... respecting your parents is a major thing—how you treat others is another thing—and ... all these are ... guidelines that are set by God for me and so it defines ... how I act with others."*
> —Inaara, 18-year-old Sunni Muslim student

It was beyond this definition, which was not particularly different from those of the other three groups of students, that their understandings of this term began to vary. The Muslim students uniquely considered religion as the expression of their daily lives, what Sabur called "the daily grind of being a Muslim." They also discussed the relationship between religion and morality, what Suha called "kind of a code of conduct." This topic, interestingly, although hardly of note to the Christians and Jews (with two comments each), was also considered important among atheist/agnostic students. Finally, in a nod to the current state of the world, they also saw religion as being inextricably linked with politics and government.

In terms of spirituality, the Muslim students defined it mostly in a similar way to the other religiously affiliated students as a connection to something greater than themselves. They did push back on this term, however, some rejecting what they perceived to be a false dichotomy between religion and spirituality. For example:

"It is difficult, as a Muslim, to consider religion and spirituality on two different poles. Islam very much integrates these two things."
—Suha, 19-year-old Muslim student

In addition, Shashi and Sabur described finding spirituality as problematically linked with "fuzzy, New Age, hippie" behavior. Perhaps if spirituality truly was completely interwoven into the Muslim religion, defining it as separate or outside the purview of religion lent an air of fuzziness or vagueness to it.

The Muslim students described themselves as strongly believing in God. They depended on God in daily life, had a personal relationship with God, and did their best to be "God conscious." Shashi described her challenges with the latter:

"I keep God in my mind throughout the day, to some extent for selfish reasons when I am in a tough spot. I remember God; I pray ..., you know, 'Help me through this.' ... It's probably not the best thing because [you] probably should remember Him regardless."
—Shashi, 18-year-old Muslim student

The Muslim students expressed no doubt in God's existence. Despite reservations about specific Islamic beliefs and practices, God was never questioned. In addition, the Muslim students did not offer any negative definitions of God, here matching the Christian students. Many of their positive God images also paralleled those of the Christians. Despite the differing theological constructions in the ways Muslims and Christians relate to God, the God concept itself was highly overlapping. A quotation from Inaara demonstrated the sheer incomprehensibility the students felt over questioning God's existence:

"I've always ... tried to think, what would it be like if I didn't believe in God? I tried to put myself in that mind frame, but it's always so difficult for me, and I've never really been able to understand that. I guess my faith is ... so driven within me that ... I never could really understand the whole questioning one God and such."
—Inaara, 18-year-old Sunni Muslim student

The Muslim faith frame is comprised of additional common understandings. In addition to their desire to distinguish their conceptualizations of religion and spirituality from those more commonly utilized in society, the students were focused on the ideas of proper behavior and humility. The topics that they discussed most heavily included prayer, dietary restrictions, anti-Islam sentiments, immigration and immigrant status, race and racial identity, and wars around the world. Their areas of concern were timely and highly pressured. These were five young Muslim adults who were concerned with behaving in ways that were in accordance with the guidelines of their religion. This included both personal acts, such as frequently praying to God, as well as the public acts of demonstrating to society the types of people that Muslims truly are. Yusuf explained the latter point to his fellow participants in an interfaith discussion:

> "And then I guess an ideal,... as a member of the Muslim community,... just enhancing the community,... especially here in America where there's so much bad PR for Muslims—it's really emphasized,... as a responsibility of every Muslim to ... be a good image ... to the world around, like act right, don't be disrespectful, know that ... you can ... affect how people perceive your religion."
> —Yusuf, 19-year-old Muslim student

As for whether they did and should question the beliefs handed down to them through Islamic theology, the students were in favor of it, especially during these politically trying times:

> "Before then you would go to Islamic school on Sunday, just take in all the information you got, you know, blindly accept it, but ... with 9-11 you were forced to not only defend yourself, but also know exactly what you thought and where you stood."
> —Shashi, 18-year-old Muslim student

Although it was not one of the most talked about topics with any of the groups of students, it is important to note that the Muslims did mention the events of September 11th and its aftermath a handful of times.[14] When accompanied by topics related to immigration, race, and war, one can clearly see that the Muslim students were thinking quite heavily about their status in society. Interestingly, none of the students mentioned any incidents of being on the receiving end of prejudice after September 11th. They were much more circumspect about the impact of that day upon their lives:

---

[14]For context, note that these conversations took place during the winter and spring of 2007.

*"The beginning of my freshman year [of high school] was when 9-11 hap-
pened,... So ... the way we talked about Islam would be a lot of the time students in the class asking me specifically questions.... 'Cause I was well-liked
in high school and it was nice that I felt good that my peers could be able to
talk to someone ... about, you know, 'I'm seeing this kind of stuff on the TV
and why is it that you're so different?' "*
—Suha, 19-year-old Muslim student

These Muslim students were quite concerned with living their lives
according to their religion. Like other religious students, they more easily discussed this lifestyle among each other, rather than with diverse
peers. For example, Arabic words or phrases were used nearly three
times as much in the Muslim discussion group as they were across all of
the interfaith groups combined. It was, however, perhaps due to the
heightened awareness of religion and status that made talk among
Muslim peers more tense, as the students risked alienation from the
group if they overstepped commonly agreed on boundaries around belief
and practice. Yet this situation also offered high reward, as they were able
to utilize the familiar language of their people. As with the other students
of religious backgrounds, they may have felt more comfortable being
open in the mixed setting, but they were more easily able to build communities of understanding with other Muslims. The following quotation
illustrated the bind felt by one student:

*"I'm Muslim so I tried joining ... the Muslim Students Association, and I
didn't like it very much ... because of how conservative they were, and I feel
that I don't want to be labeled in that kind of conservative atmosphere as
much.... I want to be labeled as a more liberal Muslim and I feel that my
horizon's really limited inside the Muslim Students Association, especially
this past year.... Well the thing is, with ... conservative religion, it seems
more fanatical at times across the board, like, conservative Christianity, conservative Judaism, conservative Islam, seems kind of radical, not really mal-
leable to ... social changes and things of that nature. And I feel like if you're
part of a more liberal crowd or more of ... a centrist crowd you can have more
of an opportunity to bend to the social times a little bit better than what a
conservative base would be able to do."*
—Sabur, 19-year-old Muslim student

Despite the consensus around displaying proper, humble behavior to
boost the social standing of Muslims in the United States, the students
did disagree over the priority of having a religious life in a secular society and the overall value of having a spiritual identity. In fact, this lack of
prioritization by some students came into direct conflict with that overriding desire to live as a valuable representative of Islam. It is possible to

say that, for some, this was the main motivator, and personal benefit would not otherwise be enough of a catalyst to lead to religious and spiritual expression.

Finally, the Muslim faith frame was also comprised of certain Islam-specific issues that arose in the students' dialogue. The students felt their peers were highly influential in the securing of their places in the Muslim community. This was apparent in their dialogue, as the students utilized their statements of faith to appear to be in conformity. They also modified their language to reach understanding with non-Muslims. There were different motivations for this, either conforming to the secular norms around them or the more complicated choice to present oneself in a diplomatic manner that better facilitates conversation. One woman surprised herself by editing her language to reach out to an atheist student:

> "I notice actually ever since I sat here [in the interfaith discussion] ... I didn't say 'God' once, even though I'm very much a believer in ... monotheism, and that there is one God behind everything and that we must submit solely to Him. But ... I don't view it as a completely singular view."
> —Suha, 19-year-old Muslim student

Summary. The concept of a Muslim faith frame adds to the preexisting knowledge about these students from previous research and theory. Like the rest of the students in the study, the Muslim students heavily discussed the ritual aspects of religion. However, they defined it somewhat differently, as the manifestation of daily life and a moral imperative, in addition to the standard understanding. Their definitions of spirituality incorporated the usual connection to something greater, as well as the less favorable labeling of it as fuzzy. They described God in wholly positive terms as one they depended on, had faith in and a personal relationship with, and who remained in their thoughts constantly. They were interested in speaking about important topics to their faith and culture: prayer, proper behavior, how to best represent Muslims to the rest of society, whether to question their beliefs, and various anti-Islam sentiments and political situations occurring throughout the world.

The Muslim students seemed to be the most highly attuned to the fact that they resided in two distinct worlds, the religious and the secular, or they at least had the strongest perception that this duality existed for them. All of them distinctly experienced their minority status, although some saw this status more strongly and usually more negatively. This important connection between the different faith frames and religious privilege and marginalization will be discussed more fully in Chapter 4.

Extrapolating beyond these specific students, we can see that embedded within the Muslim faith frame is an awareness that Islam must be in dialogue with other religions in order to be accepted and understood. Even more so than with Jews, Muslims perceive themselves to be in the spotlight socially, so they experience pressure, both externally and internally motivated, to represent Muslims positively to others. They focus intensely on proper behavior (including restrictions on drinking and smoking) because these are both religiously prescribed and easily observed by others. They also wonder about the appropriateness of questioning one's beliefs, as if any reconsideration would be taken as a sign of ideological flaws in their religion.

ATHEIST/AGNOSTIC FAITH FRAME

Perhaps the least understood of the four types of students, this last group features atheist, agnostic, and otherwise heterodox students—those who reject God, struggle with an unsettled decision about God's existence, or perhaps have no inclination to even consider God. Their unique faith identities have received comparably little attention in the literature and practice of student affairs. Despite what is generally known about them, this absent or conflicted view of God does not preclude a full and complex belief system that incorporates the many nuances of faith. Quotations from the students with whom I spoke highlight their distinct feelings of separation from the religiously committed. Carl described other people's lack of understanding of where nontheistic morals originate from:

"I get frustrated to no end with the sort of prevalent cultural idea that, 'Oh ... you don't believe in God so you must not have any morals. You must not ... look at the world in any sort of systematic way whatsoever. You just go around doing whatever you please because you don't fear any sort of punishment or whatever.' And ... obviously, I think, ... most people here [in the intrafaith group] wouldn't agree with that."
—Carl, 23-year-old unaffiliated, atheist student

Misty set up her spiritual identity partially as a reaction against her mother's Christian identity:

"The only way I would define myself as spiritual is when I'm defending myself against my mother when she says that I have no religion, that I'm going through a phase. So I had to come up with something to kind of counteract that."
—Misty, 21-year-old unaffiliated, agnostic student

Rick also defined himself partially against external worldviews to help understand his own beliefs as they had changed over time:

"I've been thinking about ... the knee jerk reaction I had to religion for awhile when I started going to [the Unitarian Universalist group], and how I wasn't willing to call it worship to myself because I didn't like that. Worship always connoted worshipping something, other than being and being with one another, and so I've gotten over that a bit. But religion, I still can't say that religion is something that's important to me, because to me religion still has some sort of meaning to it that it's set, it's defined, and it's static. And that's the antithesis of my religion at this point. So, it's still kind of just a knee jerk reaction to growing up a Roman Catholic and not really finding that to work out and things like that."
—Rick, 20-year-old multispiritual,[15] atheist student

These students' words demonstrated that so many elements of their identities diverged from those of students' with religious commitments. Their disbelief in God was related to separations from religious establishments and what the students associated as the negative qualities of those institutions. Their moral codes originated from a different source, one that did not rely on the ruling of an ultimate judge. Their moments of spiritual connectedness emanated from alternate sources as well, as they placed emphasis on the personal and internal and questioned the influence of institutional channels of inspiration. They also struggled with their places relative to religion, and their comfort levels with the religious around them, splitting from the religious in their lack of belief in God and usually, lack of involvement in organized religion.

Atheism/agnosticism and religion/spirituality/faith/belief in other literature. According to Nash (2003), who has written on fostering religious pluralism in higher education, religious and spiritual observances of all varieties have become highly tolerated on college campuses. The revival of religion has also been noted in the higher education literature. But, Nash says, atheists have not been accorded the same respect on campus or attention in journals.

Their lack of God belief has earned them some condescension from the developmental theorist Fowler. He stated in an interview early in his career that nontheists tend to advance through the early stages of faith in his model more quickly than do theists due to the rational, critical environments in which they usually grow up (Kuhmerker, 1978). However,

---

[15]Rick is described throughout the text as "multispiritual." This is being used to represent his self-definition as "Druid, Unitarian Universalist, Secular Humanist, Zen."

he has not spoken positively about their ability to move beyond his Stages 3 or 4:

> When teaching college sophomores and freshmen, I encountered a number of Stage 3 atheists and agnostics. At present our society seems to be populated by a substantial number of Synthetic-Conventional adherents of what might be called a "low" civil religion that involves mainly tacit trust in and loyalty to a composite of values such as material success, staying young, and getting the children out successfully on their own. (Fowler, 1981, p. 249)

This dismissal of nonbelievers as not being able to advance beyond a strictly rational worldview has hardly been directly challenged in other literature. There is no American theory on the faith development of atheists. Markus Achermann's (1981) theory was described in Chapter 1.

There is some additional existing literature that helps complete the picture of the varied identities of atheists and other non-God-believing college students. In a study of 150 college students in Glasgow, Scobie (1994) found that 40% of students declared ideologies that were a negation of some aspect of religion or politics. This either occurred because these students' own worldviews were not highly organized and personally understood or because their beliefs were systematized against a targeted, rejected belief system.

Hunsberger and several colleagues examined the patterns of doubt and fundamentalism among 348 undergraduates. They found that doubters have different ways of thinking about religion, being low on measures of religious fundamentalism. Unlike those scoring high in fundamentalism, they tend to respond to divergences between their beliefs and those of religious authorities by moving away from religion, as opposed to conceding that the religious teaching is the correct interpretation. The authors conclude with the suggestion that thinking about "religious issues may precede a drop in religiosity for some people" (Hunsberger, Alisat, Pancer, & Pratt, 1996, p. 211).

According to the Higher Education Research Institution (2005), students marking their religious affiliation as "None" had the highest levels of Religious Skepticism of all faith groups and the lowest levels of Religious Commitment, Religious Engagement, Spirituality, and Equanimity. Their scores are rough mirrors to the students in this large study who have chosen the most religiously involved lives, the Mormons, Baptists, and "other Christians." They rarely pray, do not follow religious teachings, and do not believe in life after death.

Finally, the atheist student and the agnostic student in a qualitative study by Mayhew (2004) had quite "cerebral" (p. 657) understandings of spirituality. They have not had the chance, through religious participation, to develop "emotion-based vocabularies" (p. 667) to describe their spiritualities.

In summary, researchers and theorists describe them as trusting in humanity instead of God, as skeptical or negating of established religious ideologies, as intellectualizing spirituality, and as wholly conceiving of religion in ways quite different from the religiously committed. Based on my own discussions with atheist and agnostic college students, I would add much to these ideas and findings. I believe that the faith of non-God-believing students incorporates many additional elements, such as a disdain for Christianity, internal conflict about acknowledging the value of religion in other people's lives, and the complexities of stretching beyond one's comfort zone to connect with religious others. In addition, there is a very important growing awareness of their minority status in a country dominated by religious believers and of the ways they choose to address this marginalization. The special circumstances of these students deserve a more detailed examination, one that can promote a more knowledgeable and equitable treatment of them on American college campuses.

Getting to know five atheist/agnostic college students. Before I describe the complexities of their faith frame, I offer introductions of the final five students who informed me of their understandings of religion, spirituality, and faith—those students who did not have a relationship with or belief in God. In addition, I include information on their perspectives on religious privilege in society.

- Melanie, age 20, was a White, Unitarian Universalist woman and an atheist. She had a religious and spiritual life with which she was comfortable. Melanie came the closest to employing the label religious, calling herself "a little bit of a nomad religiously" because of her background in the Unitarian Universalist movement. She employed the term spiritual as more of a convenience because it was readily accessible to and relatable by those of religious backgrounds. Melanie opposed the privilege of the religious and the other forms of discrimination that are tied in with it. She saw power in holding a minority position, explaining that "the person who was … in the minority was empowered to be the spokesperson for that." She was not, however, always willing to use this to work against privileges in her own surroundings.
- Rick, age 20, was a transgender White, atheist student who was raised as a Catholic. He listed his varied religious/spiri-

tual affiliations as "Druid, Unitarian Universalist, Secular Humanist, Zen." Like Melanie, he labeled himself as spiritual mainly for the convenience of the term. Rick was beginning to move past the anger that often characterized his relationship with religion. As he did that, he was able to offer internal validation to his beliefs, which often did not receive that from external sources. He opposed the various forms of privilege, including that of the religious, but was not always willing to engage with the system.

- Misty, age 21, was a biracial White/African-American woman. She described herself as "agnostic/no religious affiliation," although she was raised a Christian. Misty accepted that she could develop her own form of spirituality that was free from religion. Like Melanie and Rick, she utilized the term spiritual mostly as a convenience. She was also letting go of her anger and was accepting that religion may be right for other people. She was still learning much from atheist peers about potential beliefs to embrace, rather than merely finding beliefs to reject.

- Meghan, age 21, was a woman of Chinese and Mexican descents. She was an atheist with no religious affiliation, although she "definitely would consider [herself] spiritual." She was beginning to develop a full set of beliefs, but many of them remained tacit and not well understood by her. Meghan knew she only needed to validate herself and was working to build her confidence. She experienced the religious as having power in society, although her understanding of how this worked was not complex.

- Carl, age 23, was a White man who was settled in an identity as a science-based and humanistic atheist. He was raised as a Roman Catholic. He had comes to terms with the religiosity of others and accepted the potential benefits of such a life. His thinking about his own identity was complex, and much had been shaped by his religious upbringing, but he no longer experienced doubt or confusion about his beliefs. Carl was the most averse to describing himself as spiritual, preferring to think during potential spiritual moments that, "Ah! Oh my mid-lobe is firing a lot." He was opposed to religious privilege but also preferred to avoid direct confrontations surrounding it.

These five students were far from a monolithic representation atheism/agnosticism despite the fact that none of them was willing to define themselves as religious and only one (Misty) had not totally concluded that God does not exist. They were quite different in terms of their spiritual beliefs and their comfort level with the terminology and labels that originate in religious institutions. Some were raised in religious denominations that they later specifically rejected. They demonstrated varied states of security with their own faith identities.

Faith frame. As with the other three groups of students, I describe the faith frame for the atheist and agnostic students through explicating the three major components—their common understandings, points of disagreements, and the faith-specific issues that arose in dialogues on these topics. The first elements of the non-God-believing faith frame were their common understandings of the meanings of the words religion and spirituality and their interpretation of the concept of God. They tended to describe religion in a negative manner, particularly with regard to what they perceived was a false connection to morality. They were highly concerned with what they felt was an erroneous connection between the two:

> *"So you got the main point there which is the ethical code ... does not ... in any way tie to religious beliefs or lack thereof, right.... You know, [for] secular humanists ... the idea is that you believe to lead a good life and do good without a promise of reward in the afterlife."*
> —Carl, 23-year-old unaffiliated, atheist student

Their understanding of spirituality was quite different from that of religious students—not a connection to something greater or out of the ordinary but instead a manifestation of living one's daily life in a heightened manner. They described spirituality in terms of self-reflection, noticing or being aware, and being outside the everyday. They distinctly avoided linking spiritual expression with religious institutions. Meghan described how religious expectations limit spirituality:

> *"When I think of religion I think of something very ... structured and ... it's already been ... put together and you have to follow it and it's more ... rigid and stuff. But, when I think of spirituality, I think of ... a way ... that's just more liberating that ... you could just ... do it yourself or ... you're not bound to these certain rules and things like that."*
> —Meghan, 21-year-old unaffiliated, atheist student

These students rejected nearly all understandings of God, describing external God concepts mostly for the purpose of disagreeing with them. They did not believe that God is a source of tests, that humans should depend on God, or that God is a creator. The following was an example of one student explaining her lack of belief in God:

> *"I identify as agnostic, and my personal definition is that I don't know there's a God, I can't disprove or prove it, and regardless, it really wouldn't change the way that I behave or my actions."*
> —Misty, 21-year-old unaffiliated, agnostic student

Interestingly, for many a disbelief or doubt in God was paired with a current or past desire to *have* a religious faith or to believe in God because this was perceived to be the more accepted way of living in American society. They may have viewed religious affiliation as being a comfort mechanism or a social lubricant, going so far as to test out religious participation to see whether they could convince themselves that religiosity worked. Invariably, these students experienced these religious exercises intellectually, perhaps feeling frustrated that they did not share the same emotional connection to religion as did some of their friends. A student told this type of story:

> *"My best friend was ... Evangelical Christian and ... I just really wanted to be Christian in middle school and ... I think that the point at which I just gave up was when ... probably I'd been going to her group probably a couple of months, and ... I was like, 'Yeah you know,... I really like your group,' and you know, just really trying to be there with her, and she was like, 'Well you know Melanie, you can't just believe in God 'cause you say you believe in God. You have to really believe in God.' And I was, like, 'Darn it I'm trying!' So, at that point, I was like, 'Well I guess it's just not meant to be. I'm not, I mean, it's not there.' ... Apparently she saw that ... I wasn't that into it, so. I don't know, at that point I just let go, and kind of moved on with my spiritual life, I guess."*
> —Melanie, 20-year-old Unitarian Universalist, atheist student

The students who expressed wanting to have a religious faith or belief in God tended to describe high school as a time when they tried to fit in religiously. They found, however, that they could not simply will themselves to believe in God. This passage from Carl described a multifaceted internal battle:

> *"I've had friends tell me that for someone who says he's an atheist I really seem to believe in God a lot.... Especially back in high school ... I would ... curse God for not letting me believe in Him. Right, that I pretty much wanted God to exist but ... you can't just say that I believe in God, you actually have to believe in God. That it's two completely different things. It seems to*

me to undermine ... the whole free will argument for condemning people to hell. I didn't freely choose to reject God. I tried to believe in God, He just didn't let me. But I guess in terms of how I've changed over college,... one thing is that I've mellowed out and I am not so angry at the God I don't believe exists anymore."
—Carl, 23-year-old unaffiliated, atheist student

Besides the core definitions and beliefs, there were additional common understandings inherent within the atheist/agnostic faith frame. Beyond the overriding disbelief in God, they shared a conviction about their own religious minority status within the U.S. culture (discussed in depth in Chapter 4) and their related desire to avoid religion and the discomfort that arose during conversations focused on the topic of religion. This intertwined pair of concerns led them to feel frustrated at the presence of Christian missionaries on their college campus, to consider residing in portions of the country that they perceived to be more welcoming to the nonreligious, and to choose nonreligious friends. A quotation illustrated elements of this dilemma:

"Outside ... university circles,... it's kind of surprising how much of the ... American population is religious, and so then [you're] kind of like, 'Oh, where am I going to settle down?' And like, 'Am I going to find friends?' ... At least for me, it is kind of hard for me to be friends with someone who ... completely is fervent in their beliefs.... You kind of think at least, 'I can only be in these certain places where people do or at least are more likely to ... share my beliefs.' "
—Misty, 21-year-old unaffiliated, agnostic student

Alongside their concern for finding accepting peers, these atheist and agnostic students were worried about meshing with their own families, many of whom practiced religions long since abandoned by the students themselves. It was not easy to find harmony with family members who still attended the students' childhood churches, still believed that God holds influence in their daily lives, and thought the students were merely going through a doubting phase that would someday pass.

But these students often had firm ideas about their identities and were unlikely to return to God belief. They also cared to delineate their own explorations of alternative avenues for spiritual expression, partially to demonstrate that religious organizations do not hold exclusive rights to them. One important spiritual influence for these students was art and music. Another opportunity for a spiritual moment came from the absence of activity:

"And so, a lot of that kind of connection actually came from not doing things, as in deliberately taking time to just stop and that's been really important to me as of late. To be able to be idle, I guess, and I'm not talking about meditation per se, but just when I'm do—I'm cooking dinner, like just right before I came [to the discussion group]. I'm thinking about the smell of the sauerkraut, listening for the oil to heat up and just being very attuned to these details that otherwise are really trivial. And that's where I've taken on spirituality and that's how it's meaningful to me—to have time to see and experience what I normally don't."
—Rick, 20-year-old multispiritual, atheist student

Interestingly, one of the unique features of this faith frame, relative to those of the religious students, was the ease of communication between atheist and agnostic students. Although all three of the religiously affiliated groups of students found their talk with each other to be more challenging (despite the communities they were building), these students did not. They found it refreshing and relaxing. It was comfortable (if novel) to discuss their beliefs with an all atheist/agnostic group; in contrast to the religious students, they felt no pressure to justify their opinions about religious topics. On the other hand, the interfaith conversations, in which they solely represented non-God-believing perspectives, were highly stressful. In an interfaith setting, atheists indeed are a minority, even if all of the other students harbor different religious identities.

In addition, the speech patterns of the atheist/agnostic students with whom I spoke differed from the three groups of religious students, in that they did not reserve the majority of their talk on within-group themes to their intrafaith discussion group. The Christians spoke most frequently of Jesus Christ during their own session, the Muslims spoke most frequently of proper Islamic behavior in their session, and the Jews spoke most frequently in the Hebrew language during their session. The atheists/agnostics, however, were more evenly divided across multiple settings in which they spoke of their core beliefs. They were equally likely to discuss in the intra- and interfaith groups their lack of belief in God, their tendencies to avoid religious conversations, and their desire (past or present) to have a religious faith—in order to fit in better or simply to see what the fuss was all about.

The feeling of insecurity that occurred in mixed-faith settings also prompted these students to keep a safe distance between themselves and the religious establishment. This avoidance was conducted as an act of self-preservation. Depending on the intensity of this behavior, and particularly if it includes diverse peers in higher education settings, avoiding contact with the religious establishment can limit students' learning during the college years. For example, a student who sought out experiences with religious diversity told this story:

"There just such a mix of people here [at the University] that I've just felt ... a lot more comfortable because I didn't have all the pressure from just the huge amount of people who were just ... a certain religion ... I've learned a lot from just everything.... I went to a mosque ... two weeks ago and it was really, really interesting to see ... everything going on there, and ... learn about the religion. And ... it just feels like a nice learning environment really."
—Meghan, 21-year-old unaffiliated, atheist student

In contrast, a student who avoided a similar situation told this story:

"I don't find myself in the situation where I actively challenge myself. I'm not around and engaging with people that have very different religious beliefs than myself. And so sometimes I've gotten too comfy.... I shut down, as from the outset of the conversations there are a lot of things set up to set me on the defensive. And so I tend to let other people handle it."
—Rick, 20-year-old multispiritual, atheist student

A reason for the students' continued avoidance of the religious was because they perceived themselves to be minorities in a country full of religiously committed people. This acknowledgment of their minority status was intriguing when coupled with their conflicted thoughts on using "atheist" as a label to describe themselves. In combination, they illustrated that atheism truly is not an organized body of believers, or even nonbelievers, but instead a category of convenience used both by the religious, to set them apart, and atheists themselves, to band together in support. Meghan explained the "atheist" label in the following way:

"Ok, yeah, in terms of ... putting a label on it. I'll say just ... 'agnostic/atheist' whatever, but I don't know. I don't really ... have a name for ... my own ... spiritual thing. It's just, it is what it is.... I'll just say it because it's easier for people. They're just, like, 'Oh, ok.' "
—Meghan, 21-year-old unaffiliated, atheist student

This ease of conversation in the intrafaith setting did not mean the atheist and agnostic students were in full agreement with one another. Certain points of disagreement were involved in shaping the atheist/agnostic faith frame. Within the group, they harbored very mixed emotions about religion and the perspectives of others. Some of the students were willing to acknowledge that religion does play an important role, both historically/socially and within individual lives. Others harbored so much anger toward religious institutions and the people within them who have wielded ideologies as tools to harm them that they simply could not allow room in their minds for religion to have any positive associations.

Sometimes these points of disagreement led to issues arising in dialogue that were specific to viewing the world through this faith frame. The students who were willing to acknowledge that religion may have some value were likely in interfaith dialogue to stretch beyond their usual comfort zone to connect with religious students. This happened with Rick, for example, who surprised himself by finding common ground with Suha, a Muslim woman. The phenomenon was particularly heightened for atheist/agnostic students, who even in a mixed-religious setting remained outsiders. Some students found this easier to do than others depending on their confidence levels and how well formed their beliefs were. If an atheist herself was not totally sure of her beliefs, she may have been quite wary of opening herself to any influence from someone who was secure in a belief in God.

Summary. The nonbelieving students with whom I spoke were distinguished from their religious peers by more than simply their lack of belief in God. The ways they spoke about their beliefs and their basic definitions of religion and spirituality were all unique. They cared to speak a lot about their differentiation from the religious practices of family members, their prior interest in having a religious identity, their minority status and the "atheist" label, and the various means they now employ (art and music, focusing on one's goals and dreams) to experience spirituality. Their shared bond of lack of belief in God and of being a minority was strong in the moments of their interactions.

This bond, unfortunately, is unlikely to last. These students shared in no community of like-minded thinkers, such as a Hillel Foundation for Jewish students. Other than those who affiliated with a nontheistic religious community, such as the Quakers or Unitarian Universalists, they did not gather on any regular basis with people who had shared similar life experiences involving religion and spirituality and who could reaffirm their ideologies. There existed no home community to which to retreat for comfort and reassurance, which is an ironic consequence for those students who were directly rejecting what they perceived to be the negative influence of religious institutions. In this sense, these students were much more isolated than their religiously affiliated peers.

Due to their uniqueness, it is in the best interests of all students for educators to be inclusive of the faith identities of atheist, agnostic, and nonaffiliated students when considering the role that faith plays in the critical college years. Including these students in interfaith dialogues and identity-building educational programs benefits those whose religious affiliations limit their interactions with students unlike themselves in faith. The students with whom I spoke had complex inner lives that would be overlooked by theories, such as Fowler's, that truly reserve such complexity for the religious and God believing. The inner workings of spirituality play an influential role in life and educational decisions for these students as well, and they deserve to be included in campus conversations. Yet when working directly with these students, educators should be sensitive to their feelings of marginalization, their inclination to avoid contact with the religiously committed, and the usual absence of a community of support.

FAITH FRAMES COMPARED

Although the previous sections presented similarities that bind together all of the students, I cannot make the leap to conclude that faith identity is universally experienced. It is clear to me through my work that there are frames through which the students see the world, which they use to make meaning, and which allow room for growth over time. I was able to witness the in-process construction of the students' understandings of these frames due to the group interaction fostered through the intra- and interfaith dialogues.

As I have already said, Fowler's (1981) original theory focused on the structures of people's faith as they developed over the lifespan. He did not include the contents of those faiths, such as the spiritual paths, beliefs, and values inherent in religious and nonreligious faith systems. However, in the context of the current work, these contents are actually quite relevant and illuminating about the students' faith identities. Although the frames represent a group level of identity, they also allow room for the natural variations of individual people. Due to the frames being so multifaceted, it will be helpful to have a working summary of each one to utilize in a future discussion. In addition, when they are compared directly with each other, each one's distinctions become clear:

- The Christian frame is concerned with the tenets of Christian ideology, discrepancies in beliefs and practices surrounding them, and Christianity's relationship with other world religions. Embedded within this frame is the implicit understanding of Christianity's dominance, although this is somewhat tempered by the apprehension of trampling other religions.
- The Jewish frame is focused on religious rituals and the choices people make to practice them or not, as well as Judaism's place in the world in comparison to other religions. Embedded within this frame is a sense of insecurity, as if Jews are not entirely established in society and that deviation in practice may weaken the group's solidarity and strength.

- The Muslim frame centers around living a religious life in a secular world, including the distinguishing of Muslim conceptions of spirituality from the beliefs of other religious groups, as well as a focus on fundamental ritual practices. Embedded within this frame is an awareness that Islam must be in dialogue with other religions to be accepted and understood.
- Finally, the atheist/agnostic frame is concerned with the core disbelief in God, mixed emotions about religion, and the exploration of alternative avenues for spiritual expression. Embedded within this frame is a deep insecurity over atheists' position in society, which is actualized by conflicted interactions with religious others.

Although perhaps slightly tangential, I would like to now point out that three of the students being discussed in this text did not fit exactly into the four designated worldviews being analyzed, or by extension, into the homogenous focus groups into which they were assigned. Joanna defined herself as a Jewish atheist, which is actually a self-definition shared by up to 25% of all Jewish college students (Sales & Saxe, 2006). Brooke considered herself to be an agnostic Christian. Melanie was affiliated with Unitarian Universalism, which is a religious movement, although one that does not require a belief in God. She therefore had interacted with institutionalized spirituality during young adulthood in a way quite different from the other atheists in this study, all of whom had abandoned religion much earlier in life.

These three students' definitions of self complicate any discussion of their talk, in that each one was slightly discrepant from their reference group. For example, Joanna did not feel that her responsibilities in the world had anything to do with extending God's work, and therefore she had a lot in common with the atheist students who believed that social justice transcends association with God. Brooke's near break with Christianity in high school and her continued questioning of it resembled the disappointment with God described by other atheists and agnostics. Melanie was highly communal in orientation due to her affiliation with Unitarian Universalism, which gave her similarities with the religious students.

This characteristic of not quite fitting in with one particular group also enabled all three of these women to speak across the usual boundaries of faith. Brooke, once considering a conversion to Islam, had a strong understanding of the commonalities between that religion and Christianity. Joanna explained in her interfaith group that she could "represent both sides" of her dual identity. Melanie exhibited similar skills in her interfaith session, employing religious language with Sam and Yusuf that differed markedly from her talk in the atheist/agnostic student focus group.

For students like these women, this bridging likely does not always occur with the greatest ease. Dual identities can also correspond with vulnerability or a reactionary attitude. Such students may be forced to confront their own beliefs earlier in life yet take longer to feel confident about their identities. Therefore, they occupy tenuous yet valuable positions within their faith communities and within college campus communities. They have the ability to speak across difference as long as they feel that their unique perspectives are respected.

CONCLUSION

Looking at the four faith frames together, it becomes apparent that the ways students view the world are sometimes similar or overlapping and at other times vastly divergent. Muslim and Jewish students share a focus on ritual practice, although for Muslim students, these obligations take on a greater social urgency. Muslims and atheists/agnostics have concern over the uniqueness of their religious and/or spiritual activities, although atheists/agnostics shoulder the burden of their practices being considered by many as wishy-washy and ungrounded. Christian and Jewish students both wonder about the appropriateness of showing tolerance or acceptance of the beliefs of others. Christians, however, come to this view from the position of social dominance, whereas Jews come to it from a place of insecurity. Christians have the luxury of debating denominational distinctions in beliefs without worrying that division will undermine the strength of their group, whereas Muslims and Jews must worry that a lack of unity will weaken them socially. All of these emotional undercurrents—worry, insecurity, concern, and urgency, plus still others—color students' daily lives and interactions, their ways of being in situations that seemingly have little to do with faith, religion, or spirituality.

When students operating from within the same faith frame talk with one another, they establish what I call a "familiar community." The communities are familiar because they resemble the students' own affiliation groups, either at houses of worship in their home towns or in campus religious organizations. This concept of a familiar community features shared terminology (such as religious vocabulary or the use of Hebrew/Arabic), shorthand descriptions for foundational concepts, and detailed presentations of beliefs. These familiar communities demonstrate that there is a level of group interplay involved in identity building, and that educators can capitalize on situations of group participation to reach out to individual students.

As I will show, these familiar communities were powerful enough during my research study that they extended even to the handful of students who consistently broke with the norms of their religious groups. Jasmine, with her opposition to political support of Israel, and Joanna, with her disbelief in God, both conversed with equal facility using the key terms of Judaism. Brooke, questioning God and Christian theology, also employed Christian language with ease. In this sense, the familiar community is a robust concept because it transcends the particularities that distinguish believers even within their faiths. In Chapter 6, I discuss examples for utilizing the faith frames, and related concepts such as the familiar communities, as educational tools.

The new concept of the four faith frames provides an important tool for student affairs practitioners and other campus educators to employ in their work with college students. The frames can help us to understand how people view the world and interact within it. They demonstrate that people of the same faith share some elements of their outlook, which vary markedly from those of differing faiths. They also demonstrate that there are important elements of identity that can be contentious between students of the same background. Finally, the frames help to explain why a Christian-centric perspective in research and practice is inappropriate for addressing the needs of non-Christian students.

The faith frames make it possible for practitioners to conduct intrafaith dialogue on college campuses. By this I mean addressing students within their faith communities of choice and with their fellow community members. I also mean that educators can utilize the concept of familiar communities, in which students connect through shared language and topical congruence, to help students think through their issues of concern.

The implications of the faith frames on morality and equity are profound. To act morally as educators, we need no longer overlook vast swathes of our student population. To treat all students equitably, we can open our awareness to ways of being in the world that do not operate out of a place of Christian privilege and dominance. We higher education leaders, researchers, and other professionals can change our understanding of spirituality and faith identity. The moral imperative prods us to no longer be complacent in this arena of diversity.

3

THE RELATIONSHIP BETWEEN FAITH FRAMES AND DISCOURSE IN INTRA- AND INTERFAITH DIALOGUE

The college students with whom I worked in intra- and interfaith discussion groups reflected on their experiences and then shared their reactions in interviews and written questionnaires. Some quotations highlight these reactions. Suha felt she could have a more honest discussion with her non-Muslim peers:

> *"I felt that my experience with Islam was very different than ... my fellow Muslims. I felt more as though my peers responded as though they were on TV interviews saying, 'Islam is basically 1, 2, 3,...' I felt I related in a different way to those of the mixed religion identities in that I could speak more about the way religion or spirituality structures one's life and also general beliefs. I feel that in the similar religious identities group, there was already some sort of unsaid 'agreement' about general beliefs so this could not be discussed. I appreciated that we could talk about it in the mixed group because it is the very core of the way I live my life as a Muslim. What was interesting, though, was that my beliefs were similar to those, especially many atheists, in the mixed group."*
> —Suha, 19-year-old Muslim student

David was more cautious in the interfaith group, feeling that his non-Christian peers would not understand all of his terminology:

"Okay, I tried ... being professional, ... in the [interfaith discussion] because of ... the different religions, and the [all Christian discussion], I think because we were all Christians and it was understandable that ... we could say 'God in heaven' and 'Jesus Christ', but in the [interfaith group], because it was with an atheist and the Jew and Muslim, I just didn't want to offend anybody."
—David, 18-year-old Lord of Light Lutheran Christian student

Meghan had vastly different experiences in her two discussions, strongly preferring to converse with the atheists and agnostics:

"I felt extremely uncomfortable and threatened in the ... [interfaith] group. But I absolutely loved the [all-atheist/agnostic] group.... I was surprised how people in my first focus group were proud to be who they were. I felt at home in mine."
—Meghan, 21-year-old unaffiliated, atheist student

Jasmine, in contrast, preferred the interfaith group, which lacked any perception of competition between the students:

"I was much more at ease in the [interfaith] group, and felt much more accepted as whatever I wanted to be.... I felt a certain amount of exclusivity in the [all Jewish] group—even though people were really nice—and I'm sure this was coming from me too. A sort-of I'm-more-Jew-than-you attitude."
—Jasmine, 21-year-old Reconstructionist Jewish student

Language is a powerful entry point to understanding identity. When we speak, we make statements through our word choices, tone of voice, and how much we reveal. When we converse with different people, we make language selections specific to our discourse partner. All of these choices reveal our intentions, our comfort levels, and the ways that we situate ourselves with respect to others. In doing so, the strategies employed offer a window into our identities.

This expression of identity through language is especially true for students in the campus setting because they are experiencing a time of life filled with self-exploration and growth. They are also likely to be interacting with other students from a variety of backgrounds that are new to them. In both intra- and interfaith settings, students will employ various language strategies (or discourse moves) to find common ground with one another and distance themselves from unpalatable ideals. As educators, we can come to better understand students through witnessing their use of language with each other. By doing so, we can also gain the ability to improve our practice to become more in tune with how our students want to be identified.

In this chapter, I will discuss the ways students from specific faith groups used language to negotiate their relationships with each other during dialogues about their faiths, particularly in dialogue with those who share them. To describe my understanding of these topics, I will introduce the method of discourse analysis, which is applied in qualitative research to observe this language in use. I employed discourse analysis to consider the words of the 21 undergraduate students who participated in focus group conversations about their faith identities, as well as in interviews and written questionnaires.

These usages of language are critical for deeper understanding of the four faith frames I introduced in the previous chapter of this book. The discourse strategies selected by the students shaped relationships in conversation; they also reflected the identities of the students utilizing them. In addition, they provided another lens through which we can understand who these students are and how their faiths shape them. Therefore, in this chapter, I will carefully reflect back on the material about the faith frames already discussed and use this additional material to continue to build my case for the importance of recognizing the frames in our work with diverse college students.

My discovery of these language techniques was possible because I employed discourse analysis as my tool to describe the students' group-level interactions and faith identity-building. Discourse analysis takes as a given that identities are subjective and are developed in situated moments; they do not exist or grow in a vacuum. With its emphasis on the way language passes between speakers, discourse analysis is uniquely able to capture that development, as identities are expressed and refined contextually. Discourse analysis has infrequently been employed in higher education research,[16] but my success with it demonstrated to me its inherent value.

As I described in the previous chapter, the students who considered themselves to have religious identities, generally speaking, were more comfortable engaging in dialogue about religion and spirituality with those from different backgrounds from themselves, rather than with peers from their own religious groups. Consequently, I will focus on the more complicated, sometimes contentious, intrafaith interactions and the related strategies typically employed by the four faith groups being discussed in this book. This is an expansion of the concept of "familiar com-

---

[16]An initial review of four major journals in the field of higher education (*The Journal of College Student Development, The Journal of Higher Education, Review of Higher Education,* and *Research in Higher Education*) found only 13 articles making use of discourse analysis techniques between 2001 and 2008.

munities," communities built through conversation that resemble students' home religious groups.

I will also include information on students' interactions during the interfaith dialogues. The familiar communities established by the students in their intrafaith conversations existed relative to those within the interfaith discussions. I came to understand the language strategies employed in the latter as being due to the influence of a "discourse community" (Johnstone, 2002, p. 114), a group that engages in similar ways of speaking about a particular topic. In contrast to familiar communities, discourse communities do not involve students coming together in ways they are used to and comfortable with. In fact, it strongly has to do with the rareness of the situation that the students work hard to forge connections, unable as they are to fall back on established methods of communication. While in the process of conversing, they create conversation rules on the fly, establishing these discourse communities. I will expand on this concept in the second half of this chapter.

Over the course of the students' time in my study, I was able to witness how particular interactions exemplified the discourse techniques through which students achieved their goals. The following are examples of language strategies that became apparent in analyzing the groups' interactions. I include extensive excerpts from the dialogues through which I became aware of these strategies. I also include this information to be useful for other practitioners who wish to conduct intra- and interfaith dialogues, and I will further discuss implications for practice in Chapter 6.[17] Although in my research I considered more than I have presented here, I have selected those that will be of most use when purposefully observing students' communications to inform practitioner mentoring.[18] The ways that students chose to speak to one another are a direct revelation of the topics that were important, controversial, or confusing to them, and these topics were reflections of their faith frames.

DIALOGUE AND THE CHRISTIAN FAITH FRAME

We will begin by examining a transcript from the intrafaith Christian conversation, utilizing discourse techniques as additional lenses into the

---

[17]See Watt (2009) for information on establishing the conditions to "create the emotional and intellectual space for difficult dialogues" (p. 71) around religious privilege. See also Nash, Bradley, and Chickering (2008) for perspectives from faculty and administrators on conducting "moral conversations" on campus, as well as a "step-by-step how-to guide for facilitators and participants when doing moral conversation."

[18]See the Appendix for additional information on how transcript elements were selected and analyzed.

Christian faith frame. I have chosen this segment in particular to high-light the ways that Christian students' conversations with one another demonstrate interdenominational competition and acceptance of varying levels of literalism of belief. In addition, it spotlights the students' usage of familiar, valued language when they speak with one another.

This conversation took place between David, an 18-year-old White man affiliated with the Lord of Light Lutheran church, and Will, a 26-year-old Asian-American Episcopalian. Julie was the Christian co-facilitator for the session.

1 Jenny: Let's try to warm things up a bit more just talking about our own lives, so
2 ... since you guys all seem to have working definitions of what you think
3 "religious" means to you, can you talk about what a meaningful religious
4 experience has been in your lives? Or, if there hasn't been one, you can say that.
5 Yeah, go ahead.
6 David: ... I think in the Christian experience, when you are a Christian, or if you
7 claim to be a Christian, I think the most religious experience for you is, well,
8 more of a spiritual significant time for you was when you decided to become a
9 Christian. Because in the Christian faith, it is you deciding to become a
10 Christian. And I don't know necessarily about other religions, but that, most
11 definitely in the Christian faith, it is one of the most significant days that we feel.
12 'Cause it's that day where we, where we realize that Jesus Christ was ...
13 our Savior who took away our sins so that we could ... be in heaven ... for all
14 eternity. And that, for me,... and I hope for all Christians, is a very significant,
15 ... most religious time for us.
16 Will: Actually, many Mainline—that's probably true for almost all Evangelical
17 Christians—but many Mainline Christians are born into their, born into their
18 denominations. They probably grew up hearing about, they probably grew up
19 around Christianity, so ... they may have had an experience like that at some
20 point in time but ... they may not have used exactly the same language that you
21 used.... I actually grew up Evangelical. I later became Episcopalian.... So yeah,
22 I would characterize that as an awakening, but ... I would not use the same
23 language that ... Evangelicals use to describe it. It's just, it's kind of the same thing,
24 but it's different....
25 Julie: So what language would you use, just out of curiosity, for the more non——
26 Will: Well,... like I said,... I would have characterized it as an awakening....
27 Julie: [to David] Can I ask one more clarifying question? When did you feel like
28 that experience happened for you? Was that ... when you were younger?
29 David: That was about when I was in tenth grade,... at church, one night at
30 youth group.... I mean, I understand what you're [Will] saying. I was raised in a
31 Lutheran church and also in a Baptist church. My parents both took me, my
32 parents were separated and both took me. But ... I know what you mean,... by
33 being raised, in a ... family of Christians. I understand where you're coming
34 from. But would you also agree with me that ... you kind of, you need that day,

35 that, your own, realization of that. I mean, you can go throughout life ...
36 knowing the Bible stories, and knowing ... the Bible through and through. You
37 know,... knowing the stories and ... knowing the reasons and knowing the
38 workings of the faith, but *accepting* the faith for you own, wouldn't you say that
39 you kind of have to accept that?
40 Will: ... For me it helped, definitely.... I don't know that I'd say—I mean, for
41 some people it may not be a ... lightening strike kind of experience. It may be
42 ... more gradual. I mean,... it kind of depends on the person. I agree.
43 David: Ok.
44 Will: I think we're talking about the same thing, just the specifics,... are not
45 really the same.
46 David: Ok, I agree with that.

This interaction occurred extremely early in the Christian focus group. David led off the answers to my question by immediately declaring a standard for one to "claim to be a Christian" (line 7), which was that one has had an experience of being born again, or having a personal realization that "that Jesus Christ was ... our Savior who took away our sins" (lines 12–13). David was utilizing a discourse technique of establishing a *norm*, which is the standard operating procedure held in common by the speakers for each conversation. They are so standardized, in fact, that they often go unnoticed by the people employing them. Sometimes it takes an outsider to a situation to point out the existence of a norm and how it functions to encourage conformity.

In making this statement so boldly, David seemed to assume that he was stating the obvious, and that his experience was normative for Christians. This assumption emerged directly from the Christian faith frame, an element of which is that there are certain core ideologies at the core of Christianity. Due to the concern within the frame for denominational discrepancies, David asserted what he believed those core ideologies to be. At the very least, he "[hoped] for all Christians" (line 14) that this type of conversion experience had happened. However, not all students in the group were Evangelical, so the norm David attempted to establish never had a chance to take root in the discussion. He was unable to transcend the power of competition among the varied Christian denominations.

The next speaker was Will, who offered the clarification that Christians of "Mainline" (line 16) denominations were not required to have an experience of being born again to be considered Christian. Although the term Mainline does have an official definition as including specific Christian denominations (Roof & McKinney, 1987), its usage by Will had the effect of positioning Evangelical Christians as outside the mainstream of U.S. Christianity. Will underlined this by pointing out that he "grew up Evangelical" and then "later became Episcopalian" (line 21), presumably converting to a denomination more suited to his belief system. Although he took the time to martial his thoughts through the use of several hedges (i.e., repeating "born into their" [line 17] and "they probably grew up" [line 18]), Will's turn had the dual effects of blocking David's attempt at establishing a norm for the group and positioning David's belief system as being on the fringes.

Positioning is a discourse term that describes the attempts of individuals in conversation to define someone else's identity. This occurs because people feel compelled to determine their relationships with those around them. Often, positioning connotes a power relationship in a conversation; if an individual is successful in positioning someone in a negative manner, he gains the upper hand. As related to the Christian faith frame, Will's positioning of David during their dialogue had the effect of reducing David's influence in the discussion of the core ideologies of Christianity. Will had a strong motivation for doing this. His opposition to Evangelical Christianity was evidenced more clearly in his questionnaire from the study:

> "I have a temptation to say nasty things around Christians who I perceive
> to be Evangelicals."
> —Will

Will, however, did not seem to hold on to any negative feelings from the Christian group, which demonstrated his overall maturity and ability to explore conflicting opinions in an open manner. He said in his interfaith group:

> "I felt there was actually a fair bit of diversity of thought in the Christian
> group, so that was, that was some, that was good conversation.... We were
> all definitely Christians, but we ... came from ... a big religion."
> —Will

After Julie, the co-facilitator, sought minor clarification from Will, she turned to David to learn more about his experience. Although her follow-up question specifically addressed David's personal story, he quickly turned to address Will's points. He began by attempting to regain some footing in his discussion with Will by trying to bridge the gap between their beliefs, saying, "I know what you mean" (line 32) and "I understand where you're coming from" (lines 33–34). However, these hedges quickly led to the "but" (line 34), where David attempted to call for solidarity to convince Will to agree with him. At the conclusion of his turn, he also turned the question back to Will, twice trying to persuade him to agree, saying, "Would you also agree with me that" (line 34) and "Wouldn't you say that you kind of have to accept that?" (lines 38–39). (The discourse strategies of *footing* and *solidarity* will be discussed in depth using other transcripts in this chapter.)[19]

David also got a final chance at positioning Will himself by emphasizing the word accepting (line 38) in his attempt at persuasion. In this way, he positioned his version of Christianity as higher because, by extension, Will's version did not go far enough beyond the baseline "knowing the reasons and knowing the workings of the faith" (lines 37–38). Will deftly defused this, however, by saying that they were "talking about the same thing" (line 44), even though their readings on the topic were quite different. David was left with little more room in the discourse than to say that he agreed. In David's moves to bridge the gap between them and Will's final deflection, both men demonstrated a less-than-full sincerity with each other, another element of the faith frame.

Despite the familiarity of the topics they discussed, David was not pleased with this interaction. He retained the negative elements of his experience in the conversation with his Christian peers, mentioning them later in his questionnaire and personal interview:

> *"I found it most challenging to participate in the focus group with other Christians while some of their ideas differed some than my own and in some cases I was saddened by what they said because it appeared they had a religious experience with God and not a spiritual 'personal' relationship with God."*
> —David

> *"The one guy who sat to my left [Will] ... it sounded to me that he accepted ... Episcopalian Christianity and he had ... no intention of creating his own ... belief about ... what's out there."*
> —David

One reason that David was more affected by this experience with Will may simply have been age, as David was 18 at the time of the study and Will 26 (and the oldest participant). In addition, the weighty nature of conversing with a dialogue partner of particular value (another Christian) imbued the talk with a higher chance of disappointment around a failure to agree.

---

[19]Footing: Acts to establish alignment with other speakers, by making relational statements. Solidarity: Uses of discourse to express commonalities with other speakers.

Interfaith interactions among Christian students. From the Christian students with whom I spoke, I learned that their conversations with religiously diverse peers tended to be simple, forging broad connections across groups but without much self-conscious reflection. My students did not make themselves vulnerable to having their ideas changed by their diverse peers. None of them told me that criticisms by non-Christians caused them to reevaluate their beliefs.

This type of self-preservation may have related to an element of the Christian faith frame, in that students diverged over the legitimacy of non-Christian belief systems. Some could make allowances in their beliefs for those of other religions, understanding that ideological discrepancies did not threaten their own authenticity. Others could not make these allowances, perhaps feeling that only one religious truth can possibly exist. The students who were more concerned with self-preservation made moves to save face for themselves in the interfaith dialogue setting. They also, however, utilized positioning as a means to express their disagreement with members of other faith groups, in an attempt to make those students' beliefs appear more tenuous than their own. This type of move was exemplified at the beginning of this book in the interactions between Kristin and Meghan.

Concomitantly, I witnessed students expressing less-than-full candor in terms of their willingness to be open to others. A brief excerpt from an interfaith dialogue seemed to indicate a certain level of agreement between Jada, a 23-year-old nondenominational Christian student, and Jesse, an 18-year-old Jewish student:

1 Jesse: This is going to sound really bad, but it's something that came to my
2 mind,.... a smartass comment, but when you said you wanted to ascribe to be ...
3 exactly like Jesus, the first thing that came to my mind was, Jesus was Jewish....
4 Jada: And actually he, I mean—well I actually agree with you because,... Christ
5 basically lived out the law and ... he was the perfect Jew.
6 Jesse: Yeah, so I was just....
7 Jada: But the thing is is that, you know, I'm not a Jew, I'm a gentile, you know
8 what I mean—I mean I need a solution and that's Christ. So that.
9 Jesse: And I respect that. I was just, that was the first thing that came to mind.
10 Jada: Either that or marry a Jew. No, I'm just kidding.... So there's a new ...
11 solution, so, but yeah you're right.
12 Jesse: Alright.

Although this certainly does not read like the smoothest conversation, it is clear that Jesse and Jada did go out of their way to avoid overtly insulting one another. Each did make an effort, however discretely, to position the other in the wrong. Whatever Jesse's motivation was for raising the topic, he immediately lost any type of ground he had in the inter-action with Jada when she agreed with him and raised his statement a degree. In fact, she turned Jesse's own religious affiliation somewhat against him by pointing out that Jesus was something that Jesse himself could never be, "the perfect Jew" (line 5). Not only that, but Jada had "a solution" to that imperfection, "and that's Christ" (line 8). By saying all of this, she positioned Jesse as something lesser. A later quotation from Jada demonstrated the ways in which she maintained the generality of her answers to keep up the veneer of agreement with others:

> *"And in truth, we've only tapped the surface. Just out of propriety and how-ever people just kind of skirt around the deeper, deeper, deeper issues. If you were* really *to get down to … the … issues that … are really* very differ-ent,… *I'm sure we would differ. But on a very superficial level, of course, we do agree."*
> —Jada

In this short piece of conversation, Jada deflected any criticism of her beliefs. One interpretation for this type of behavior is that students may be working through their own commitments and understandings, and opening up that thought process to those outside the Christian frame-work may feel too risky. They prefer not to be challenged or asked to jus-tify their beliefs because they may be afraid that they will not be able to do so sufficiently enough for their own liking. Another reason for this masking of true opinions may be students' willingness to stifle their harsher opinions to foster ecumenism. They may feel confident in their beliefs and know that those beliefs are offensive (at worst) or perplexing (at best) to those of other religious or nonbelieving persuasions. Again, this is the less-than-full sincerity when talking with others that is mani-fested through the Christian faith frame.

Despite these complications, Christian students may find interfaith dialogue to be an enjoyable experience. In contrast with intrafaith situa-tions, they do not need to worry about challenges to their denomination-al legitimacy or disagreements about ideology. They can speak freely about Christianity, knowing that they are the experts on the topic. If con-versations do not progress exactly to their liking, they can utilize dis-course strategies to reposition themselves and others.

What do these examples of interactions say about how Christian stu-dents use language to create meaningful representations of their faith identities? First, it shows that in my intrafaith conversations with Christians, it was much easier to locate instances of negative relationship building between Christians than it was for positive ones. Second, there was evidence of students utilizing external sources (such as family or denominational members as a whole) as reference points, particularly to support classifying a fellow discourse participant in a less-than-kind manner. Third, it demonstrates the ways that students will feign agreement, only to illustrate later through other comments that true open-mindedness did not actually occur.

DIALOGUE AND THE JEWISH FAITH FRAME

This next interaction took place toward the end of the Jewish focus group and especially highlights the focus within the Jewish faith frame with normative Jewish beliefs and practices. The conversation had begun with a lot of agreement between the participants as they answered the first question: How do you define the word religious? Sam responded first, and the others worked off his response, leading with phrases such as, "I think also" (Joanna), "I kind of agree with" (Jesse), "…when you said that I was thinking" (Judy), and "It's interesting to hear you say" (Jasmine). The students seemed to be establishing a norm around a particular topic. However, their responses to my second question created a division between them:

1 Jenny: Can you guys talk about a meaningful religious experience that you've
2 had in your lives?
3 Jesse: I'd say going to Israel was pretty powerful for me.... I just felt really
4 connected to everything 'cause everything is kind of … made for you when
5 you're Jewish, and … visiting the Western Wall on *Shabbat* was just … an
6 experience that I was happy for—everyone's all festive, and dancing around,
7 and happy and so nice, and everyone's, like, "*Good Shabbos, good Shabbos!*"
8 Perfect strangers and I were just all … coming together. It's really cool so.
9 Judy: Mine's just like that. Mine was actually *landing*,… when the plane landed
10 when I went to Israel for the first time. I went with … a big mission with my
11 whole synagogue. And everyone on the plane was … singing and … praying
12 and … old women were … crying in the corner, and … it was just very
13 emotional. But, that's what I thought of.
14 Sam: … I'm gonna use the Israel thing too. But mine was,… we spent a week
15 on the trip I went on in the Israeli army and … probably the … most powerful
16 religious experience I had was seeing … from Friday night to Saturday night
17 over *Shabbos* even the army stopped,… the amount of people watching went
18 down, training stopped, it was just—even … the defense force of … a …
19 country stopped … out of respect for religion was a very powerful religious
20 experience for me.
21 Joanna: I don't consider myself religious at all. I consider myself Jewish
22 culturally, so I can't say I've ever really had a religious experience,… at least
23 not from my perspective, but I also have gone to Israel and … something that

24 touched me as a witness was,... well on Masada, we got there very early, just in
25 time to see the sunrise right over the Israeli flag and ... people just kind of
26 stopped in awe and ... something about that.
27 Jasmine: ... At services every week, I definitely feel very—I mean, not every
28 single week, but definitely most weeks, I feel really connected to ... —I don't
29 know, I love the *Amidah*, so every week ... I feel really connected to that. And
30 ... I also really like studying *Torah*. I don't read Hebrew, I mean I can read it
31 but I can't understand all of it, so ... reading it in English, it's not quite the same
32 but I really ... feel really connected in that way. And it's interesting that you say
33 that about Israel 'cause I went to Israel and felt *absolutely* no connection, as a
34 Jew, to Israel. I think, being in Jerusalem, I was blown away, just 'cause ...
35 there are so many people that have lived there and so many that ... have loved
36 Jerusalem. But Israel itself, I was just like—well I would love to go back but I
37 was, like, "Whatever, why are Jews all so obsessed with Israel?" [laughs]

In this segment, Jesse, Judy, and Sam created a dominant norm by all
naming Israel as the location of their most meaningful religious experience. They used the words "pretty powerful" (line 3), "very emotional"
(line 12), and "very powerful" (line 19), respectively, to describe the experience of traveling to Israel. Judy and Sam also expressed their solidarity
with the norm originally established by Jesse by stating "mine's just like
that" (line 9) and "I'm gonna use the Israel thing too" (line 14). This norm
was built strongly around a key element of the Jewish faith frame, the
presumed agreement over Israel's place at the center of Jewish ideology,
which would be a typical boundary of the religion.

Joanna's declaration of not having a religious identity was the first
breach in the norm established by Jesse, Judy, and Sam, who all had a
powerful religious moment at the tip of their tongues, ready to provide.
Breaches are, in a way, the flip side of norms. They occur when someone
specifically subverts or calls attention to a norm, particularly one that is
boxing someone into a way of being that he or she is not comfortable
with. A breach can be disconcerting to conversation participants because
it helps to highlight the very existence of the norm. Breaches may occur
when students attempt to locate themselves in relationship to each other
and because they do not have time to think before they speak.

In this case, Joanna's breach stemmed from disagreement over the
place of a particular belief (the importance of Israel) at the center of
Jewish ideology, a disagreement that is inherent in the Jewish faith frame.
Her statement that she considered herself to be "Jewish culturally" (lines
21–22) was new information in the discussion. Joanna's self-definition
enabled her less-than-powerful agreement with the others to be a bit
padded. She was distancing herself from the need to have any kind of
meaningful religious experience by placing her self-definition as nonreli-

gious first. Understanding the traditional boundaries of the Jewish observances, she chose to distance herself from them, as opposed to looking for
concession from the other students.

In addition, in stating the *face saving* phrase, "at least not from my
perspective" (line 22–23), Joanna offered permission for the others to
come to their own conclusion about her religious experiences. Face saving during dialogue, both for oneself and for one's conversation partners,
is done to avoid embarrassment. Here, it came as a concession to the faith
frame at work in the conversation, which continued to presuppose the
place of Israel at the center of Jewish ideology. Joanna additionally saved
face by succumbing to the norm, offering a trip to Israel as somewhat
meaningful. She noted that there was "something about" (line 26) witnessing others' moment of awe, although she did not find words to
express what that "something" actually means to her.

Jasmine's turn diverged from the norm much more dramatically, pos-
ing the first major breach in this discourse and establishing her footing in
the conversation as someone who connected to her Judaism in a very different way from her peers. She began by establishing her credentials as a
Jew by stating that she attended worship services weekly, referring to a
prayer with a Hebrew name (*Amidah*, line 29) and mentioning her love of
studying *Torah*. This all functioned as a sort of preemptive face saving
before she breached the norm of deep religious connection with Israel.
When she finally did address Israel, she emphasized her disagreement
with the rest of the group, saying she had "*absolutely* no connection" (line
33) to the country. Then, she again tried to soften the blow of this breach
by strongly indicating the she "loved" Jerusalem (line 35), just not the
country as a whole. Like Joanna, she conceded to the traditional boundaries of Jewish belief and behavior, but she more pointedly demonstrated
that there was a lack of agreement within the Jewish faith frame at work.

Notably, Jasmine's laugh at the end of her final turn was not shared
by the others in the session. She attempted to deflect from her breach by
making a joke, but the humor was not mutual. Perhaps the others felt that
she had positioned them as "obsessed" (line 37) with Israel, which may
not have played to them as a compliment. Quotations from the students
in other texts provided some insight:

> "I remember in the Jewish one, all of us basically said Israel and, like, going to
> the Western Wall and everything, so that was, that one was, like, very similar."
> —Jesse

> "The first group re-affirmed to me that Jews really are similar. I easily under-
> stood where everyone was coming from when they answered each question,
> and our experiences on campus seemed to all be fairly similar."
> —Judy

"The most challenging part of this experience was the first focus group. I felt like there was more to argue about and more to disagree upon among members of my own faith."
—Sam

The responses provided on questionnaires filled out by Jesse and Judy depicted their lack of reflection on the differences demonstrated in the Jewish group, and neither mentioned at any point noticing that one member of their conversation did not believe in God and one did not support Israel politically. Although Sam did mention in passing during his interfaith group that there had been a Jewish atheist in the first group, he made no further comment about it.

Joanna reacted strongly to being so different from her Jewish peers, which she seemed to have experienced much more so than did Jesse, Judy, or Sam:

"In that setting it was four very Jewish students; they really valued their Judaism, they valued God, they valued going to Hillel and being active in Hillel and ... just this higher level of Judaism. And so even though I was raised Reform, which is the lowest level of Judaism, but still isn't atheism, I felt just so far apart from them, that I might as well have not been raised Jewish. And here, I actually feel more Jewish than I felt, then with those other Jewish students."
—Joanna

Jasmine also had a lot to say about the matter. She took me aside immediately after the focus group to confess how difficult it had been for her to admit her feelings about Israel. Additionally, her concern of being marginalized within the Jewish community stayed with her throughout the study:

"I don't rely on Israel in terms of my ... spiritual—that doesn't relate to how I'm religious. And to be in a room of Jews and to think that doesn't usually go over very well. So I think people were being fine, like, I didn't feel threatened or anything, but I just ... feel much more comfortable talking about it with non-Jews than with Jews..."
—Jasmine

In addition to Jasmine and Joanna's personal feelings of disenfranchisement, their situation reflected the complex nature of familiar communities, and how these dialogue-created communities are imbued with the consequence of great disappointment if one's beliefs are not embraced by important others.

Interfaith interactions among Jewish students. I learned from the Jewish students in my study that they had a high level of concern for establishing the place of Judaism in a Christian-dominant culture. There was a sense of insecurity embedded within the Jewish faith frame, as if Jews were not entirely established in society and that deviation in practice may weaken the group's solidarity and strength. This was especially the case being at a time when the students were learning that they could be authority figures who stand up for the rights of their group. This insecurity tied directly in with the minority status of Jews in this country.

The keen feeling of being separate from the religious majority seemed ironically to enable the Jewish students to speak more freely when among non-Jews. As outsiders to Judaism, their religiously diverse peers had less influence on how the Jewish students understood their own identities. The impact of this condition was that the young adult Jews may have felt less compelled to extend themselves in dialogue. They may have instead simplified their talk or avoided direct conflict to protect their own feelings or those of others. Like their Christian conversation partners, the Jewish students also employed face saving and positioning when talking with religiously diverse peers.

A brief excerpt from an interfaith conversation demonstrated one Jewish woman's willingness to go along with the normative discourse at work:

1 Jenny: Well, you guys have had a high level of agreement tonight, or at least
2 saying, "Yeah that's not surprising," or "I totally expected you to say that" ...
3 Or someone can say, "I believe my religion is the ultimate truth" and nobody
4 really blinks at that, and yet you're pretty much all from very different
5 backgrounds. Why so many common answers?
6 Carl: We're trying to play nice with the other kids.
7 Jenny: Is that really what it is?
8 Carl: I guess.
9 David: We're not aggressive people. We don't believe in violence. [laughter]
10 ...
11 Inaara: You guys kind of basically just said it, that ... it's not so much playing
12 nice, I guess, but ... I figure that we all just have this common understanding
13 and respect for each other and ... nobody's trying to force their beliefs on
14 anybody else, it's more of ... we just understand where everybody else is
15 coming from and that's respectable.
16 Jenny: Want to add anything?
17 Judy: Um, no, I definitely just agree. I don't think that I'm right and I don't
18 think that other religions are wrong. I just think that my religion's right for me,
19 and it could be just because I was brought up that way and was taught that ...
20 these specific beliefs are *good* and they should be valued and so I do. But, I've
21 also been taught that everyone else has been brought up ... in very different

22 ways than I have and it's not a means to ... judge them by or criticize them.
23 It's just different and how they were brought up.
24 Jenny: I mean, it sort of sounds like you're saying "Anything goes. It's all up
25 to you, whatever what you want to do is fine with me. I don't really care." Is
26 that sort of an accurate or semi-accurate reading of what you guys are saying?
27 Judy: I think as long ... as one religion or one person doesn't take their religion
28 to go against another person or another group, I think it's great that there are
29 different religions, so there can be different views and different ideas and
30 beliefs, and that once one is targeting another and saying "They're wrong" or
31 that "They shouldn't exist" ... then I think there's a problem.

This conversation, throughout, was marked by a distinctly high level of agreement among the students and a lack of questioning or critiquing one another. The students did not make great efforts to connect with each other. Many of their answers were brief, and reactions to each others' comments were minimal. Afterward, Judy explained how the members of her interfaith discussion group diligently avoided conflict:

> "My [interfaith discussion] group wasn't as successful, I don't think, because it seemed that everyone was afraid of offending another.... In [this] group I learned that people can be sensitive to others and people fear bringing up potentially uncomfortable conversation topics in order to dissuade an argument.... I found myself censoring what I was going to say before I actually did, in order to not offend anyone."
> —Judy

To me, this passage demonstrated that Judy was pleasantly surprised by how interfaith students spoke selectively to avoid offending one another. The act of censoring herself before speaking was a particularly important discourse technique that I will discuss further in the next section of this chapter. The unintended consequence of this move was a lack of true critical discussion. As with the Christian students, however, the Jewish students also found interfaith dialogue to be a positive learning experience. Spending time with students from other religious minority backgrounds bolstered them. In addition, they were aware of their own expertise about Judaism and did not need to concern themselves with challenges to the legitimacy of their ritual practice.

I also witnessed hedging in this group when a student wanted to make a criticism of a Christian missionary but felt compelled to separate himself from that criticism in case it was received harshly by others. *Hedging* is a discourse technique that occurs when dialogue participants try to separate themselves either from their speech moves or from each other in a situation of conflict. One method for doing this is to use hedges, such as inserting words of indecision or delayers like "um" and "I don't know." These help the speaker gain more time to think about what to say but can also give the impression that she is not secure in responding to what has been said. Hedges are a trade-off in a way, moves that reveal in this case the layer of insecurity inherent in the Jewish faith frame.

What do these examples of interaction say about how Jewish students use language to create meaningful representations of their faith identities? Although they are not illustrative of all Jewish college students, they do demonstrate a level of internal struggle within the Jewish campus community as students work to figure out what are acceptable beliefs and what are too far outside the norm to be considered tolerable. They also show a level of concern for the judgments of those outside the faith, and particularly if and how Judaism is perceived and legitimized by Christians.

DIALOGUE AND THE MUSLIM FAITH FRAME

We turn now to a transcript from the intrafaith Muslim conversation, in which extreme delicacy was utilized by the students who disagreed with the normative behavior that was occurring. The students were verbally demonstrating an important element of the Muslim faith frame, the concern for proper behavior, as well as their feelings about the inaccuracy of using standard terms to describe their identities.

1 Jenny: Do you guys consider, currently consider yourselves to be religious or
2 spiritual or both or neither?
3 Sabur: ... I don't think of myself as a very religious person or—alright, I don't
4 have a definition for spiritual, so I'm going to leave the spiritual out of this, just
5 because I have a lack of definition for it. For religious in my mind, I don't find
6 myself a religious person in Islam.... I don't pray nearly enough, and I'm not—I
7 don't drink, I don't smoke, I don't do those things. I don't eat pork. But that
8 doesn't make me a religious person. I find that to be religious, I need to go
9 through the daily grind as being a Muslim. I don't do that nearly enough to be
10 considered a religious person. But I find myself to be a good person. I don't find
11 myself to want to harm anybody, but I live by the tenants of my religion.
12 However I don't really, I don't find myself practicing the religion nearly as
13 much as I should. That's how I look at it.
14 ...
15 Inaara: ... I guess I would *not* define myself as religious or spiritual, but rather,
16 just God conscious,... just ... this constant remembrance of God and ...
17 sometimes we let that go when we get caught up in so many other things, but ...
18 at the end of the day, you come back to that. Or ... during the five daily prayers.
19 I remember, "Oh wait a minute, hold on, rewind,... let's just get back to me and

20 God and that whole relationship real quick." And I guess ... when I think of
21 religious I think of the example of the prophet Mohammed, and ... kind of
22 epitomizing the *Koran*. And I obviously don't even come close to epitomizing
23 that at all. And it's ... this constant struggle, so I wouldn't necessarily say that
24 I'm religious, but at least that I attempt to try to always be in remembrance of
25 God and ... I have all these inner struggles and everything in overcoming that is
26 ... going to take a long while. But ... religious, I don't—I wouldn't really use
27 that label... I wouldn't like to use that label. It's kind of ... a dangerous term to
28 just shove onto someone.
29 Yusuf: Well, I guess I've kind of felt what Inaara was saying about it being
30 relative,... comparing yourself to the prophet, who was ... obviously the
31 epitome of religious, or ... perfect man. But ... I guess I compare myself to ...
32 friends I know or people from community who ... I define as religious, and ...
33 the stuff they do compared to the stuff I do—which ... I don't.... But then you
34 compare yourself the people that aren't, the people who might not pray or ...
35 fast or ... have God consciousness, so ... it's really hard to define ... yourself as
36 religious. Or ... it's very, it might even be arrogant in a sense, to say "Yeah I'm
37 religious." Oh, 'cause religions or religious, I guess, depending on who you ask
38 would have ... a positive connotation. So, I don't know, you'd be ... attributing
39 to yourself a quality which by doing might be ... considered arrogant and
40 therefore you wouldn't be religious. Know what I mean? I don't know if that
41 makes any sense but, yeah, so. [Laughter]
42 Suha: Yes, that does.
43 Shashi: I like the way that Inaara actually put it, being God conscious.... I
44 myself am not ... religious in the sense that I also go through what Sabur had
45 mentioned.... I don't pray five times a day. I try to—I do pretty much
46 everything else. I fast during *Ramadan*, I try to pray at least once a day.... But I
47 don't go to the Friday prayer, that kind of thing.... But at the same time, I keep
48 God in my mind throughout the day, to some extent for selfish reasons when I
49 am in a tough spot.... I remember God, I pray,... you know, "Help me through
50 this." ... It's probably not the best thing because you probably should remember
51 Him regardless,... so dare I say I'm selectively spiritual? I don't like that term
52 though because of ... the connotation it has.

In this segment, the students were performing what they perceived to be the complicated task of defining their religious and spiritual identities for their interviewers and for each other. They were declaring their *identities/presentations of self*, in which individuals situated within discussion groups use language to construct their identities for one another. People are necessarily made up of multiple identities and understandings of self, and certain of these elements come to the forefront based on the nature of their interactions. Conversation partners affirm these presentations of self, establishing them as the salient points of identity in the discussion.

The current presentations of self related directly to the Muslim faith frame. In the first place, several of them pushed back against the very terms religious and spiritual, which we had just worked on defining through previous questions: "I don't have a definition for spiritual, so I'm going to leave the spiritual out of this" (Sabur, lines 4–5), "It's kind of … a dangerous term to just shove onto someone" (Inaara, lines 27–28), "It might even be arrogant in a sense" (Yusuf, line 36), and "I don't like that term though because of … the connotation it has" (Shashi, lines 51–52). After these succeeding dismissals of the main terms in use during the study, it seemed quite difficult for any of the Muslim students to use them with confidence.

However, each student was then able to take his or her replacement term for religious or spiritual and provide a definition of self based on this. Sabur did not "find [himself] a religious person in Islam" (lines 6–7) because, although he did observe some of the necessary behavior restrictions, he did not adequately perform the "daily grind as being a Muslim" (line 9). Sabur did not specify exactly what identity he was utilizing while performing that daily grind, but if that identity was not as a Muslim, one possibility is that he considered his daily life to be secular in nature.

Inaara, quite opposed to utilizing the "dangerous term" (line 27) to describe herself, instead selected "God conscious" (line 16) as being more appropriate. She was much more comfortable owning her description, as she tried "to always be in remembrance of God" (lines 24–25). This was clearly a statement of a religious identity even if the label had been modified. Inaara also declared that she modeled her religious life after the prophet Mohammed, which set a high bar for the students who spoke after her turn.

Yusuf tagged onto Inaara's turn by supporting her idea of comparing oneself to Mohammed; however, he lowered the stakes by comparing himself to members of his community, the religious and "the stuff they do compared to the stuff [he does]" (line 33) as well as "the people who might not pray or … fast or … have God consciousness" (lines 34–35). The latter was a list of tasks likely considered definitional for being religious. Yusuf found himself somewhere in the middle of the continuum.

Shashi moved through several potential definitions of her religious and spiritual identity before settling on one. She first tried out ideas presented by others. Her definition of "being God conscious" (line 43) was a bit more utilitarian than Inaara's, as she admittedly relied on her relationship with God to get her through when she was "in a tough spot" (line 49). The "sense" (line 44) she used to determine her religiosity was based on what Sabur had said, and she agreed that she was not religious because of the things that she did not do. Finally, after some hedging, "it's probably not the best thing" (line 50) and "so dare I say" (line 51), she defined herself as "selectively spiritual" (line 51) despite her lack of affinity with the word. At the end of her turn, despite all the covers she had taken under others' definitions and her own hedges, Shashi found her own voice, albeit one she was quick to say she did not readily embrace.

All of the students' declarations about their identities, their presentations of self, spoke to the Muslim faith frame: the common understandings over the inaccuracy of using standard terms to describe one's identity and the importance of humility and proper behavior; the points of disagreement over the priority of having a religious life in a secular society and the value of a spiritual identity. There was also a norm in play, which had become defining oneself in comparison to something: a living role model, Mohammed, or some sort of ultimate standard of what one was supposed to be—and clearly could not achieve. The norm was to depict oneself as humble—again, a key element of the Muslim faith frame.

The students each made moves to determine their *footing* relative to each other during this interaction. The concept of footing can assist us in viewing how speakers assume positions in opposition. Students act to establish their footing, or alignment with other speakers, by making relational statements. They may define themselves as opposed to, as overlapping, or in contrast to something or someone.

Although Suha's narrative was somewhat out of synch with the rest (and thus not excerpted here), the others all covered similar bases in a pattern: redefinition of "religious" or "spiritual," statement of role model or idea catalyst, and declaration of one's identity in relation to the new definition and model. When examined through the lens of this outline, one can more readily identify Inaara as the strongest embracer of a religious identity, with Shashi and Sabur distancing themselves from that world, and Yusuf falling somewhere in between. Again, there was some disagreement over the priority of having a religious life, and this was a topic very much in play in this dialogue.

In addition to Inaara being somewhat more willing to declare herself religious than the others, Yusuf and Shashi also both referred back positively to Inaara in their turns. Inaara, who wore the *hijab* head covering and was the younger sister of the campus Muslim Students Association (MSA) president, may have occupied a seat of certain respect during the session. Incidentally, she was also acquaintances with N'Mah, the co-interviewer for the session; although N'Mah was a graduate student, they had taken a course together titled "Muslims in Black America." These factors potentially combined together to make the others even more careful of what they said around Inaara.

Sabur and Shashi, who were actually good friends before taking part in the study, shared similar experiences of having their religious commit-

27 Misty: Oh no, I was going to say that your guys' comments, was it you two who
28 said that "I don't have religion, oh but I'm spiritual" is a hippie thing?
29 Shashi: Yeah, that's another thing I wanted to say. I hope I didn't offend you by
30 saying that.
31 Misty: No you didn't. Actually that's, like, one of the biggest thing, there's so
32 many misconceptions about atheists and agnostics but that's understandable.
33 Shashi: Well, and I think that's one thing that's, you know, like, just as an
34 American culture we've grown to associate with that era—you know, pot
35 smoking, and peace signs.
36 Misty: Oh communists, and yeah.
37 Jasmine: Communists. [Laughter]
38 Shashi: Yeah, exactly. I mean, the fact that it's so ingrained in our culture now,
39 that's what first comes to mind. So.
40 Misty: I'm not a communist. [laughter] Just so you guys know.

During this dialogue, Shashi joined with Jasmine to establish a norm—that spirituality without a basis in religion is "really wishy-washy" (line 3), deserving of a "whatever" (line 8), and reserved for the "hippie" (line 11) segment of the population. As well, it is outdated because it had its heyday in "1970, when spiritual was *the thing*" (line 12). Misty breached that norm, "[taking] out [her] card" (line 17) as an agnostic, and calling the others out on making an assumption about the nature of their discourse community. That faulty assumption around which the religious students have established their norm was actually a "stereotype" (line 18).

Shashi got her chance to save face on her potential insult of Misty toward the end of the conversation. Misty brought up the previous comment, and Shashi effectively offered an apology, saying immediately, "I hope I didn't offend you by saying that" (lines 29–30). Unfortunately, Shashi's interjection of this cut off whatever it was that Misty "was going to say" (line 27).

A later quotation from Shashi described her stance during this conversation, as opposed to her intrafaith discussion with all Muslim peers:

"We all still came to similar conclusions, however I felt much more open and able to speak my mind with those that were not of the same faith. With other Muslims, I felt I had to prove myself in some way and that if I didn't meet their expectations, I would be judged for it. With the mixed group though, I felt a sense that we were all learning from each other without the judgmental facet."
—Shashi

As with Christian and Jewish participants, the Muslim students reporting experiencing interfaith dialogue in a positive manner despite any specific challenges they had while the actual conversations took place. This reaction was possible because, unlike when they spoke with their fellow Muslim peers, they did not need to worry about their ritual observance or their relative level of conservativism. Face threats were easier to avoid, and they could find ways to connect around similar commitments to God or their feelings about their religious minority status.

What do these examples of interaction say about how Muslim students use language to create meaningful representations of their faith identities? For one, they show a greater level of concern for one's reputation among peers who have high potential for being seen again and impacting one's status in the community. They also demonstrate the variety of discourse forms available to students when speaking about their religious and spiritual identities. The students can speak using the language and references of their religion or they can utilize common, secular words. The choice depends on who the listeners are.

DIALOGUE AND THE ATHEIST/AGNOSTIC FAITH FRAME

This segment took place at the end of the atheist/agnostic student focus group and highlighted the disdain for Christianity inherent in the atheist/agnostic faith frame. Ethan, who appears toward the end of the segment, was the atheist co-facilitator for this session. The conversation also demonstrated that these students had no familiar and established in-group language to employ when alone with each other. Because they could not utilize the language of their cultural predecessors in the ways religious students could, they had to create their shared understandings on the spot.

1 Jenny: Well, we have a few minutes left. Is there anything else that you guys
2 wanted to say or is there anything that you didn't have a chance to say about
3 spirituality or your belief systems or how things have changed over time?
4 Melanie: We've made references to people's backgrounds, but I mean,
5 obviously full disclosure's unnecessary, but it would just be interesting to know
6 like, where we're coming from so that I could get the impression that there's
7 like.... I don't know about you, but the rest of you came from Christian families.
8 Carl: Yeah, I mean I was raised Roman Catholic.... I did my first communion
9 and then after the first communion, I couldn't find my parents and I started
10 crying. My grandparents decided I was crying because ... Jesus was making
11 me cry. [laughter] ... But ... by the time I got around to confirmation, I was
12 doing the confirmation because not doing the confirmation would make my
13 mother cry. [laughter] It was a little different that time.... But, yeah,... I was

14 raised Catholic, fell away from that.

15 Rick: I quit right at the time of my confirmation, like one day before I was

16 supposed to go through with it I was, like, "No."

17 Carl: See, I just did, the part where you're saying, "I do" to all the tenets of

18 belief, and I just said, "I don't." [laughter] Nobody listens.

19 Misty: ... I guess my dad wasn't really religious but my mom ... is ... Dutch

20 Reformed.... So she, I don't know necessarily how religious she was but it was

21 always, it's very much part of the tradition, you go to church every Sunday.

22 And my dad would only go on Christmas, but then he would always get into a

23 fight with my mom about how Jesus was Black and he wasn't blond haired and

24 blue eyed and that would just piss her off to no end. [laughter] It was really

25 funny.... I would always go but I never really, I just liked the music, that's why

26 I went. But, and my mom I guess turned—my dad died when I was about

27 fifteen, so then my mom turned more religious after that, and then she started

28 asking, "Misty, why don't you go to church with me, you know, are you

29 religious, blah blah."

30 Melanie: Well, I'm a third generation U.U., so I didn't really—

31 Ethan: Unitarian Universalists, for those who don't know.

32 Melanie: Yeah, Unitarian Universalists, which is basically, because I only have

33 two seconds, "Believe what you want" [laughter] and I'll just, I mean,

34 obviously it's not that, but that's another one of those half hour things, so.... So

35 yeah,... my uncle who I mentioned is kind of ... the odd one out and my ...

36 grandma, neither of my grandmas really seem to care. Actually, my grandma

37 wrote me a Christmas card, wrote us a Christmas card this year that had like,

38 she needed to use up religious cards that she had received so she had this one

39 with a Bible quote and then said "Yeah right!" And I was like, "Grandma!"

40 [laughter]

This interaction demonstrated students' presentations of self. These presentations of self pointed directly to a critical element of the atheist/agnostic faith frame: the common disdain for Christianity. This negative feeling was complexly intertwined with how these students self-identified. Melanie, having discussed personal issues with the others for an hour, sought out additional information about their identities, wanting to know "where [they're] coming from" (line 6) religiously. Intentionally, I had not asked the students for "full disclosure" (line 5) within the sessions about their faith identities so that they would be able to decide how much or how little they were comfortable telling each other. Melanie perhaps asked for additional information because she found this discussion to be a learning experience, which she later explained in her mixed-faith session:

"I think in a lot of ways since I'm still searching, … the first focus group was really helpful, in that … I could kind of take the ideas I and be like, 'Do I like that?' … It was more of a learning [experience.]"
—Melanie

The others responded to Melanie's request to describe their identities with similar presentations of growing away from a Christian upbringing. Carl said that he "was raised Catholic, fell away from that" (line 14). Rick, also raised Catholic, "quit right at the time of [his] confirmation" (line 15). Misty, who described herself on her initial demographic paperwork as "agnostic/no religious affiliation," discussed how she maintained her participation in Christianity to appease her mother. She would "always go [to church]" but did not get anything more out of it than "just [liking] the music" (line 25). Melanie, uniquely in this group raised in the Unitarian Universalist faith, presented herself as well. Her explanation was brief, her belief system summarized as "believe what you want" (line 33).

Meghan's explanation of her religious upbringing came later in the discussion and was not included here because it turned the group's conversation in a new direction. Her story was of being enrolled in a Jewish private school by her lapsed-Catholic father so that she would get a leg up on "[going] to Harvard one day or whatever." Her family put on the trappings of Judaism to fit in with the school community, and Meghan emerged as a young adult without interest in organized religion.

At the end of all of their turns, they had presented themselves in similar manners, as people who realized at a certain point in life that religions with strictly literal or illogical belief systems were to be abandoned (or practiced for strictly utilitarian purposes) without remorse. This was despite the fact that each of these five students had experienced a time when he or she had wanted to have a religious identity, usually to fit in with peers. At this point in their lives, that desire no longer resided within any of them. It remained, however, as a common point of their faith frame that bound them together.

These five students depicted a high level of *solidarity/situational co-membership* with each other throughout their homogenous session and a greater level of comfort and enjoyment than did the students from the other faith groups. The discourse strategy of solidarity/situational co-membership is utilized when participants in dialogue realize their commonalities, and they choose to express their solidarity with each other. In addition, feeling as if their identities relate to one another, they may perceive themselves to be members of a group. This co-membership is situational, however, as different aspects of identity are expressed and relationships within dialogue are fluid.

In this interaction, the students' solidarity was based on their shared disregard for Christianity. Some had abandoned it; in Melanie's case, it had been a topic for mockery within her family. The first to establish this norm was Carl, who joked about his grandparents erroneously thinking that "Jesus was making [him] cry" (lines 10–11). In a different setting, where students who believed in the divinity of Jesus were present, this statement might not have been received positively; here it invoked laughter among the others. They continued to laugh as Carl mocked his mother's potential distress if he had abandoned the faith prior to his confirmation ceremony.

Rick supported this norm by showing solidarity in rescinding Catholicism at the point of confirmation into the religion. This move allowed Carl to continue his ridicule of the belief system they both had abandoned, revealing another act that would have been insulting to some Christians, saying "I don't" (line 18) during a sacred religious ceremony.

During Misty's turn, she responded to the request for presentation of identity and then took up the joking about Christianity and Jesus. In a twist on the narrative, she revealed her father's irreverent teasing of her mother about Jesus' racial identity. Misty tolerated her mother's requests to accompany her to church while maintaining her distance from the beliefs; however, since her father's death, she had not been on track with her mother. Her final comment, reducing her mother's imploring her to attend church to a "blah blah" (line 29), indicated that the trappings of religious observance continued to have little meaning to her.

Melanie, differing from the others in her religious upbringing, was able to close the circle in the situational co-membership by joining in on the mockery of Christianity. She also revealed that her grandmother was actually in on the joke, having written "Yeah right" (line 39) over a Bible quotation on a Christmas card. In retelling this incident, Melanie was able to bridge the gap between herself and the religiously unaffiliated in her focus group.

The peppering of laughter throughout this interaction was typical of the entire session. The atheist/agnostic students described feeling extremely comfortable in this session:

> "...that same you know warm, squishy feeling of being in a room with a whole bunch of other atheists."
> —Carl

The intrafaith atheist/agnostic session made an interesting counterpoint to the other three intrafaith conversations due to the fact that it did not reflect back on a previously established faith community. It was likely due to the lack of peers who might later appear at a worship service, club meeting, or religious educational program that these students did not have to worry about alienating valued intrafaith others. This comfort would not continue for the atheist/agnostic students in the mixed group perhaps, in part, because their shared irreverence toward religion could no longer be revealed outwardly:

> *"As the non-religious representative in the mixed group, I felt especially guarded in my responses as to not offend anyone. I found this difficult because I find my agnosticism to have two parts. One is the 'spiritual' side … and the second is a disassociation with organized religion. Although this second side wasn't expressed a ton in the [all atheist] group, I think it was a point that was silently understood by most there. So the second side I don't think I really even mentioned anything about because it would have absolutely offended people."*
> —Misty

Interfaith interactions among atheist/agnostic students. Finally, I learned from the atheist and agnostic students with whom I talked that some were holding an internal debate on whether to go beyond their comfort zones to connect with religious believers. In the mixed-faith settings, the atheist and agnostic students tended to remain outsiders because there was a lack of balance between the number of nontheists and the number of theists. Some students found this easier than others depending on social confidence levels and the strength of their beliefs.

In addition, the atheist and agnostic students had to decide whether to conceal their true opinions to avoid conflict. Their beliefs about the nature of religion and its impact on its adherents fanned the full range from indifferent to hostile, and expressing these beliefs put them at risk for offending others or becoming a target of criticism. Therefore, these young adult atheists and agnostics had different motivations for hiding their opinions. One reason was to conform to the religious norms around them and not make waves. Another was to present themselves in a diplomatic manner that better facilitated conversation. These motivations were not so different from those described by the religious students.

I observed atheist/agnostic students going out of their way to build solidarity with their religious peers, as well as conceding to the norms of getting along and not causing disagreement in the interfaith setting. As previously shown, however, I also saw Misty, an agnostic woman, defend the term spiritual from being deemed fuzzy and wishy-washy by the religious students who attempted to define it (and therefore her) in that way. Mostly, however, these nonbelieving students went along with the norms established in their groups, and even Misty made her points civilly.

An excerpt from another interfaith discussion group demonstrated one of the stronger moments that solidarity built among students of different faiths:

1 Suha: I wanted to respond to Rick's comment.
2 Jenny: Sure.
3 Suha: Because you said ... what I thought was really interesting, you said that
4 it's kind of like, as a human we're constantly creating things, and kind of, am I
5 maybe quoting you right, that as a human being we are constantly creating
6 things, and for that reason, we have to be kind of knowledgeable of our action,
7 is that what you said?
8 Rick: Yeah.
9 Suha: So, I ... reacted really strongly to that because I actually, I'm Muslim,
10 and I went to Catholic school in high school. So that was ... the place where I
11 was able to reflect a lot on my own beliefs and kind of see what other people
12 believed ... about Catholicism and their idea of God, and just different
13 viewpoints.... That's something that I really reacted to because that's how ... I
14 feel a lot of the time. Like, when you create something,... you have to have
15 complete ownership over it and be very responsible. It puts yourself in a lot of
16 responsibility. So that's something I thought about when you said that.
17 ...
18 Rick: I was surprised that we could connect in that way in that I found out
19 through the [all-atheist/agnostic] focus group, the first time here, just how much
20 not believing in God was important to me, and so the idea that I put something
21 forth that—I guess I don't want to assume necessarily that God may be your
22 [Suha] driving force—but just the idea that since we come from such a different
23 understanding about maybe why it's important to take responsibility for our
24 actions that I just find myself surprised that we could understand that together.

One of the more surprising connections to be established between two participants in my study was the one between Suha, a Muslim woman, and Rick, a multispiritual transgender student. Rick, like the other atheist/agnostic students, was somewhat concerned by society's erroneous judgment that, because they did not believe in God, they also did not live by a moral code. It was perhaps due to this concern that Rick was pleasantly "surprised" to find that he and Suha "could connect in that way" (line 18) over taking responsibility for one's own actions. Perhaps because of his upbringing in a Catholic family, Rick utilized religious speech to address Suha, musing briefly on the idea that "God may be [her] driving force" (lines 21–22). He was, however, quite careful not to "assume necessarily" (line 21) the nature of her identity, which exhibited respect toward her.

Afterward, Rick expressed the ways in which common ground was discovered:

"I was surprised that the Muslim woman found commonalities in our spiritual experience, even though I come to religion without god. Our commonalities focused around the importance of self-reflection and mindfulness in daily life. I found this situation much more exciting to be in."
—Rick

This was another case in which atheist/agnostic students significantly differed from their religious peers, in that their experiences in interfaith situations were unlikely to foster a positive emotional response. Externally, these students seemed similar to their religious peers—that is, any student may have concealed an intensity of opinions or reactions to foster smoother conversation. Internally, however, the atheist/agnostic students were much more likely to feel a negative burden because each was the only nonbeliever in a room full of the religiously committed. This may have led them to concede to the norms established in diverse conversation groups or even to extend beyond their true beliefs to find solidarity with the religious students around them. To make a breach and offer a true criticism was a risky proposition.

What do these examples of interaction say about how atheist and agnostic students use language to create meaningful representations of their faith identities? One result emphasizes again the unique reaction of atheist and agnostic students in this study—that they found it a meaningful, reassuring experience to converse with like-minded thinkers. They minimized any differences within their group and perceived a large span between them and the religious. However, once interacting with those religious peers, they tended to dampen the critiques and mockery they would have liked to express in favor of avoiding overt conflict.

EXCEPTIONAL DISCOURSE MOVES: POST-HOC POSITIONING AND POST-HOC FACE SAVING

We have now seen examples of how students' discourse moves both illuminated the faith frames at work in their worldviews, as well as how those faith frames shaped how they interacted with one another, in both intra- and interfaith discussions. Not all discourse moves, however, are immediately apparent. The strategies of positioning and face saving both have the important feature that they can actually be invisible to the conversation participants at the time and not be revealed until later. For example, some of the students I talked to admitted later on that they deliberately omitted facts or softened their opinions either for their within-group peers or for their peers of diverse faiths. This type of situation may take place when a student has concerns about the reactions of his or her conversation partners. It may be the case when a student feels he or she may be judged by a peer or when something said may cause emotional distress to a peer. If that peer is someone of consequence who will be encountered in the future, there may be little discourse evidence revealed within that initial conversation to elucidate the student's opinions.

These types of time-delayed discourse moves are what I call *post-hoc positioning* and *post-hoc face saving*. After the conclusion of a dialogue, students may describe situations in which they had omitted information or softened their true opinions. When this occurs for the primary reason of continuing to define another student, I call the act post-hoc positioning. When this occurs for the primary reason of protecting oneself and one's interests, or of not offending one another, I label the move post-hoc face saving. The employment of these strategies is noteworthy for practitioners because students' statements of harmony and agreement are not always the complete story.

In my work with the students, I witnessed some clear and informative post-hoc moves. The Christian students made these types of moves both in their own interest and in the interests of others. Their motivations were tied into the Christian faith frame, either due to denominational competition or the ability to make allowances for the beliefs of others. Jada and Brooke, two Christian women whose mutual antagonism I have already described, exemplified the former motivation. They developed a strong opposition to each other, fueled by disdain for one another's worldview. In post-hoc settings, they continued to act out their feelings for one another, describing for me and their interfaith peers how wrong the other one had been. They remained mired in their denominational competition with one another, as well as their passionate disagreement about the appropriate level of literalness in their beliefs.

In contrast to that, Will and Karen exemplified the latter motivation, revealing post-hoc face-saving moves that they had made for themselves and their fellow participants. Will's comment, presented earlier, about his "temptation to say nasty things" about Evangelical Christians demonstrates how he saved face for himself and his peers as he "managed not to" make offensive statements about others. Karen indicated in her interview that she saved face for herself and others in her interfaith focus group by neither expressing her disagreement with atheism nor allowing the views of atheists to influence her own beliefs. Instead, she made allowances for other beliefs:

> *"If somebody say is atheist, but they're still a very good person, they make*
> *good decisions, they help others, they do ... the right thing the majority of*
> *the time.... I don't see ... any problem with that as long as there's ... a jus-*
> *tified reason for why they feel that way.... If they're just like, 'Oh well, God*
> *is dumb' or something, then I can't really see that as justifiable, but if they*
> *say 'Well, this happened and this happened and I was always told this and I*
> *believe this, and this leads to this,' and there's ... a logical thinking process*
> *behind it as to why they believe that, then ... I don't necessarily agree with*
> *it, and it doesn't necessarily change my opinion about God, but I don't see*
> *them as any less of a person or wrong.... I wouldn't just say 'Oh you're*
> *wrong,' but in the back of my mind I'm not going to agree with them or*
> *change my mind."*
> —Karen, 19-year-old Methodist Christian student

The Jewish students also utilized post-hoc moves in relation to their faith frame. These instances of post-hoc positioning and face saving related to a disagreement inherent within the frame (the place of certain beliefs in the core of Jewish ideology) and a faith-specific issue (the legitimacy of Judaism in a culture dominated by Christianity). In the first case, Jasmine expressed several times how she attempted to soften her uncommon opinion on Israel so that she would not be judged harshly by her peers. She also defined her fellow Jewish participants as an exclusive, competitive group, with an "I'm-more-Jew-than-you attitude." I interpreted this post-hoc positioning as protecting her from the judgment she felt from them; if they were discredited, she potentially would feel their criticism less sharply. In addition, because there was a point of disagreement within the Jewish faith frame over the place of certain beliefs (i.e., Israel) in the core of Jewish ideology, the post-hoc move worked to shore up Jasmine's position at least from her own perspective.

In the second case, Jasmine's Jewish peers Jesse, Judy, and Joanna all described after-the-fact instances during the study in which they saved face for themselves and others by not expressing potentially offensive opinions. Their face-saving moves had kept conversations less conflict-ridden. They also served to protect the legitimacy of the Jewish perspective in a Christian-dominated culture by not opening it up to too much external (or internal) criticism. Joanna described the motivation behind her face-saving moves as trying to balance honesty with sensitivity:

> *"I wanted to speak candidly without offending anyone, but I have very*
> *strong opinions on this subject which can easily offend people. Particularly*
> *in the Jewish group, this was a problem."*
> —Joanna, 20-year-old atheist/cultural Jewish student

Judy felt that the cautions people took in her interfaith session caused the group's conversation to be less successful:

"My second group wasn't as successful I don't think because it seemed that everyone was afraid of offending another. When it was people of the same religion, we didn't censor ourselves, and when we had a disagreement we said it bluntly."
—Judy, 18-year-old Conservative Jewish student

Just as with the Christian and Jewish students, the Muslim students' usage of post-hoc discourse strategies related to particular elements of their faith frame. These students revealed information on their true feelings about the peers, having hidden these sometimes to avoid causing offense and sometimes for self-protection. Interestingly, cases of both of these motivations related to the significance of peers in the securing of one's place in the Muslim community, a core element of the Muslim faith frame.

Based on the former motivation, Sabur and Suha positioned the other Muslim students similarly to each other—as people who were judgmental and did not allow dissenting opinion to be expressed. The fact of this positioning being post-hoc and not conducted in person suggested an impetus from a faith-specific issue that arose in dialogues with Muslim students, the significance of peers in the securing of one's place in the Muslim community. They did not want to be made outcasts by making their opinions of their peers known. In addition, Inaara positioned the students in the mixed group as being "politically correct" and "walking around glass" to the point of ineffectiveness in dialogue. She clearly took issue with other students' inclination to change their language to more effectively converse with interfaith peers, which was an additional element of the Muslim faith frame.

Additional examples relate to the latter motivation, self-protection. On the campus where I held my dialogues, the MSA was a closely knit group, where most students knew each other to some degree. Sabur and Shashi described protecting themselves by not revealing the true nature of their feelings about the MSA in the discussion with Muslim students. These instances of post-hoc face saving also strongly related to the significance of peers in the securing of one's place in the Muslim community. Shashi's experience highlighted this situation:

"I feel like to some extent ... because we were in ... the same religious groups,... I myself didn't really want to voice my frustration because I guess ... these are the people you see occasionally at MSA events, so I don't want them talking about me, like 'There's the girl who hates MSA but she's still

here.' ... And also,... one of the people that was here,... she's the sister of the president."
—Shashi, 18-year-old Muslim student

Finally, the atheist and agnostic students made post-hoc discourse moves that related to three main elements of their faith frame: the place of atheists as a minority in a religious society, stretching beyond one's comfort zone to connect with religious students, and concealing one's true opinions to avoid conflict. Carl and Meghan, both engaging in acts of post-hoc positioning, made fairly opposite moves, with Carl painting his mixed-session peers as "respectful of each other to a fault" (a similar move to that made by Inaara about the same group), perhaps an indictment of a lack of critical thinking. His move was conducted to avoid conflict. Meghan instead pinned her dialogue partners as "very judgmental" and uncomfortably questioning of her beliefs. She strongly experienced the place of atheists as a religious minority within the microcosm of the conversation and was therefore unwilling or unable to stretch beyond her comfort zone to connect with them. Meghan's relationship with the atheist/agnostic faith frame had direct consequences for her discourse moves.

Melanie and Misty made post-hoc face-saving moves, concerned that they would have offended religious students if they had expressed their full opinions of the others' beliefs. Although this basic sentiment was present among students from all four faith groups, it was particularly salient for the atheists and agnostics (and thus what I considered an element of their faith frame that colors their worldview) because their opinions on religion had the greatest perceived likelihood of causing offense. Misty reported feeling "especially guarded in [her] responses as to not offend" any of her mixed-faith peers. In addition, a quotation from Melanie described the lengths she took toward avoidance:

"I was afraid to express my full religious views in the second [discussion], especially any biases I had towards the other two religions. I avoided bringing up feminism or problems I see in the legitimacy or holiness of the texts. There are some things in their holy books I sharply disagree with, but I was more comfortable highlighting the similarities, especially because the other two interviewees were really nice."

—Melanie, 20-year-old Unitarian Universalist, atheist student

Examining the four groups of students, their post-hoc discourse moves, and the relationship of those moves to their faith frames, it appears that individuals from all of the backgrounds had a basic tendency to keep their true opinions inside. Although the students did not express feeling competitive over religion in the interfaith groups, they also expressed a great many times that they censored themselves from saying what was really on their minds during those sessions. This was compared to a much lower instance of such censoring in the intrafaith groups. Still, despite the lower level of competition in the mixed sessions, which also corresponded with a slightly lower perception of being judged, the students felt compelled to gloss over or conceal their true opinions. They were more comfortable "[working] around" than "[working] through" (Heft, 2004, p. 3) their interfaith issues.

SUMMARY OF RELATIONSHIP BETWEEN FAITH FRAMES AND DISCOURSE

To conclude this section of the chapter, I would like to draw some comparisons among all four groups of students and the ways their discourse moves offer windows into their faith frames, as well as the familiar communities and discourse communities they constructed during conversation. Although I pointed out uses of particular discourse techniques with speech excerpts from students of particular faith groups, it is important to note that those techniques were not necessarily exclusive to that one faith. So, for example, while I spoke mostly about breaches in the section about Jewish students and the Jewish faith frame, there was also an important element of a breach in the Muslim intrafaith conversation.

Looking at the linkages among the techniques, the people utilizing them, and the contextual piece of the faith frame, I see clear relationships between students' discourse in both intra- and interfaith dialogues as a means to understand their distinctive faith frames. In the intrafaith sessions, the religiously affiliated students had a high level of focus on utilizing their talk to establish their places in the group, often in contrast to the others. This tied in with insecurities inherent within faith frames or discomfort with denominational distinctions. The atheist/agnostic students, instead, used their talk to build on the religious aversion inherent within their shared frame. In the interfaith sessions, students from all four groups utilized their talk to ascertain the differences between themselves and their diverse peers; their attitudes toward these gaps depended somewhat on the groups' perspective on their social position (discussed in depth in the next chapter).

I also conclude that students from all four faith groups expressed some difficulty at truly extending themselves in interfaith dialogue. I infer that students on other campuses may also be sincerely interested in talking about religion and spirituality and be genuinely willing to hear the opinions and viewpoints of others. These conversations, however, may be plagued with playing nice, speaking in broad universalisms, or exhibiting a general unwillingness to come into direct conflict. Students may save their true criticisms (constructive or not) for later report, thereby preventing hurt feelings but also avoiding a truly deep analysis of difference. These conversational issues are part and parcel of the faith frames: For Christians, they may be about recognizing the legitimacy of non-Christian faiths. For Jews, they may be related to being a religious minority in a Christian-dominated society. For Muslims, they may be about building a positive face for their people. For atheists/agnostics, they may be related to the perceived risk involved with connecting to religiously committed peers.

Because of these difficulties, sustained contact between students from diverse faiths will likely be necessary for any true breaking down of assumptions and stereotypes to occur. Such hard work, however, can have great benefit. Students may gain a more complex understanding of their own beliefs through the need to explain them to others. They can learn how someone's upbringing influences his or her religious commitments. They can connect through their commonalities with those who are purportedly quite different from them. Students from mainstream faiths can learn how social positions impact those from alternative faiths, a situation that I will discuss more fully in the next chapter.

CONCLUSION

The language employed by students when they interact in intra- and interfaith settings can be a useful window into their identities and how those identities function in the complex environment of a diverse college campus. These moves demonstrate students' level of comfort with disagreement, their tendencies to conform to the ideas of those around them, and their desires to distance themselves from potentially controversial viewpoints. They can let facilitators observing a dialogue and other campus professionals know more about students' faith identities.

Awareness of discourse strategies and their connections to the faith frames can be a useful resource for educators. A dialogue facilitator will have an advantage if he understands that two Christian students may be scrambling to position each other due to an inherent disagreement over literalism of beliefs. A faculty member will be better equipped if she realizes that an atheist student may be more likely to conceal his true opinions due to his heavily perceived minority status.

Educators who come to understand these discourse moves, and the ways in which students employ them in their day-to-day lives, can in turn make them tools for building connections between students.

Students may not be fully aware of how they are utilizing language in the ways I have described. Pointing out their acts of face saving and positioning, in plain words, can be a means for moving conversations forward and making them more productive. In Chapter 6, I will further discuss methods for using knowledge of discourse moves as an educational tool.

4

THE RELATIONSHIP BETWEEN FAITH FRAMES AND STUDENTS' AWARENESS OF RELIGIOUS PRIVILEGE AND MARGINALIZATION

I next raise for your consideration the linkages among faith diversity, awareness of religious privilege, and social justice imperatives on college campuses. Moving beyond the confines of previous literature on the religion and spirituality of college students, it is important to realize that educators and researchers are not the only people considering the roles of religious privilege and marginalization in society. Individual students are tuned in to these phenomena as well. The students with whom I spoke had a range of awareness of the ways that religious privilege operated in their immediate surroundings and larger society. This awareness, coupled with their faith frames, shaped their faith identities. It was also evident within the frames, yielding some of the faith specific issues in dialogue discussed in Chapter 2.

I have selected student remarks to illuminate their perspectives on these linkages. First, a young woman described her growing awareness that being a non-Christian caused more questions to be raised about someone's beliefs:

> *"Well, I think it's pretty easy for me, especially ... the town I'm from because ... nobody questions like, 'Oh, you're Christian?' It's not a big deal. And nobody questions it and everybody almost expects it. And so,... it's never*

really been ... anything major. It's always just been, I'm Christian and that's it, whereas, I don't know, I guess it almost seems like, for other religions, it would be more of a defining feature of ... their personality in a way ... because it's more like, 'Oh, really, you're Jewish' or 'You're Muslim' or whatever. And so,... I guess that's me just not really knowing because I've never been in the situation, but it seems like ... you would get ... asked more questions about it if you're a minority religion or you would get questioned more about it or not accepted possibly, depending on where you're at."
—Karen, 19-year-old Methodist Christian student

A Jewish woman reflected on a stereotype of Jews from Long Island, New York, which she felt limited people's understanding of her personal struggles. She experienced a seemingly affirmative image of her life as having a strong negative consequence:

"When I came here, it was kind of horrible ... If someone I knew found out I was both from Long Island and Jewish, they're like, 'You don't seem it. Are you really from there?' No one could tell. And I sort of resent the stereotype now, and unfortunately, most of the Jewish girls I knew at home fit the stereotype. And ... I can't completely deny the stereotype, but I don't feel like I fall into it and I think my entire family has sort of suffered due to Jewish stereotypes ... I mean I think,... along with the well-educated there's this whole stereotype of Jewish families being very ... together, they don't have this sort of ... dysfunctionality that a lot of other religions do. And yet,... my parents just separated a few months ago and it wasn't an amicable separation ... and people are just shocked and part of it is because we're Jewish. So I just find that ... the stereotype of Judaism,... of Jewish people, Jewish families, Jewish girls,... has had a very negative influence on my personal life."
—Joanna, 20-year-old atheist/cultural Jewish student

This Muslim young man reacted to a perceived victimization of his people by aiming to live as a positive role model:

"I kind of feel like, today Muslims are very victimized in American society. And I guess that makes me, personally,... kind of want to set the best example ... as Muslims ... just, I guess, act right, be a good person, and be kind, good, I guess, PR. Yeah,... you're under a microscope, like, 'He's Muslim,... examining how he's acting.' ... So, I guess, I feel like we have to have good PR and then we also have to ... look at the potential for what we could be, of what our status could be."
—Yusuf, 19-year-old Muslim student

Finally, an atheist student expressed anger over his family's religiously prescribed belief that God could be the only solution to depression:

"I think my lingering anger with religion can best be described as the idea that for a lot of people that I know, specifically family, it's completely arbitrary. I was born into it, therefore it's the right one. And so that would probably summarize any sort of lingering resentment towards it, is the illogic of it.... Having depression ... coming into adulthood, fifteen to twenty,... wanting to have a belief in God really did nothing and since I had read a lot about how it was blasphemous to be depressed,... I [didn't] know what to do about it, and I didn't tell my family. I didn't tell my extended family about it because I didn't want to hear 'Pray to God and God will make it better.' So ... there was just a lot of sort of bitterness about it all."
—Rick, 20-year-old multispiritual, atheist student

These concerns demonstrate that even as each student held a specific perspective on the relationship among faith, religious organizations, and social norms, each perspective was in response to different social positions for Christians, Jews, Muslims, and atheists/agnostics in the United States. As a Christian, Karen recognized that her religion was considered the default belief system around her, and that religious minorities must explain or even defend themselves to others. In the literature, this has been described as the difference between having an "optional choice identity" and having your identity ascribed to you by others (Markstrom-Adams, Hofstra, & Dougher, 1994, p. 456). As a Jew and a Muslim, respectively, Joanna and Yusuf struggled with those ascribed identities in the form of other people's prejudices and assumptions. As an atheist not affiliated with a particular organized religion, Rick was at a disadvantage even within his family because those who remained connected to his childhood religion held an emotional power over him.

Knowledge of the four faith frames provides additional nuances to these students' quotations. These students were concerned about the faiths of others, in particular which faiths were legitimate and how their own beliefs measured up. These four students, despite attending the same prestigious university and being in the same age bracket, differently perceived the experience of having a religious and/or spiritual identity in today's American society. Their awarenesses of their faith-based social positions interacted with their faith frames to influence their spiritual lives. Together, the perceptions of privilege/marginalization and the faith frames offer instruction to educators about how to engage students in social justice imperatives on college campuses.

THREE-TIERED STRUCTURE OF RELIGIOUS PRIVILEGE IN AMERICAN SOCIETY

As students instructed me in our conversations, they perceived a three-tiered structure of religious privilege in American society, one that impacted their day-to-day experiences on the college campus. At the top of the structure are the Christians, who hold the mainstream worldview in this country. In the middle are the other religious groups, who fit in with a religious society but differ from the dominant ideology. At the bottom are the atheists, who do not concur with the highest value of those religions, God belief, and generally do not participate in organized religious institutions.

This perceived hierarchy impacts interactions between people at disparate levels. It leads to feelings of disempowerment among some of the marginalized, as well as attempts by others to dismantle privilege. For example, in one of the interfaith discussions I conducted, which did not include a Christian participant, the atheist student was able to join with the Jew and the Muslim in criticizing Christianity. The students who spoke here were Melanie, a 20-year-old Unitarian Universalist, atheist woman, Sam, an 18-year-old Conservative Jewish man, and Yusuf, a 19-year-old Muslim man:

1 Melanie: In terms of ... campus climate ... the most frequent thing I run into is...
2 the Campus Crusade for Christ and ... first of all, I find that ... a very offensive
3 name,... and they'll be ... giving out granola bars at the bus stops and getting me
4 to fill out surveys that are always, like, "Are you interested in Bible school?"
5 "No." ... And then ... I'm always like, "Should I feel dirty for eating this granola
6 bar?" And I don't know.
7 Sam: I eat their granola bars and they think I'm going to hell.
8 Melanie: That's the thing ... should I let this group nourish me? I don't know, and
9 I guess it just makes me a little bit uncomfortable but, but I don't think it has
10 anything to do with ... maybe strengthening my own beliefs but ... it puts me in
11 the position where I'm not able to really think of what I believe in a productive
12 way.
13 ...
14 Yusuf: I guess I feel what you guys were saying a lot ... especially about [feeling
15 that] ... you get disrespect from other groups or ... a lot of imposition from other
16 people's beliefs.

In this conversation, the Campus Crusade for Christ (Cru) served as a means for two participants to build solidarity with each other. Their talk was quite dismissive of the student group. Melanie recounted turning them aside with just one word "No" (line 5), although the interaction left her pondering a new way of "strengthening [her] own beliefs" (line 10). Sam, inciting laughter, was not visibly concerned that "they think [he's] going to hell" (line 7), and he would "eat their granola bars" (line 7) without a second thought.

The ways in which Sam and Melanie bonded through their shared opposition to Cru was also quite reminiscent of how the atheist/agnostic students found solidarity in bashing Christianity with each other. Indeed, Sam even noted at one point in the session how the conversation would have been different "since kind of Christianity isn't represented" (due to the vagaries in assigning students to the mixed focus groups). Likely, they would have had to be more delicate in their critiques of Cru. Yusuf, although he did not comment on Cru itself, was understanding of the experiences that Melanie and Sam had described; he joined in the solidarity by saying, "I guess I feel what you guys were saying a lot" (line 14). The power in this conversation was obviously in the hands of the minority students.

Contrastingly, in other settings where Christian students and students from other religions discussed their faiths in a shared positive manner, the atheist/agnostic students were left on the outside of that talk. Here, Jesse, an 18-year-old Jewish student, worked to forge connections among religions, necessarily excluding Meghan, the atheist participant in the conversation:

> "We all pray to the same source,... I mean besides,... not necessarily you [Meghan]. I mean ... Judaism and Christianity and Islam are all ... the Abrahamic religions, they all pray to the same God, just ... have a different name for God and have different views on who Christ was."
> —Jesse

Jesse's desire to forge connections among Jews, Christians, and Muslims (despite the fact that there was no Muslim student participating in his interfaith conversation) caused him to affiliate his group with those of the other religious students, even the socially dominant Christians. The power in this dialogue lay with the religiously affiliated, not with the minorities.

In combination, these two scenarios demonstrated that Jews and Muslims were able to straddle privilege and disadvantage depending on the context, putting them in a boundary-spanning role in a diverse community. This even extended to a student like Melanie, who affiliated with a nontheistic religion and fell somewhere in the middle of religious believers in God and unaffiliated nonbelievers. Although Melanie preferred her spiritual life to be strictly without worship, she understood both sides of the religion/atheism divide:

"I do have a religion in a sense,... Unitarian Universalism, but ... I see that as my spiritual home.... There is a group called ... Young Religious UU's, and so religion is right there,... but I never actually remember enjoying the events I went to for that. So I think that ... my fear going in was that, they had worship and ... things that I wasn't comfortable with, because ... worship and religion go together for me. So I guess I see it as something that some people maybe need or ... can benefit from but that I would rather ... keep separate."
—Melanie, 20-year-old Unitarian Universalist, atheist student

Students such as Melanie can help to swing the power in conversation between the two poles, to that of the socially dominant Christians or to that of the atheist/agnostic outsiders. There are two possible interpretations of why this may be. On the one hand, this indicates a dominance of Christianity in American society, as students perceive this group's place at the top of the structure as a fixed fact of life. They might consider the United States to be a "Christian country" or suspect that an avowed atheist could never be elected president, as the atheist/agnostic students told me directly.

On the other hand, Christianity, particularly its conservative denominations, is often criticized by outsiders as being insular and ignorant. These critiques from the outsider perspective lend an important counterpoint to Christian cultural dominance, affirming minority students' opposition to Christian privilege. Such critiques indicate that students from religious minorities are not necessarily complacent about their marginalized statuses in society, and their growing understanding of the privilege/marginalization dynamic enables them to empower themselves to act against it. In essence, their outsider stance lends them some power of their own over what may otherwise seem like the fixedness of Christian social privilege. This is a parallel situation to the "social status ambiguity" of Evangelical Christians, who are "both privileged and oppressed in the same setting as a result of the same aspect of social identity" (Moran, Lang, & Oliver, 2007, p. 35).

There are elements of the faith frames that are additionally instructive on this topic. Based on my talk with students, I determined that both the Jewish and Muslim frames are permeated by some degree of anxiety and unease about social positions. From the Jewish perspective, Jewish people have to constantly negotiate their places in a Christian-dominant society; deviations from the norm in religious behavior are felt to weaken Judaism's united front, perhaps also diminishing their battle for legitimacy. From the Muslim perspective, the entirety of society is watching their every move, and they must behave to the highest social standards to prove that Muslims are good people.

Elements from the Christian and atheist/agnostic faith frames shed further light on this three-tiered structure of privilege and power. On one end of the continuum, the perspective of Christian college students demonstrates a power position, as they question whether they should consider other faiths to be legitimate. Due to their dominance, they have the luxury of accepting or dismissing these other worldviews. On the other end, the perspective of atheists and agnostics may include a strong disdain for Christianity, but that disdain does not translate to power. Instead, they must be the ones exerting the most effort to connect with those unlike them, the religiously affiliated and God-believing.

There is also an interesting contrast, for the three types of religious students, between their claims of feeling more comfortable in the interfaith conversations and the tiered power structure they described. It begs the question of why a Jewish student such as Jasmine would indicate feeling "much more accepted as whatever I wanted to be" in her mixed group when Jewish social status was not quite secure. The answer in this case perhaps lies in the complicated relationship between interdenominational competition within Judaism and Jewish students' ability to swing their allegiance away from minority status to the social dominance of the religious in general. To support this supposition, the atheist and agnostic students, of all the groups, clearly experienced the greatest alignment between their perceived overall social status and their status in the interfaith dialogues. They do not hold the same ability to shift positions as do adherents of minority religions. They always remain at the lowest power level.

This perception of a tiered power structure has implications for issues of moral and equitable treatment of students, in that it is sufficiently real in students' minds to be detrimental to their feelings of well-being and respect on campus. When people feel marginalized in their surroundings, they are less likely to engage in positive and knowledge-building interactions with others. In the microcosm of interfaith dialogue settings, those experiencing this feeling might employ more face-saving moves, attempting to avoid making themselves vulnerable to the pressures exuded by those they judge to be in the religious majority. In the broader campus environment, they may isolate themselves from situations in which the privileged are actively involved or where religious affiliation is not reflected on as a significant element of social power. Further implications for moral practice will be discussed in Chapter 6 of this book.

In addition to students' awareness of this power structure being connected to their faith frames, I learned that their understanding of religious marginalization tends to increase over time, particularly due to exposure to diverse others during college. Because it is a general trend,

the relationship between age and awareness level should not be regard-
ed as always parallel, nor can it be considered prescriptive due to vari-
ability in the ways individuals come to understand privilege and develop opposition to it. Some students, not faced with challenges to their status quo, may never come to oppose religious privilege at all. In addition,
there are specific ties between this growing awareness and the four faith
frames that we have been discussing.

RELIGIOUS MARGINALIZATION AWARENESS AND THE CHRISTIAN FAITH FRAME

Christian students are in a unique position because they are the bearers
of religious privilege in society, and therefore they must come to terms
with being perceived by others as oppressors or instigators of the marginalization of religious minority groups. This coming to terms is not an easy
process, and not even one that occur for all Christian young adults. It is,
however, one that may transpire on college campuses rich with students
of diverse faith backgrounds.

At first a young adult Christian may not recognize the presence of
Christianity's dominance in society, especially if he or she was raised in
an environment where few people of other religious backgrounds were
present. Some such students even feel that they are on the receiving end
of bias, as the media in the United States tends to look down on conservative Christianity. The nonreligious especially are seen as trying to tear
down Christianity's societal influence and not for positive reasons.

Three of the Christian students with whom I spoke fitted this description. Jada, a conservative, nondenominational Christian, felt pressure to
be "less vocal" about her beliefs so that she was not judged by society as
being "some kind of horrible person" for believing in Biblical inerrancy.
David was emotionally affected by what he felt were attacks against
Christianity in the public sector of this country, which were prompted by
Christianity's majority status. Kristin claimed she was not really affected
by the social status of Christians, as she basically attempted to avoid the
type of conflicts being raised by Jada and David. A quote from David
illustrated this mindset:

> "Now because today [Christianity is] also a predominant religion … in the
> United States, … you get a lot of battles between … Christianity and …
> atheists, … taking 'under God' out of the Pledge of Allegiance, and taking
> the Ten Commandments out of … court houses, and things of this nature.
> It's … just simply a battle … for us Christians,… and it's a shame that it
> goes on."
> —David, 18-year-old Lord of Light Lutheran Christian student

During college, when exposed to the life experiences of diverse others, some Christian students experience an increased awareness of their privilege. This may be a profoundly painful event for them, as they realize they are benefiting socially from a position that they themselves did not work to acquire. They may feel guilty over having inadvertently benefited from the marginalization of others. In this early stage of developing awareness, students are unlikely to actively work to negate their social position because they mainly exist in a reactionary state.

I spoke with two Christian women who expressed similar feelings. Like Kristin, Karen claimed she did not think much about the social position of Christians, except when tuning in to the news. Her awareness of people's differences in faith had been raised, however, by the diversity of the population at her university. Brooke was surprised that other people felt "attacked" for being Christian, which she believed clearly dominated politics and policies in this country. She had not, however, moved to address the situation through her own actions. A quotation from her contrasted directly with David's:

> *"I feel like people feel threatened by the influx of people in this country who maybe aren't Christian. And they feel like Christianity's being attacked. And … separation of church and state—I feel like people don't even understand what that really means. And … you ask them about it, they're like, 'Oh yeah, I'm for separation of church and state.' But … if they take the ten commandments off, everyone's just like, 'Oh my gosh, they're trying to do away with Christianity! And they're attacking us!'"*
> —Brooke, 19-year-old agnostic Christian student

After prolonged exposure and learning about religious marginalization through intentional workshops, academic classes and one-on-one teaching, Christian students may come to oppose privilege so as to ensure the equitable treatment of people from all backgrounds. Positive growth can be catalyzed by constructive interactions in college, whereas intolerance toward other groups and undirected anger toward one's own group seem to hinder such growth. This is a key time for student affairs practitioners to work with students, so as to help them find positive outlets for their emotional reactions and constructive ways to actualize them. As with minority students, Christian students can benefit from educational sessions and direct interventions, and from encounters with professionals who can guide and support them.

One of the Christian students I met held a constructive attitude toward Christianity's place in society. Will opposed all forms of Christian privilege throughout the world and believed there has been a social confusion of Christian theology with "militaristic nationalism." Locally, his awareness of Christian privilege had been enhanced by his recognition of the marginalization of "the Lesbian, Gay, Bisexual, and Transgender community," which prompted him to search for a more accepting denomination. His explanation of belief illustrated what opposition to privilege from within the Christian community could look like:

> "My experience has led me to believe that diversity is one of God's gifts to humankind... That's shaped my view of spirituality by, I guess, making me a universalist ... I recognize that other people have their own ways to God, or however they define God.... So ... I recognize the diversity of spiritual practices.... And ... on the other side, Christians are called to preach the Gospel to all nations,... so there's, there can be a bit of tension there.... For me I just ... try to live out the Gospel, and social justice is a huge part of what Jesus taught, so I'm ... trying to commit myself to that, and I'm trying to be in fellowship with Christians who do that. So, you know, we'll just live out the Gospel and God will sort things out in the end, I hope."
> —Will, 26-year-old Episcopalian Christian student

Drawing together the opinions of the students about the status of Christians in U.S. society, they reflected back on the mainstream, or majority, position of their group. The comments made by David, Jada, Kristin, and Karen all generally illustrated that, due to their majority status, they did not feel compelled to contemplate their social standing. In extreme cases, they even worried that being in the majority made them the subject of unwarranted scrutiny. Of the four, Karen expressed the most recognition (in her interview session) that being a religious minority in the United States would make one's life more complicated.

Brooke and Will's comments did differ from those of the other four, in that both called out Christian privilege. They expressed particular concern about the work of missionaries both locally and globally. They worried that missionaries gave a bad name to devout Christians by preaching on street corners, knocking on the front doors of non-Christians, and traveling around the world to locate potential converts. As already shown, Will had taken the strongest step toward dismantling privilege, converting to a Christian denomination that operated using "liberation theology." He also weathered a round of questions from his peers in the homogenous focus group about missionary work, which he believed was "fraught with problems of ... cultural colonialism." All told, these six Christians exhibited a range of understanding of how their privilege of religion operated in this country, from total lack of awareness to active opposition.

Generally, Christian students' rising awareness of religious marginalization in society is also a critical component of their faith frame. Most directly, it relates to the issue of the contested legitimacy of non-Christian faiths arising in dialogues. When these two strands of changing Christian identity are examined in concert with each other, it makes sense that those students who are younger or less aware of their privilege will also be more likely to question the legitimacy of other faiths. They do not necessarily view their ability to safely question others (without threat to their own social position) as an effect of their religious privilege. As a student gets older and more exposed to diversity, he may be less likely to feel insecure over the presence of non-Christian peers.

As well, Christian students' religious marginalization awareness is linked to their discourse strategies. For example, a student may feign agreement, only to reveal her true opinion in a post-hoc move, due to her understanding of her social position. She may be choosing to avoid conflict to assuage her own guilt or confusion over privilege that she does not feel she deserves.

RELIGIOUS MARGINALIZATION AWARENESS AND THE JEWISH FAITH FRAME

Jewish students are in some ways in a privileged position themselves. Among minority religions, they seem to face the least amount of pressure to represent their people or to advocate for their own religious rights in the United States. This may be due to Jewish students' fairly successful assimilation into prestigious institutions of higher education (Synnott, 1979). At the same time, they acutely recall a long history of oppression and remain wary of their apparent security. This dual position leads to a duality in behavior, as they are caught between action and inaction relating to religious marginalization. None of the Jewish students I met with presented an empowered embracing of Jews' social status.

Those particular students had a variety of ways of understanding their social status, ranging from relative ignorance to a sort of passive acceptance. As they enter college, Jewish students may feel a vague sense of marginalization with no detailed understanding of how this is operationalized. Some are content to blend in with their minority crowd, walling themselves off from the diversity (and challenge) around them.

Two of the Jewish students with whom I spoke fitted this description. Both were members of Jewish sorority or fraternity houses, which contributed an additional layer of insulation between themselves and their non-Jewish peers. Judy deemed herself affected by stereotypes of wealthy suburban Jews, although she did not specifically address what effect that had on her life. Jesse felt proud of the status of Jews in America, that they were stereotyped as being successful and well adjusted:

"The fact that Jews have a stereotype of being wealthy, and Jews have a stereotype of being educated,*... those are* good *things. We should be proud that we built ourselves up from ... the immigrant status ... back in the day, to now ... —we're at the top.... I think that's ... a pretty good stereotype for the most part. I mean besides there's resentment for that, but everyone's going to hate the guy with the biggest house on the block."*
—Jesse, 18-year-old Jewish student

Additionally, Jasmine considered herself to be more "White American" than Jewish and felt that Jews were highly assimilated in U.S. culture. This disconnect from Jewish social status may have also related to her lack of political affiliation with Israel, which in turn she felt drove a wedge between pro-Israel student groups and other groups on campus.

As they progress through the college experience, Jewish students may become more aware of their social status, understanding that there are harmful ramifications involved. They may feel anger or other negative emotions about this status. At this early stage of developing a complex awareness, they are unlikely to begin taking action around it.

The other two Jewish students I met were experiencing anger around stereotype awareness. Joanna believed herself to have been adversely affected by stereotypes of Jews because of how "shocked" people were that her Jewish parents divorced. However, she accepted the stereotype of Long Island Jewish girls as truth, saying that *"most* of the Jewish girls I knew at home fit the stereotype." She was not herself tolerant of others, in particular the Christian practices of her roommate. Sam was more connected to stereotypes faced by Jews around the world than locally and felt the need to transcend them with his own positive commitments to Judaism. This was likely because he lost three cousins to a terrorist act in Israel. A quote from Sam explained his point of view:

"I've experienced and my family has experienced anti-Semitism on ... a world political level. I feel like it's the world overall really objects to the Jewish place in the world, that I feel ... the less than complementary stereotypes ... that the Jews control the media and there's this whole big Jewish conspiracy for the world's money and ... all that other crap—you know, the Jews made up the Holocaust—... those other stereotypes that fortunately aren't prevalent where I'm from and really overall aren't prevalent in this country, but are prevalent throughout the world. I feel like ... that really affects me,... that makes my observance,... my ... connection to Judaism even stronger because I feel like I need to identify more, because of the negative stereotypes I feel like I need to prove them wrong."
—Sam, 18-year-old Conservative Jewish student

I surmise that, by the end of college, many Jewish students are clearly aware of their social status. Although none of the students with whom I worked demonstrated this, others may be interested in taking action to combat negatives in the situation.

Looking at these five students together, the Jewish students' talk about how social status was related to the perceptions other people have of Jews was interwoven with their identities. The idea of stereotypes was high in their consciousnesses despite the fact that such stereotypes tended to depict Jews as wealthy and positively assimilated into American culture. They perceived themselves to be marginalized; however, any details about the realities of this status were vague and hard for the students to operationalize. They had trouble describing the consequences of status. In order for these students to feel any urgency about the situation, some type of catalyzing event would have to cause them greater understanding. It is only then that they would gain the willingness to take action to change their group's social standing.

Looking beyond just these Jewish students, their rising awareness of religious marginalization in society is also a critical component of their faith frame. It clearly relates most directly to the common understanding that Jews are a minority in society, as well as to the issue of negotiating the legitimacy of Judaism in a Christian-dominated culture. Holding these three strands of Jewish identity together, it is logical that despite a continual awareness of their marginalized position, Jewish students must work at varying points in their young adults lives to make themselves feel secure in a society permeated by Christian privilege. A student like Joanna, who harbors a great deal of anger toward those who stereotype her, may herself be questioning just how legitimate is the status of her people.

In addition, the Jewish students' religious marginalization awareness ties into their discourse strategies. For example, a student may be concerned with a breach in the normative agreement in dialogue about proper Jewish behavior because he is worried about maintaining Judaism's uniformity and, therefore, legitimacy. He may try to smooth over a breach so as to protect his marginalized group.

RELIGIOUS MARGINALIZATION AWARENESS AND THE MUSLIM FAITH FRAME

Muslim students tend to perceive their religious marginalization more acutely than do Jewish students due to what they feel is a precarious position in this post-September 11th American society. They place a high level of pressure on themselves to demonstrate to others that Muslims are good, humble people who behave properly. Interestingly, the students with whom I spoke did not harbor resentment about this situation; rather, they saw it as an opportunity to promote their position socially.

In terms of level of awareness, Muslim students seem to have an earlier understanding of the negative aspects of their place in society than do their Jewish peers. They are similar, however, in not necessarily feeling compelled to advocate for their own rights. Their relatively heightened understanding does not necessarily lead to an individual burden or action on it.

Three of the Muslim students with whom I spoke were highly aware of Muslims' marginalized social status and the various internal complexities of the situation. Each addressed it through a certain level of political activity, scholarship, or good behavior. Shashi felt that Muslims were closely scrutinized by the rest of society, but that her social position enabled her to work politically to defend her people. She did not, however, offer examples of how she had taken a political stance. Suha felt encouraged that her parents were able to immigrate to America so she could "enjoy this privilege" of living in a place in which Islam could be analyzed, rather than it completely subsuming the culture. She worried about the divisions caused within Islam by the various denominational differences and factors. She also thought critically about Islam in relation to other world religions. Sabur, who "[found himself] to be a good person" through his behaviors, was very influenced by African-American Muslims and the fight for freedom in the African-American community. A quotation from him described his feelings about a comparative lack of action:

> *"Muslims nowadays aren't really in those culturally sensitive areas.... Some of them live in very posh societies or have surrounded themselves with other Muslims where they don't feel ... the confusion the Black Muslims felt when they converted.... We don't have that history now. We don't need to stand up like that anymore.... If there is a sense of violence then it's addressed but ... there's no ... definite power structure."*
> —Sabur, 19-year-old Muslim student

As they develop a more complex understanding of their marginalization, Muslim college students may be motivated toward positive action. Newly coming to understand the complexities of Muslims' social status could lead to empowerment from this new perspective. Throughout their expansion of awareness, the Muslim students I spoke to generally did not express their understanding of social status in terms of the specific privilege of Christians. Rather, they seemed to see their community as being scrutinized by all other Americans.

Two students most clearly fitted this description. Yusuf believed that Muslims were mistreated in American society, and that he had a responsibility for modeling the positive ways of acting as a good Muslim. He enacted this through his personal religious behaviors, as well as through political involvement. Inaara did not consider herself negatively affected by social status, only fortunate that she had been exposed to other belief systems. However, she had concern for the plight of impoverished Muslims in the United States, who she felt were overlooked as a social cause. She and Yusuf both treated their minority status as an obligation. This perspective was illustrated by a quotation:

> *"I guess I have to explain more and ... so ... it's more of a obligation upon me to represent my religion than it would be if I was a Christian then, since I'm a minority and there's less ... information out there and stuff about minority groups, obviously so. It just puts me more in a spotlight as a Muslim, I guess,... which isn't necessarily a bad thing.... I guess it's a pretty good thing 'cause then it dispels a lot of ignorance that could be out there."*
> —Inaara, 18-year-old Sunni Muslim student

Looking at the five Muslims students together, they demonstrated smaller differences along the continuum of awareness. These students were highly alerted to their societal status, no surprise given the influences of immigration, war, and terrorism on the lives of Muslims around the globe. They all displayed relatively complex levels of understanding, and I suspect it would be difficult to find any American Muslim young adults who are completely ignorant of the impact of Muslims' marginalization in society. Yusuf and Inaara had also turned their minority status into a positive catalyst for growth.

Generally speaking, Muslim students' rising awareness of religious marginalization in society is also a critical component of their faith frame, which we have been discussing throughout the previous chapters. It relates to several points of the frame, including the importance of humility and proper behavior and the issue of the contested value of modifying one's language to reach understanding with non-Muslims. These students are concerned, even at a relatively young age, with the knowledge that they are a minority in the United States. As they get older and become more exposed to positive forms of faith diversity, they may feel more comfortable with working to dismantle privilege through constructive dialogue with non-Muslim peers.

In addition, the Muslim students' religious marginalization awareness ties into their discourse strategies. For example, students' presentations of self in dialogue as being positive role models of Islam may have to do with a sense that even as a member of a minority group, one can promote change in society.

RELIGIOUS MARGINALIZATION AWARENESS AND THE
ATHEIST/AGNOSTIC FAITH FRAME

Atheist, agnostic, and other nonbelieving students perceive that the religious are privileged in society, although like students from all worldviews, some express a more nuanced understanding of what such privilege means than others. This type of understanding may be presented through discussing the role of religion in American politics and the relationships among religion, lifestyle, and career choices. They may also rail against the assumptions made by others about what a lack of religious commitment means, particularly a falsely assumed connection between religion and morality.

Atheist/agnostic students are similar to Muslims, in that, even at a young age, they may feel vaguely marginalized in a religious society. Many, having made a conscious break from the religion of their families and communities, have already moved from an insider to an outsider position. This does not necessarily mean, of course, that they are interested in doing anything to combat that position. One atheist student with whom I spoke held a rather vague understanding of her social status. Meghan realized that the religious held the power in society but not how this influenced her life on a day-to-day basis. She described how she felt left out religiously during high school:

> *"Just as long as I can remember,... all through school,... everybody was tied to a religion. There was not one person that was like, 'Oh I don't believe in God or whatever.' Everyone had one, so I always felt so pressured that ... I need to belong to some certain religion."*
> —Meghan, 21-year-old unaffiliated, atheist student

This vague, undefined sense of marginalization is unlikely to last for atheists and agnostics within the diverse higher education setting. There may also be a strong sense of anger experienced, similar to what Jewish and Muslim students feel when they become aware of their minority religious identities. If not already actively critical of the privilege of the religious, they are likely to become so. Opposition may initially take the form of protecting one's vulnerable lifestyle, such as by choosing to reside in a part of the country where many people do not take on a religious affiliation.

Two atheist and agnostic students fit this description. Rick and Misty were both aware that their beliefs categorized them as minorities, both within society and within their own families. Rick had a strong feeling of anger against the religious, whereas Misty was beginning to let go of hers. A quotation from Rick highlighted how this can be a reactionary point in time:

"I end up talking about God as a deficiency model, somehow, like it's because of lacking something. And I think that's probably still a reaction to being told, not even that I need God, but God must exist for you. And so, I talk about it still with a little bit of harshness when all I really mean to say is that, I think that I can find more strength and more obligation to behave in a way that I consider responsible without a God."
—Rick, 20-year-old multispiritual, atheist student

Finally, atheist and agnostic students may eventually transcend the anger that characterizes their rising awareness of their social marginalization. If and when this does occur, they may eventually begin working toward dismantling Christian privilege and bolstering the social positions of nonbelievers and the religiously unaffiliated.

Of the atheist/agnostic students I spoke with, Melanie and Carl had the most nuanced understandings of religious privilege and a related intellectual/academic opposition to it. Melanie was strong in her opposition to the privilege of the religious and related discrimination. She felt empowered by her peripheral position but not necessarily to the level that she actively worked to dismantle privilege. Although Carl believed that there was "such a strong *stigma* against the word atheist," [his emphasis] he had developed some tolerance of the religious, understanding that other people's religious beliefs should not necessarily reflect negatively on them. Carl provided insight into his position:

"What has changed for me during college ... is that I've gained greater respect/tolerance for those who do hold religious beliefs. As I noticed a strong correlation in high school between the kids who questioned their faith and the kids who did well in school, I came to the conclusion that anyone who is smart enough would give up believing in something so silly as God. Coming to the University and meeting very intelligent people who nonetheless adhered strongly to their faith changed that misconception for me."
—Carl, 23-year-old unaffiliated, atheist student

All together, the atheist and agnostic students keenly felt religion as a negative force in their lives, although not all described this force as permeating their place in society. They did seem to identify a growing awareness of the complexity of the situation as they progressed through college. As with Muslims and Jews, the atheists and agnostics felt a deep insecurity over their position in society.

Going beyond these five individuals, atheist and agnostic students' rising awareness of religious marginalization in society is also a critical component of their faith frame. Even more so than with the three groups of religiously affiliated students, it permeates their entire frame, from the common understanding of atheists as a minority in a religious society to the debated issue of concealing one's true opinions to avoid conflict. A student like Meghan, who had not yet developed a complex understanding of how marginalization is operationalized, may hold Christianity in high disregard while also hiding this opinion in interfaith dialogue. A student more like Carl, with his greater confidence in his own voice, may choose to conceal this same type of opinion, but instead doing so to construct a more agreeable conversation.

In addition, the atheist and agnostic students' religious marginalization awareness ties into their discourse strategies. These students are much more likely to develop comfortable norms with each other in intrafaith dialogues due to their marginalization feeling most acute.

RELIGIOUS MARGINALIZATION AWARENESS SCALE

Drawing together the information from the preceding sections, parallels can be seen among the students of the four faith groups. Although additional empirical research must be conducted to validate and delineate a specific scale, it is clear that there is an overlap between the rising awareness of religious privilege and marginalization among students from all four faith backgrounds. Obviously, there are some distinctions: The Jewish and atheist/agnostic students demonstrated the least amount of action surrounding their status. The Muslim and atheist/agnostic students demonstrated the earliest awareness of their marginalized social positions. The Christian students, because of their unique position as the dominant faith group, had to confront their own passive or active complicity in their own privilege. But no matter the social position of the individual, there appears a general trend from lack of awareness, although developing understanding, and to an intellectual (if not always active) opposition to the marginalization of certain faith groups in society.

Students from minority faith backgrounds may come to college already knowing that they do not fit in with the dominant perspectives in society. Jews exhibit a range of awareness of religious privilege in this country. Some perceive themselves to be marginalized but fail to carry this reading of social status through into their actions. Atheists, agnostics, and other nonbelievers already perceive a negative impact of their minority status; those who harbor intense anger toward the religious may be unable to use their social status as a form of empowerment. Muslim students seem to be the most highly attuned to the fact that they reside in two distinct worlds, the religious and the secular, or they at least have the strongest perception that this duality exists. Those with a less complex outlook on their faith may see their minority status more strongly and more negatively. Christian students, the majority group, follow a similar path. Each individual's willingness and ability, however, to accept the position and implications of privilege will impact his or her likelihood of progressing to the place of working against the marginalization of others. It takes a strong concern for justice to work, in some sense, against one's own group.

Of course, within these groups, students understand their faith marginalization to varying degrees, more strongly for minorities if they have had to directly confront their status during their high school years. Even if they are aware of their social status, they may not know how to act to deal with it. Nevertheless, periods of developing understanding and opposition may be stressful for students as they come to realize that they are either among the privileged or among the marginalized. This type of exposure may occur during discussion of a different form of privilege/oppression, such as race or sexuality, triggering a consideration of a student's own faith minority position. Reactions to this development may include confusion, guilt, anger, frustration, sadness, futility, or denial. Eventually, these feelings may wane and be replaced by more constructive perspectives, and educators can play an important role in this growth. Exposure to the language and concepts of faith privilege allow students to potentially take steps to combat its negative consequences.

I have taken to calling the trend of generalized growing awareness the Religious Marginalization Awareness Scale, although *scale* is perhaps a term that connotes more of a quantifiable measure than would be appropriate here. I use the term more as an indication of change over time, leaving specific numerical identifiers to be determined at a later date through quantitative studies. Nonetheless, this observable increase in religious marginalization awareness is noteworthy for educators, and a generalized way of viewing it may be helpful when working with students on campus. Based on the experiences of these 21 students, I extrapolate that young adults who are constructively challenged to learn from both intra- and interfaith peers will progress toward an attitude of ecumenism toward other faith groups. Although awareness and ecumenism are different constructs, I see ecumenism as an end-game consequence of a fully realized awareness. Individuals with this level of development will be prompted to both speak out and work (be it interpersonally, politically, academically, or in other arenas) to level the balance of privilege and marginalization among Christians, religious minority groups, and the atheists/agnostics and unaffiliated.

It would be counterproductive for higher education specialists in this area to overlook that among college students there is a growing awareness of religious privilege and marginalization in society. The growth I have noted in these 21 students, the similarities among them, and their movement through awareness toward ecumenism all denote an important trend, which, while not having been previously addressed in the literature sounding faith development, is similar to ideas found within a variety of racial identity development models.[20] Although a body of quantitative research and more focused qualitative research would be required to fully demonstrate these parallels, an understanding of the similarities can be a useful tool for campus practitioners.

BENEFITS FROM A CLOSER EXAMINATION OF RELIGIOUS DIVERSITY AND ITS RELATIONSHIP TO PRIVILEGE

Constructive challenges faced in the arena of religious marginalization can be seen as assets toward increasing the likelihood of students working to defeat religious privilege in their campus communities. If, however, the challenges are emotionally grueling, and the students do not receive the support of the campus community, they may retreat into their affinity groups and avoid addressing the situation. Therefore, this is a critical time for professionals to ensure that students are not addressing religious marginalization all on their own. Educational sessions such as dialogue programs and direct interventions with students such as counseling should become a part of practitioners' regular campus agenda so that students have appropriate outlets for support. Seifert (2008) also offers a beginning list of Christian privileges on college campuses that can be examined by educators and students.

Although both Christian students and students from minority backgrounds move through the process of becoming more aware of religious privilege during the college years, it may not be until afterward that a person reaches the point of believing in a true ecumenism for all people in society. This type of growth takes time, perhaps beyond the years spent on the college campus. It is the task of responsible practitioners to lay the groundwork, to support those students who are ready to work for ecumenism, and to encourage those students with less awareness of the situation to consider the topics of privilege and marginalization.

Educators can use this notion of a growing awareness of religious marginalization in combination with the faith frame of the individual.

---

[20]Minority students' growing awareness that they are separate from the dominant culture, and their dealing with the fallout from that understanding, may be akin to the development in Black identity described by the Cross Model of Psychological Nigrescence (Cross, 1995). The development of Christians' awareness may be similar to the abandonment of racism and defining of a nonracist White identity described by Helms's White Identity Development Model (Helms, 1993). For a more detailed presentation of these and other racial identity development models, see Evans, Forney, and Guido-DiBrito (1998).

Again, a student's perspectives on key topics within the faith frame may change over time. However, they will still tend to address a topic such as marginalization from within the frame. So, for example, a student who does not participate in organized religion may feel marginalized by the simple utilization of the term atheist by a religious peer, feeling as if she is being labeled as lacking in something. A Christian student may struggle with coming to terms with the acceptability of other religions' belief systems as he realizes that Christianity occupies a place of privilege throughout much of the world.

Interestingly, being of a marginalized faith may actually pose some benefit to students as well.[21] Nonmainstream religious followers are more frequently forced to confront their beliefs than are those of the dominant religion in society. Their "misfit [with the environment] may encourage creativity, independence, and a personal sense of control in life" (Pargament, 1986, p. 681). Although a secular voice can often find room for expression in the classroom setting, the rest of the campus environment may be much less welcoming. These students, therefore, necessarily spend more time in self-exploration and in negotiating their identities in the context of others'. Practitioners should thus be careful not to think of religious minorities as helpless victims of societal circumstance. They should, of course, be considerate of the struggles and challenges these students face on a daily basis.

In addition, this examination of Christian privilege can benefit Christians themselves, as they receive the opportunity to learn from diverse peers and gain a fuller understanding of their own religion. Self-examination can actually honor Christianity in a way that the unexamined allowance of privilege does not. This could occur through focusing on the unique position and viewpoint of Christianity, rather than assuming it to be the generic, universal mindset of everyone in American society. Once again, however, caution must be used so that Christian students are not left feeling attacked on campus. It will take some time to move them from their comfortable position of privilege to one where they are ready to consider how they may inadvertently (or purposely) be contributing to the marginalization of others.

As traditional-aged college students develop their awareness of religious marginalization, they are likely to begin seeking out ways to make

---

[21]In a longitudinal study, Alyssa N. Bryant and Helen S. Astin (2008) found that struggling spiritually correlated with a growth in tolerance toward other religions and that those students who adhere to minority religions, such as Islam and Unitarian Universalism, exhibit higher levels of struggle. They explain this as being due to the fact that "being a member of a minority religious group may present challenges that those identifying with majority traditions do not typically face" (p. 19).

their campus environments more equitable for religious minority groups. Campus professionals have the responsibility for creating opportunities for such activism and for supporting the actions of students, as well as for raising their own awareness of how Christian privilege permeates their institutions. Doing this will make college campuses stronger learning environments for students of all faith identities.

CONCLUSION

The utilization of students' religious marginalization awareness as a window into their faith identities is a new notion, one that is quite different from the conceptualizations of faith and spirituality existing in previous literature. This is a major revision that takes into account social position and therefore ascertains that a person's identity is not being described solely by his or her internal understandings of self. An individual's place in society, as related to faith, has a bearing on identity growth. It also relates to how he or she converses with others and what he or she may try to accomplish in both intra- and interfaith settings. Therefore, students' religious marginalization awareness can be understood by practitioners to be both an important identity element as well as a lens into other facets of their worldviews.

The relative positions of faith in American society, as well as students' varied understandings and levels of opposition to religious privilege, indicate that campus professionals should create opportunities to educate students on these topics. Unlike conversations about race and other forms of diversity, those about diversity of religion and faith have been infrequent and perhaps lacking in information from supporting literature. Certainly, there has been little discussion about relationships among religious privilege, faith identity, and students' use of language in interactions with diverse peers. Campus professionals who come to understand the convergence of these topics, however, can become more effective than ever before in their work with diverse college students.

5

THE IMPACT OF THE COLLEGE ENVIRONMENT
ON STUDENTS' DIVERSE FAITH IDENTITIES

I would now like to bring the focus of this text back onto the college and university campus. The 21 students with whom I spoke were very specific about the situations they felt had caused them to grow in faith during their college years. Listening to their stories, I noticed that some of those situations were characterized by constructive challenge, which prompted growth in self-understanding and greater tolerance for diversity. Other situations did not challenge the students but rather allowed them to remain in their safe, unchanging identity spaces. Some situations even inhibited growth by causing students to withdraw. Undoubtedly, there were other experiences that shaped the students' identities; the ones I highlight, however, were the ones they chose to bring to the forefront of our conversations. The examples that I provide in this chapter are also meant to be illustrative and not taken as typical of all students.

The following influential situations were recognized by more than one student. I have divided them into two groups: those that catalyzed positive growth and those that inhibited growth. I have left out a few experiences that students did not back up with explanations of resultant growth or stagnation (i.e., those that had a neutral or unrelated impact). The influential situations are particularly noteworthy for educators interested in fostering growth in faith (and tolerance) in their students, as well as for helping students to push through situations that might otherwise cause them to withdraw or hold back from identity growth. As well, I will note a couple of examples of how the experiences related to respective faith frames. The experiences will act as a bridge to the final chapter of this book, in which we will examine implications for practice and research.

CATALYSTS FOR POSITIVE GROWTH IN FAITH

The following four situations are those noted by students that promoted their positive growth in faith.

Interactions with religiously diverse peers. Students reported experiencing a positive growth in faith when they interacted with religiously diverse peers, usually in informal situations. This type of experience seemed to be a common and also effective means for engendering genuine respect toward other faiths. That is, development toward plurality could occur when individuals were open to other faiths. One student who had embraced these interactions was Sabur. He described his biggest influence for change on campus as being interactions with religiously diverse peers:

> *"Back home [in Saginaw, MI] I don't really like hanging out with other Muslims 'cause I felt that they'd always judge me ... and I didn't really like that feeling. So ... a lot of my friends were non-Muslims. They were Hindus, one was a Jain who became an atheist, a couple were Christian.... I didn't have any Jewish friends because there's really no Jewish [students] in my high school, but now I find myself befriending Jews in my hallway or in my dorm which is very nice 'cause I get to learn about another religion.... And then I get to talk about religion with atheists, friends that are atheists and friends that are not of my religion that I didn't have access to back in Saginaw. So I feel like, perhaps maybe I don't pray five times a day, but at least I get pretty interesting discussions, pretty good discussion times around dinner..."*
> —Sabur, 19-year-old Muslim student

Sabur, although clearly already open to a diversity of religious and nonreligious ideas as a high school student, had continued to make room for this type of learning while in college. Interestingly, he hinted at using peer-to-peer conversation as a replacement for requisite Islamic rituals such as daily prayers. Also, because Sabur remained sensitive to the judgments of fellow Muslims, he accessed this learning through non-Muslim friends.

Beyond Sabur, four other students described similar experiences. Karen (19-year-old Methodist Christian student) portrayed the situation that altered her beliefs to be when she was exposed to a group of friends with a broader cross-section of religious identities. Coming from a town where one could "count the number of diversities … and, like, on one hand," religious diversity was a positive revelation for her. Jesse (18-year-old Jewish student) found the religious diversity of the campus to be a positive inspiration, where students were told, "Make up your own decision based on what these books say." He ascribed this supportive environment to being on a secular campus, where students came from a variety of backgrounds. Misty (21-year-old unaffiliated, agnostic student) faced the initial challenge upon arriving at college of discovering that students tended to find friends and communities through their religious and ethnic identities, something that was not possible for her personally. She felt forced to ask herself, "Oh, well, what am I?" and truly consider her faith identity. Finally, the main challenge for Carl (23-year-old unaffiliated, atheist student) was interacting with people with religious convictions and realizing that religious faith and intelligence were not mutually exclusive character traits. Carl was quite open to his growth in tolerance despite the steadfastness of his own beliefs. He was confident of his own voice.

These five students, from all four faith backgrounds, had each taken the diversity around them and turned it into a positive learning experience. Some even sought out diversity as an intentional way of accessing new knowledge. They did not shy away from the personal reflection that observed differences caused them to undertake.

Academic courses on religion. Several of the students discussed having taken classes in religions. Suha was unique, having taken courses on Eastern religions, whereas the others all studied the monotheistic religions of the West. In each case, however, the students experienced a marked growth in understanding, tolerance, and openness to other religions, and sometimes they even gained greater knowledge of their own religions. For example, Melanie was a committed atheist. However, she let herself be more open to the existence of monotheistic religions when information about them was delivered through academic means:

> *"I took a religions class here, the intro, the three religion tripartite kind of class. It was … so great,… I learned a ton, it was very non-proselytizing. I mean, it's interesting … the way the different professors approach their subjects, each one representing a single religion…. I feel like there's more variation in certain religions than others, and … the Christian teacher, for example was very much … analytical and a critical…. And I saw the Muslim teacher as … you know, he was Muslim, he was teaching Islam, and … it*

was a very different feel from him. And I also saw him as a cultural ... being because of the way that he expressed himself was different. And I think that through reading the Koran, I got an idea of where that came from, so I mean it was just a great class.... And so I guess that ... I have a lot more respect for each of the three monotheistic religions from that experience ... and I think that the tone in the class was excellent, like, I had conversations with ... Christians who were like, 'What are they trying to tell us ... in this class?' And I thought that was ... fascinating, kind of ... just a study of humanity. So, I guess that's how it started to come through to me at this institution."
—Melanie, 20-year-old Unitarian Universalist, atheist student

As detailed in this quotation, Melanie utilized her classroom experience as a way of investigating monotheistic religions and the people who adhere to them. She seems to have undertaken religion as mainly a cultural study and not an inroad to self-analysis. While remaining uninterested in changing her own spiritual beliefs, she did become more respectful of others' beliefs.

Four other students described similar experiences. David (18-year-old Lord of Light Lutheran Christian student) said he found himself being changed by exposure to other religions. For him, this took place in a religion course that explored Christianity, Judaism, and Islam. Through the class, David developed a greater understanding of the latter two, as well as what he termed the *"secular* view" (his emphasis) of Christianity. Inaara (18-year-old Sunni Muslim student) had taken several classes involving religion as a topic. One in particular was a class on interreligious dialogue that was "insightful" and helped Inaara to become even more confident in her own beliefs. Suha (19-year-old Muslim student) had taken courses on the religions of Southeast Asia, such as Hinduism, Buddhism, and Taoism. She was influenced to think more critically about the classifications people make based on religion. Finally, Meghan (21-year-old unaffiliated, atheist student) had taken courses on religion and found them to be a positive learning experience. In particular, a class trip to a mosque "dispelled a lot of things that [she] thought" about Islam, presumably of the stereotypical variety.

For these five students, academic exposure to other religions, particularly in contrast to their own faiths, was a positive learning experience. New knowledge caused the students to reflect back on their own beliefs, modifying or strengthening them accordingly.

Differentiating oneself from the ideals of one's faith group. Two of the students were undergoing separations from their faith communities around the time of our conversations and acknowledged their college experiences as significant influences in their change in religious identification.

Both used their statuses as relative outsiders to their faith communities to shape their individuality. They were not merely accepting the standard ways of thinking and being but were coming to develop their own paths. I have written about one of the students, Jasmine, whose main challenge was her realization that she was a rare Jew who did not support Israel politically:

> "... In high school ... I was ... one of the only Jewish people.... There was ... no Jews at my high school and so coming here I was, like, 'Oh my God, there's so many Jews, what am I going to do?' ... I think I shifted a lot, like, it forced me to think about a lot of things, about ... what I thought it meant to be Jewish.... I had to think about it when I was younger 'cause I was ... asked questions ... like, 'You're the only Jew in the class, like, what does it mean to be Jewish?' But then ... in this context,... suddenly it wasn't about ... me making things based on my parents or ... my synagogue or something. It was ... based on all these other people around me and how do I see myself then ... in comparison with ... this huge community. And I think specifically ... in terms of Israel ... I had never thought about it that much and then came and was, like, 'Oh my God.' I don't know, I freaked out 'cause so many people, the only way that they're Jewish was through Israel. And that was really ... scary for me 'cause that was so different than my Jewish experience."
> —Jasmine, 21-year-old Reconstructionist Jewish student

Jasmine went on to say that exposure to Zionists led her to become less Zionistic in outlook herself and to realize that she could be different from the other Jews on campus. This experience of shifting from one of the only people identifying as a Jew to being one of a large group forced Jasmine to constantly evaluate her identity and the circumstances under which she would discuss it. Instead of feeling at home in an environment with so many other people of her religion around, she had to mentally work to differentiate herself from them.

Suha (19-year-old Muslim student) was similar to Jasmine, in that she was highly critical of the status quo in Islam, including the Islamic microcosm contained within the campus MSA. She spent a lot of time analyzing Muslim life from an academic standpoint, which she found to be "stimulating." Jasmine and Suha had both shaped their identities in contrast to their intrafaith peers. Suha contrasted with the cases of Shashi and Sabur, Muslims who *did* not find themselves fitting in with the MSA, but had not expended much energy thinking about what they did believe (as opposed to what they did not believe).

Theology. Two Christian students encountered situations on campus that caused them to update their interpretations of theology. Both made modifications to their internal belief structure based on these outside influences. Will described a theological challenge that he faced in college:

> *"Well for me,... interacting with different people was—in some sense my beliefs have not changed at all, and in many senses they've changed a lot,... and interacting with ... different people was probably what changed them.... Exposure to the Lesbian, Gay, Bisexual, and Transgender community led me to think, led me to reconsider what my church originally taught me about homosexuality.... After that I was exposed to liberationist ideas like Freire and also Feminist theology, so ... that changed me a lot... But at the end of the day, I came in a Christian, and I'm going out, when I go out I'll still be a Christian. I'll have switched denominations."*
> —Will, 26-year-old Episcopalian Christian student

Will's reconsideration of his church's position led to further exploration of alternative theologies and an eventual change in denominations to one that was more embracing of all people. During this experience, Will opened himself to powerful change, and he took a strong, personal stance to find a Christian movement that would affirm these beliefs.

Similarly to Will, Jada (23-year-old nondenominational Christian student) represented her main challenge during college as a theological dilemma based on conflicting definitions within Christianity of what it meant to be "saved." To resolve the question, she spent time studying with a group of fellow students with whom she felt comfortable and, as she phrased it herself, "finally came to [her] own conclusion."

The experiences of these two Christian students (interestingly, so denominationally opposite to one other) were unique among the students with whom I spoke. The singular feature of their influence was that it emanated from something internal to their faith, rather than something solely external (such as an academic course or interactions with fellow students on campus). Both Will and Jada deepened their commitments to Christianity, albeit within a new or more specific denominational setting. Their growth through theological exploration also related to components of their faith frame, the denominational distinctions within Christianity, and the disagreement about how those distinctions impact the truth of Christianity.

Summary. These four motivators for progressive growth share a common theme: Each of the students faced constructive challenges to the tacit, familiar beliefs they brought with them to college from high school and their home communities. In each case, the students were influenced to reflect on their own orientations in comparison to some other, whether new friends, a student religious group, or a faculty member presenting academic information. Even the noting of theological variations prompted internal rumination, and those students who embraced such reflection and were willing to be flexible grew in positive ways.

CATALYSTS FOR STIFLING GROWTH IN FAITH

In addition to situations that promoted positive growth, the students also identified those experiences that tended to stifle their change and development.

Avoiding interactions with religiously diverse peers. Unlike the circumstances described earlier, wherein students embraced the opportunity to interact with diverse peers, there were several students who went out of their way to avoid such interactions. For some, this was a standard mode of operation perhaps because of a desire *not* to be changed or because of a generalized discomfort with the different and unknown. Joanna, exhibiting a bit of both motivations, described being challenged on campus by having to face and interact with people of varied religious identities:

> "I have one liberal-Christian-background-atheist-lesbian roommate, two very Christian—one is Campus Cru, I don't know the denomination of the other but also churchgoer every week, and then one Jewish girl…. One of the Christian girls puts up little signs of like … the crosswalk sign except someone kneeling and praying, and … all these little Christian things all around the house, and I'm completely unused to it…. I mean I'm … tolerant of it but I kind of wish it wasn't there…. I thought I was tolerant before, but I think it was because I didn't have to deal with the religion ever, and now … I'm discovering that my tolerance before wasn't really what it was…. I'm not going to try to convert anyone to my beliefs,… but I expect them not to try to convert me. And I just kind of wish they'd keep their religion to themselves, in a way."
> —Joanna, 20-year-old atheist/cultural Jewish student

Her roommate experience made Joanna realize that her tolerance for religious beliefs was not as strong as she had once thought. In fact, her definition of tolerance seemed more akin to willful avoidance. Joanna did not identify with the Jewish community on campus, and she found it preferable to shut out conversations about religion rather than engage in them productively.

Avoidance was the most common mechanism for stifling growth, and five other students told stories similar to Joanna's. Brooke (19-year-old agnostic Christian student) did not feel that college had challenged or changed her beliefs. Her main source of contention, however, was the "ignorant" student body on campus, which she felt did not know enough to engage in intellectual conversations about religion. Sam (18-year-old Conservative Jewish student) insisted that his beliefs had not changed during college. He listed, however, three situations that had challenged his faith: examinations that were scheduled on *Shabbat*, the global political situation, and encounters with Christian missionaries on campus. Sam's concerns all tied in on some level with the rights and legitimacy of Jews and Judaism. Yusuf (19-year-old Muslim student) indicated that he had not been challenged by anything taking place specifically on the college campus. As he pointed out, he was still living with his parents off campus, and so he had less exposure to many of the situations that encouraged identity development.

Rick (20-year-old multispiritual atheist student) had experienced a familiar challenge on campus—that of interacting with Christian missionaries. He could not bring himself to be open to conversation with "someone who [had] directly approached [him] with the intent to" convert him, and so he frequently avoided conversations even with well-meaning Christian peers. Finally, Melanie (20-year-old Unitarian Universalist, atheist student), although more willing to reflect than Rick, still had a fairly low threshold for openness to missionaries. Although her Unitarian Universalist beliefs pushed her toward acceptance of all others, she struggled with accepting those who were not open to all lifestyles, particularly to those of the LGBTA students on campus. Because of this struggle, she avoided, feeling that "interaction with that will have *no* impact so I just have to tolerate it."

The fact that students from all four faith backgrounds tended toward this type of behavior suggests that it is a highly likely scenario for many other college students. The tendency to avoid the challenging and seek the familiar, although not very productive, may be the easy and safe route.

Withdrawing from one's faith community. Three students had stepped away from their religious communities during college. Each was similarly at sea and felt the need to reconnect in some capacity to facilitate growth. When they did reaffiliate, for all of them, this reconnection would look different from their original attachments to Christianity and Islam. For example, Shashi was not comfortable in the MSA, which produced recognizable consequences for her growth:

> *"I was somewhat forced [through the research study] to confront myself and my religious views—how I am less practicing as I used to be, and my 'plans' to learn more about the history of my faith have remained unfulfilled.*

Nonetheless, I realized that plenty of others are in the same boat as I am."
—Shashi, 18-year-old Muslim student

Although the discussion groups had helped to awaken Shashi's awareness, she continued to allow herself to stagnate by invoking peers who acted similarly. She took comfort in her commonalities with others who were struggling, rather than seeking inspiration from those who were exploring their identities.

In addition to Shashi, two other students had withdrawn from their faith communities. Brooke (19-year-old agnostic Christian student) had disassociated from her family's religion, thinking that church "doesn't apply to [her.]" However, Brooke still believed herself to be a Christian and was seeking a way to connect with her faith outside the purview of church services. Ironically for Sabur (19-year-old Muslim student), the presence of a larger Muslim community than in his high school caused him to draw back from religious practice because, as he said, his "horizon's really limited inside the Muslim Student's Association." Like Shashi, he was not looking for another way.

None of these three students was very happy about the separation between themselves and their broader faith group. They remained in a somewhat reactionary state, knowing what they disliked about institutions within Christianity and Islam but not yet devising alterative avenues for expressing their beliefs. As well, Shashi and Sabur's pulling back from the MSA relates to the significance of peers in securing one's place in the Muslim community, recalling the Muslim faith frame projected from the study.

Falling in with a group of like-minded peers. Another situation that seemed to stifle growth in faith during the college years was actually the opposite of withdrawing from one's faith community. Indeed, enmeshing oneself *too* much into one's community could also be detrimental. Not being confronted by diversity of faiths, most likely the students' tacit understandings of religion and spirituality went unchallenged. Two women had chosen to establish friendship networks with people of similar backgrounds and ideals to themselves, restricting their exposure to diverse others. Newly committed to Christianity, Kristin had looked for a community that would enhance her growing beliefs and not challenge them:

> *"I sought out church. I sought out ... a faith community here when I got to school. And ... since I had really not ... fully realized who I was as a Christian or gotten it ... until my senior year of high school, it was kind of like I got here fresh.... So I found this great ... church that I really like and*

*a community of people and that has just really strengthened my faith.... So
... the fact that I'm surrounded more often now by people with ... a good
relationship with the Lord, that has definitely taught me a lot of things and
affirmed it in my life, I guess."*
—Kristin, 20-year-old Methodist Christian student

Kristin's choices had the effect of her learning from the other students
similar to herself, instead of developing her own ideas in response to difference. Similarly, Judy (18-year-old Conservative Jewish student) was a
member of a Jewish sorority and expressed that little had changed within her identity since entering college. Her biggest challenge was answer-
ing questions that people had about her beliefs, but she did not find that
strenuous in any way. Likely, this was because of her explanation that, on
campus, "every out of state Jew will find each other, and mush together,"
and because she had joined a sorority that was nearly 100% Jewish in
membership.

Although others in the study had similar experiences of joining student faith groups or Greek chapters organized around faith identity, most
differed from these two, who described their Christian community and
sorority as central influences on their identity. For example, Jesse, who
belonged to the same fraternity as his father, wished the group had more
non-Jewish members. Unlike Judy, he was critical of received Jewish
truth perhaps due to his positive interactions with diverse peers.

Summary. In contrast with students who grew and developed in their
faith orientations, the common thread running through the experiences
that stifled growth during the college years was a deliberate avoidance of
interactions that encouraged constructive introspection. In each case, the
students walked away from diversity or from the challenges that
emerged from within their own religious communities, seeking the familiar, the like-minded, or the undemanding. Students who acted in these
ways retained their current approaches for viewing the world through
their faith.

CONCLUSION

Student reports about situations that influenced developments in their
faith aggregated along two axes. Experiences that promoted growth were
characterized by critical self-reflection in the face of constructive, challenging interactions. Experiences that did not promote growth, or even
stifled it, were characterized by avoidance and withdrawal, often associated with protecting the status quo within comfortable surroundings.
This distinction between students engaging with difference and acting

like it did not exist appears key in understanding what is potentially gained or lost to students during their collegiate experience.

One not atypical campus experience that highlights this difference and its significance involves student interaction with Christian missionaries on campus. For Jesse, who chose to engage in conversation, talking with Christian missionaries was a learning experience that deepened a belief system. In contrast, those who chose to ignore the proselytizers, while disparaging them, such as Sam, Rick, Meghan, and Melanie, blocked the possibility of acquiring a better understanding of self.

Both intra- and interfaith situations appeared to be motivators for progressive growth. In each case, students were encouraged to reflect on themselves in comparison to some other—be it a new friend, a student organization, or a faculty member presenting academic information. Students who embraced this situation and were willing to be flexible grew in positive ways. They were encouraged to find solidarity with one another—to constructively breach critical social norms that threatened to dampen disagreement. They were helped to move beyond the compulsion for playing nice usually visible as face saving and hedging talk.

Alternately, students also acted in more restrained and self-protective ways that negated the positive effects of promising interaction. When the discomfort they experienced was too strong, they were more likely to turn away rather than productively persevere. Their prior beliefs informed the appropriateness of such actions and manifested as tendencies to dismiss the ideas of others as ignorant and unthinking or to listen without willingness to change. Whether polite superficial engagement or deliberate avoidance of interactions that encourage constructive introspection, such student responses sustain uniform rather than pluralistic ways of thinking about faith—one's own as well as others. Educators can help these students learn to take risks—to move beyond positioning those with whom they disagree into boxes that cannot influence their ways of thinking. Shielding students from negative encounters, although well intentioned, appears to be counterproductive to an educational mission and to individual students. They are better served with guidance on how to react during uncomfortable faith-based encounters.

Although the study that informs this book was not specifically designed as a learning intervention for the participating students, the experiences in the focus group conversations led to positive outcomes for the students. The students told me that open, encouraging interactions with diverse others from the campus helped them expand their worldviews. In this respect, the method of my interaction with the students was also an intervention in their lives, one that they reported caused as much reexamination of their beliefs as did other situations, although it had not been my specific intention to catalyze this type of growth.

Additionally, and although I did not explore it in detail in this chapter, the college experiences that shaped students' faith identities did relate to their respective faith frames. In the next (and final) chapter of this book, I return to the core concept of the faith frames and consider their application to many arenas of the higher education experience, suggesting ways that educators may use them as guideposts for effective practice with diverse students. As well, I consider broader implications for research and practice, aided by the students' considerations of the critical situations that impacted their growth in faith.

6

IMPLICATIONS FOR EDUCATORS WORKING WITH STUDENTS OF DIVERSE FAITHS

We now know that the campus environment has the potential to be a catalyst for positive growth in faith by college students. The lessons I learned from my students can inform practice on other college campuses, in classroom settings, in informal interactions, and in structured dialogue sessions. Using discourse analysis as a tool for better understanding students' talk holds great promise for practitioners, even those already well versed in facilitation. It can even be used in a casual manner to help educators key into critical moments in which students are exploring their identities, connecting with one another, or pushing off each other to get a better handle on their own ideals. After identifying these moments of heightened activity, students' motivations can be probed to enhance learning. When students make a move through their words, it is a moment of educational opportunity.

In this final chapter of *Understanding College Students' Spiritual Identities*, I turn to the implications of all that we have discussed thus far. This knowledge is only useful if campus educators can apply it to their practical work with students. In addition, it is important due to its context and relationship to the broader societal conditions I discussed in the Prologue of this book. Therefore, I take a detailed look here at several scenarios in which this information can be applied.

UTILIZATION OF FAITH FRAMES AS AN EDUCATIONAL TOOL
WITH INDIVIDUAL STUDENTS AND IN INTRAFAITH SETTINGS

The first broad arena in which to consider applying the material from this book is when working with individual college students or when working with them and their intrafaith peers. Educators can be on the lookout for cues in students' talk to key in to their faith frames, and therefore the ways in which faith is influencing their actions and beliefs. One way to do this is for student affairs professionals to tune in to keywords alerting them that a student is utilizing his or her faith frame to address a specific concern or situation. Examples of such terms include: *purpose, beliefs, ideology, identity, lifestyle, faith, philosophy, religion,* and *spirituality.* Other signals may be descriptors, such as: *core, fundamental, primary, deep, main,* and *strongest.* As well, educators can notice usages of certain discourse techniques in everyday conversations as students attempt to define themselves and others through their talk. These moments tend to be noticeable when they have an emotional resonance; when they seem to be concerning, enlightening, or stressful to the students; or when students define an incident as being significant.

For example, practitioners may become aware of students' statements of identity/presentations of self. In these instances, they can prompt students to contemplate their reasons for presenting themselves in these specific ways. They can ask why they chose to highlight certain elements of themselves in the conversation and how those elements contribute to the life choices being discussed. Or, to present another example, when practitioners notice instances of hedging, they can encourage students to take stronger ownership of their beliefs. Pushing back on a hedged declaration may have the effect of getting a student to admit an insecurity or a pressure to conform to certain norms. As well, a student may be prompted to expand on his true opinion without the protection of hedges.

As one considers the situations in which a student's faith frame may come into play and affect life choices, it becomes clear that there are many opportunities for practitioners to use the frames as an educational tool. They can be ways of reaching out to students, supporting their identity growth, and helping them understand and connect to diverse others. In addition, addressing students through the lens of frames is not all that difficult; in some cases, a student will raise this element of his or her identity as a topic of conversation, merely with gentle prodding from an interested professional. Another student who may not realize the influence of his or her faith can also be helped to notice it to make choices more consonant with his or her identity. This could foster greater satisfaction on the part of the student. Some situations in which educators may become aware of the influence of faith frames and capitalize on them include the following.

Selecting vocation. All college students are required at some point to determine how their educational endeavors will be put to use in the employment sector (even if they plan to delay employment for graduate school or some other reason). Some experience their determination as more of a calling, something that connects deeply to their sense of being in the world. These might be Jewish, Muslim, or atheist/agnostic students who find their faith communities to be precariously positioned in society, prompting a commitment to social justice through the workplace. Or these might be Christian students, refusing to take their religious privilege as a free pass, choosing instead to work for justice and equality. Inaara, a student in my study, felt that her faith guided her toward a career path:

> *"With my career I want to go into—I guess the simplest way to explain it is ... humanitarian work. I'm a sociology and psychology major, so I want to go ... and do humanitarian work and things like that and I guess my beliefs strongly influenced that because ... it's such a major part of my religion to be ... helping the needy, and changing ... the environment and things like that when it's in desperate need. So, I feel like this is just ... another way that I'm practicing my religion through my career and ... through helping other people is ... fulfilling ... something that God has recommended for us to do."*
> —Inaara, 18-year-old Sunni Muslim student

As a mentor, an academic advisor, or another type of counselor, how would one recognize this type of thinking? How could an educator capitalize on this strength of the students' conviction to help them work through their vocational options? Educators may be hesitant to question students on the role of faith in making career choices; however, this line of inquiry is similar to discussing how a female student's gender identity has influenced her choice to work politically for women's rights. A counselor could ask: What is it in your belief system that is guiding you to make this type of career choice? What are you bringing from who you are as a person to this decision-making process? How do you think that this type of job will support who you want to be in the next few years or even longer term?

Academic experiences. In the classroom, students bring many aspects of themselves into the learning experience. Although educators are primarily attuned to students' intellectual contributions, in certain types of classes they are also welcomed to tap into elements of their identities. In identity study courses, such as on gender and race, and in other courses, such as history, sociology, and psychology, students' personal experiences can be related to the material. Teachers may even expect students to utilize faith lenses when specifically discussing comparative religion or religious history, particularly if the essential truth of a belief system is brought into question. Students can experience a marked growth in understanding, tolerance, and openness to other worldviews and even gain greater knowledge of their own religions. As I have already discussed, numerous students with whom I worked shared this type of experience. Suha had the opportunity to academically learn about her faith in high school:

> *"When I was in high school I went to Catholic school, so ... that was during the time that I formed a lot of my world view and built upon my knowledge of Islam, because it was really nice that we had theology classes everyday so we were to talk about God and spirituality and these topics."*
> —Suha, 19-year-old Muslim student

Suha developed this thinking after taking a theology course. But how does a student's faith affect his participation in courses on civil rights, the economy, or physics? When might a student's religious minority status impact her views of topics outside the purview of religion? The academic setting is a key opportunity for educators to utilize the faith frames as a tool for fostering positive learning and growth among students. If a teacher is aware that a student is likely to hold a particular topic as important or to feel that another one is contentious or problematic, he can address them in a sensitive manner. He can also raise them to test students' openness to diverse ideas. A faculty member could ask: What in your own life experiences helps you to understand the social inequalities present in our country? How do discussions of the origins of our universe relate to your day-to-day life experiences? How can we bring our personal selves into conversations about literature, psychology, and history?

Co-curricular involvement. Outside of the classroom, students are making choices on a daily basis concerning which activities and organizations to offer their time. Many campus groups relate to students' faith frames and spirituality. These include groups addressing certain political or social justice topics or even clubs where students come together around their mutual love for nature, music, and art. Such organizations might foster new thinking, or they might feature unchallenging situations that do not encourage students to differentiate their own ideals from those of like-minded peers. The description Judy gave in her post-study questionnaire was an example of this:

"I have become more aware of my religion since coming to college. I always grew up Jewish and related to other Jews, but I never knew that it was such a large part of who I am. I instantly gravitated to Jewish friends, joined a primarily Jewish sorority and find myself at many pro-Israel, pro-Zionism conferences and activities."
—Judy, 18-year-old Conservative Jewish student

Students do connect to their out-of-classroom experiences through their faiths. How can a professional in student activities or events management capitalize on students' connections to their co-curricular choices through their faith frames to ensure the most fulfilling experience for them? How can they encourage students to think critically, even when surrounded by those who share similar values and ideologies? Again, faith may not be the first lens a practitioner thinks of when considering how a student is choosing to spend his or her time outside of the classroom. The rewards for addressing this, however, may be fruitful. A student who does not identify in a religious way may feel a great spiritual high during a camping trip with a nature club and perhaps will want to address that with someone who is supportive of that kind of experience. A professional could encourage such a discussion by asking: What type of emotional experiences do you have when participating in this organization? What is it about you as a person that led you to join this group? How are you tapping into the nonacademic elements of your college life by participating in this type of activity?

Student religious organizations and intrafaith dialogues. Finally, faith frames can shed some light into students' ways of being within their self-selected religious organizations, such as Cru and the MSA, on college campuses. Working with students within their self-selected religious communities may be outside the purview of many campus professionals; on secular campuses in particular, this task may be considered solely the responsibility of ministry staff. However, both ministry and other student affairs staff members should be aware of the difficulties students find with speaking to members of their own communities and indeed the anxieties they feel over being deemed lesser-than members of their own identity groups. Although not specifically labeling conversations to be "intrafaith dialogues," practitioners working with multiple members of the same religious community (perhaps on an issue facing their group, such as the installation of a prayer space for Muslim students in a student center building) should keep themselves attuned to forms of religious competition that might raise individuals' insecurities. If a student chooses to constructively differentiate from the ideals of her affiliate group, it may force her to evaluate her identity. If, however, she chooses instead to withdraw from her religious community, she may experience a feeling of loneliness or searching. These faith groups are students' "familiar communities," and it can be painful when the ethos of these groups do not mesh with students' personal beliefs:

> "I guess I'm pro-Israel, ... because I do agree with their position and it's also hard when that is all I'm surrounded by, and that's the only side I get,... but I can't stand the way most of the Jewish groups ... advocate,... not even just Jewish groups on campus, but when I went to those Conservative services for Rosh Hashanah, the rabbi's sermon was something on the ... conflict in Israel and they just all take such a 'the world against us' mentality. It's just so black and white and ... you're either for us or you're against us, and if you're against us it's—it's just too black and white for me."
> —Joanna, 20-year-old atheist/cultural Jewish student

As for members of the clergy, who are undoubtedly experts in the religious ideals and struggles of their students, bringing this new knowledge (from the vantage point of student affairs research) into their work may provide a new perspective on students' development, their interactions with fellow members of their religious groups, and their interactions with students of other religious affiliations. These campus professionals can consider inquiring about this by asking themselves: How can faith frames help clergy view students' internal religious conflicts in a different manner? Why are some topics particularly contentious among students of the same religious background? Why is it that disagreements between students from the same group are sometimes more fraught with emotion than those between students from different groups?

Summary. As these examples illustrate, certain situations are rife with opportunities for students' positive growth. In each case, students should be offered encouragement to consider their own motivations and perspectives and to gain a greater knowledge of the origins of those elements of their identities. They can learn how to put these personal elements of themselves forward in interactions with similar-minded peers to understand how these peers influence their growth during the college years.

In addition, the faith frames can be used as a method for stretching students in appropriate ways beyond their comfort zones. Educators can challenge them to address topics of contention from a different perspective, such as the literalism of the Bible for Christians or the necessity of ritual behavior for Jews. These types of positive challenges have the added benefit of encouraging students to become more aware of the faith frames at work in their own lives and to understand how they influence beliefs and actions on a daily basis. One advantage of this can be more thoughtful responses to ideological challenges as opposed to gut reactions. Another can be movement toward greater acceptance of diverse opinions. Finally, students who become more aware of their own lenses can help refine the details of an educator's knowledge, thereby helping to ensure more effective work with future students from similar backgrounds.

UTILIZATION OF FAITH FRAMES AS AN EDUCATIONAL TOOL WITH MULTIPLE STUDENTS AND IN INTERFAITH SETTINGS

The second broad arena to consider applying the material from this book is when working with multiple students of different faith backgrounds and in interfaith settings. Practitioners can be aware of students utilizing discourse strategies in these situations and how they work to accomplish students' goals of developing their own faith identities in a diverse environment. Practitioners can then capitalize on these discourse strategies to maximize student learning.

Interfaith dialogues. Cornille (2008) states that "if dialogue is to be possible, it must find its deepest reasons and motivations within the self-understanding of religious traditions themselves" (p. 8). I would add that dialogue is also a necessity in college as students grow and gain self-understanding on the individual level. Campuses that already offer students the opportunity to participate in formalized interfaith dialogues can make these sessions more effective through attention to students' discourse techniques. Campuses that may be looking to establish dialogues can benefit from incorporating the tracking of technique usage from the beginning of the process. By maintaining this higher level of awareness for students' motivations, attitudes, and behaviors, educators can take a fairly simple step toward making interfaith dialogues more effective.

Facilitators of these dialogues should consider bringing students' discourse techniques out into the open as topics of conversation. For example, when practitioners become aware of face-saving statements being made by students, they can take the opportunity to applaud efforts to keep the conversation respectfully civil while also encouraging participants to be honest with one another. If students are attempting to save face for others by not making critical statements, they can be persuaded to seek constructive methods of communicating criticism. If students are attempting to save face for themselves by not sharing their intimate thoughts, additional ground rules for establishing a safe conversation space can be laid down.

To make the most of an interfaith setting, dialogues should be designed so that students have the opportunity to hear each others' viewpoints on key topics, even basic ones like definitions of religion and spirituality and whether they consider themselves to be practicing in their faiths. Then students should be encouraged to question each other, follow up on comments, and generally lead the conversation to points that are important to them. The combination of these strategies will ensure that students have a basic understanding of each others' perspectives and that discussions will center on the most critical topics.

In addition, campus educators can learn to recognize the occurrence of discourse moves and the effects for students who make them in dialogue. Noting moves as they are made, or even shortly afterward, can positively influence practice and help foster learning. For example, when I realized that a group of diverse students was decidedly avoiding critique of one another, I asked them about it, resulting in a thoughtful conversation about why people may be afraid of insulting one another and making themselves vulnerable. Students may respond to this type of prodding by delving more deeply into their own motivations.

Practitioners should also consider using other techniques to make interfaith dialogues safe spaces for diverse students to join. Suggestions include:

- Having the faith background of at least one of the facilitators match that of the participating students;
- Having an even balance of believing and nonbelieving students regardless of the religious diversity of the believers;
- Checking the protocol for the group's conversation with clergy and/or knowledgeable laypeople to ensure that the questions are appropriately worded;
- Reminding students that no one is trying to convert them, but that bringing together people from varied perspectives is being done with the intention to foster learning; and
- Offering students opportunities to privately convey opinions that they may not want to share publicly, such as in one-on-one conversations or in written documents.

I myself incorporated these strategies in the conversations I held, although in retrospect I would have included a greater proportion of atheist/agnostic students. The students with whom I spoke expressed that they learned from their participation, both broadly and in more specific ways:

"I learned about other religions and other people's views on religion and spirituality. I also learned that people from other denominations and other religions have had similar religious experiences to mine and have some of the same beliefs and ideas as me."
—Karen, 19-year-old Methodist Christian student

"I actually have never spoken with a Jewish person with those beliefs on the Israeli–Palestine conflict. It was interesting to hear how she felt isolated among other Jews. Also, the students who were Muslims expressed how they believed MSA was very conservative. I suppose these two views drive home the point that every religious group would like to count itself as the voice of the religion and you must be careful not to generalize."
—Misty, 21-year-old unaffiliated, agnostic student

Dialogues are not the only situation in which student affairs professionals can utilize information about the ways students of diverse faiths interact. How can campus practitioners translate this new knowledge about students' use of language to better understand their faith identities? Interactions with peers of diverse faiths seem the most common and also effective means for engendering genuine respect toward other faiths. If the individual is open to it, development toward plurality occurs. Consider the following scenarios.

Roommate relationships. Conflicted relationships between roommates are situations faced by professionals and student peer advisors quite frequently. On the outside, a conflict may seem like a case of differing lifestyle choices, such as when an early-to-bed, early-to-rise bookworm lives with a late-night partygoer. But perhaps the conflict also relates to the former student's commitment to representing Muslims as studious and well behaved and the latter student's relative freedom of activity due to a lack of concern for Christians' place within peer culture. Or perhaps the students are keeping each other at arm's length, afraid of admitting their opinions about each other's choices and insulting one another, therefore using face-saving moves for protection. Sabur shared an example of a minor roommate problem in a humorous way:

"I tried to wake up for the morning prayer today. Instead I just kind of pissed off my roommates because the alarm went off really early in the morning."
—Sabur, 19-year-old Muslim student

Would a resident advisor or housing director look to the possibilities of faith impacting roommate relationships? How could these students be engaged on the level of their relative ideologies rather than the more obvious conflict over bedtimes? How could this disagreement be captured as an opportunity for both students to learn more about diverse worldviews? Real-life scenarios are certainly more complex than the simple example just described—all the more reason for practitioners to consider the influence of faith diversity. When talking with such students one on one or in their roommate pairs, questions could be asked to guide them into addressing this element of their selves and their relationship, such as: What is it about you as a person that guides you to set this kind of daily schedule for yourself? How does this type of activity fit with the rest of your lifestyle? What do you think it is about your roommate's lifestyle that guides him or her to choose to live this way? How can two people with such different outlooks live together more harmoniously?

Academic experiences. Academic experiences are just as critical for interfaith interaction as they are for the moments of faith frame recognition discussed above. In the classroom environment, students with diverse faith viewpoints may have vastly dissimilar reactions to the academic topics being discussed. This may be manifested in students disagreeing with each other or with the professor. A conflict may arise based on conflicting perspectives surrounding academic topics such as politics, history, or science. Nonbelieving students may harbor anger over the influence of Christianity in American history and try to position Christianity's existence as negative. Faith-based discomfort may also manifest in students glossing over their differences in opinion or softening the presentation of their beliefs to smooth the flow of conversation. Some may simply tune out rather than address a point that may lead to conflict. As an example from my students, Melanie wrote the following on her post-study questionnaire:

> *"In college I took a religions course and two major things stood out: (1) The cultural background of religions are beautiful and historically intricate and interesting, (2) There's a lot of built in stigmatizing of women and minority groups to the three big monotheistic religions. I perceive this as an obstacle caused by anachronism, in the sense that the texts were written a long time ago. On the other hand, this background to the texts proves an obstacle for future growth, at least as I see it."*
> —Melanie, 20-year-old Unitarian Universalist, atheist student

Educators should consider students' faith frames to be aware of how divergent tendencies in interfaith settings will impact academic involvement. As teachers, understanding and promoting this awareness will allow us to better serve our students. We can ask ourselves: How can a professor encourage students to make constructive contributions from their varied faith perspectives? How can classrooms be made into safe spaces, where students can feel comfortable making honest statements while still ensuring that discussions do not become disputes? A classroom educator could attempt to identify students' faith backgrounds. She could inquire about their willingness to share personal opinions on contested topics. She could ask her students: How can we work together to ensure this classroom is one in which everyone can comfortably share their perspectives? How can we commit to sharing controversial opinions while not insulting one another?

Cultural and political co-curricular involvement. Many campus co-curricular activities are centered on common elements of students' identities, such as their racial, national, and cultural backgrounds. Even within such groups, students will have divergent political and advocacy interests. Common areas of disagreement certainly center on reproductive rights and conflicts in the Middle East. Campus organizations formed around these interest areas may be hot-button groups, coming into conflict with others espousing opposing viewpoints. Members of these groups may breach the campus norms around civil debate. Students may resist having constructive dialogue with one another, instead wishing to hold steadfastly to their points of view without having to critically examine them. Jasmine's status as an outsider within her own community was evident in the following quotation:

> "I'm pretty politically involved in terms of ... liberal stuff on campus ... and it's interesting because I feel like ... we always do a lot by coalition. I did a lot with the Coke coalition campaign a few years ago and also with ... the affirmative action this past fall.... I think that Jewish groups do things pretty separately than a lot of other groups on campus, like other culturally oriented groups who often will ... band together on a lot of things."
> —Jasmine, 21-year-old Reconstructionist Jewish woman

How can professionals in the realm of campus activities bring students together to discuss hot topics? How can they encourage students to think critically even while continuing to advocate for their political interests? How should the situation be addressed when student groups come into direct opposition with one another? One strategy is to consider how students from different faith perspectives interacting in interfaith settings can be applicable for helping students engage one another in a positive manner. Understanding their tendencies in interactions can be instructive for establishing ground rules in dialogue. A professional could get students working constructively together by asking: What parts of ourselves are at risk when we engage in conversations with people who have different points of view than us? How can we make true extensions of ourselves without feeling anxious over the results? What positive outcomes might there be of talking with people who challenge our version of the status quo?

Summary. Interfaith dialogue can be a positive channel for growth within individual students. It can also lead to increased tolerance between groups. In addition, less formal situations in which students encounter others of diverse faith backgrounds may prompt students to reconsider their own identities or come to terms with the identities of others. For example, the Interfaith Youth Core (n.d.) brings religiously diverse young adults together around service projects and shared values. Just as in intrafaith settings and one-on-one interactions, educators can prompt students to explore their own motivations and ideologies. Students can learn how to appropriately bring forward these elements of their inner selves while in communication with others.

Special considerations must also be taken for the non-God-believing and religiously unaffiliated students in our midst. Educators can work with atheist/agnostic students, both within intergroup settings and on an individual basis, to help foster the same types of growth in their self-understanding and in their tolerance and acceptance of others. If practitioners can make themselves comfortable with discussing faith in general, they can also learn to talk about faith that is exclusive from religious belief. Educators should consider the ways in which a students' lack of commitment to a religious ideology could change the type of sensitivities required in such conversations. It may be necessary to modify some of the language to ensure a lack of bias (discussed below) or to simply be open to hearing about alternative venues for finding meaning in life.

ADDITIONAL IMPLICATIONS FOR MORALITY AND EQUITY IN PRACTICE AND RESEARCH

In Chapter 1, I introduced the idea that demonstrating, through research and practice in higher education, simple tolerance for people of differing faith backgrounds does not go far enough in terms of a moral stance. At the end of this text, the most critical assertion I can make is that individuals' faith frames make a difference in their identities. Frames are a strong determinant of how people view the world and interact within it. They are co-constructed at the group level and demonstrate that people of the same faith share some elements of their outlook, which vary markedly from those of differing faiths. They help to explain why a Christian-centric perspective in research and practice is inappropriate for addressing the needs of non-Christian students.

The implications of the faith frames on morality and equity are profound. To act morally as educators, we can no longer overlook vast swathes of our student population. To treat all students equitably, we should be willing to open our awareness to ways of being in the world that do not operate out of a place of Christian dominance. We cannot take the step backward of treating our students as if they are all the same in their faiths. We need to be sensitive to feelings of marginalization, of insecurities, and of resultant competition, withdrawal, or frustration among students. The substantial repercussion of this most vital understanding is that higher education leaders, researchers, and other professionals should drastically change their understanding of faith and spiritual identity. The moral imperative insists that we should no longer be complacent in this arena of diversity.

In this section, I assert several avenues in which the morality and equity of practices and theories around students' faith identities should be improved. The viewpoints and needs of non-Christian students can no longer be ignored by educators who purport to treat all students equitably. Theories and practices that heretofore have claimed to be universal in nature, but that truly operate from a Christian perspective, must be replaced by those that are inclusive of all faiths, religious or otherwise.

Challenging Christian privilege on campus. As traditional-aged college students develop their awareness of religious marginalization, they may begin seeking out ways to make their campus environments more equitable for religious minority groups. Campus professionals have the responsibility for creating opportunities for such activism and for supporting the undertakings of students, as well as for raising their own awareness of how Christian privilege permeates college campuses. This type of activism lags far behind the diversity initiatives surrounding race and gender: "The issue of Christian privilege and the struggle to create religiously, spiritually, faith-based, and secularly inclusive communities are still relatively new areas of diversity-related learning and action" (Clark, 2003, p. 48).

At their own individual level, campus professionals can educate themselves and their colleagues to become more knowledgeable in their leadership. They can conduct reading groups, workshops, and presentations for each other, as well as bring in outside experts to speak to student affairs staff members and faculty members. They can also attend the myriad related sessions at national conferences for professional and academic associations, and contribute to the further education of the broader field by publishing and presenting on their own campus improvements.

In working with students, educators can strategize ways to work with those at all levels of understanding. For those students with a simple perception of the religious marginalization that exists in society, practitioners can offer awareness-raising opportunities, such as lectures and workshops through existing co-curricular organizations, reaching out to students where they already are. For those students who have developed an understanding of marginalization, they can be encouraged to consider the impacts of power and privilege, and the effect of being in one position or the other. For those students who oppose religious privilege, educators can provide them with outlets to express this resistance, through campus leadership channels and political involvement.

At the institutional level, practitioners should consider a type of campus audit to determine when and where instances of religious privilege are occurring. Although at public colleges and universities it may not be a typical activity to reflect on the role religion plays on campus, it is important to ensure that a lack of attention does not unintentionally favor one group over another. University structures should be examined to consider their possible Christian-centricity. Such an audit could include examining campus rituals, the academic curriculum and calendar, the availability of diverse co-curricular options, the prevalence of missionaries or others trying to convert non-Christians, the access to houses of worship for minority students, and the diversity of worldviews among the college staff and faculty. For example, are efforts at honoring diverse religious holidays concentrated in December because of the prominence of Christmas? Or are other holidays at different points in the calendar also acknowledged on campus?

Language use. The next implication in the area of practice has to do with our employment of language when working on these topics. As I indicated toward the beginning of this book, atheist and agnostic students have unique interpretations of the typical terms surrounding their faith. Although my students provided several different definitions for religious, the only one they discussed with any frequency was the relationship between religion and morality. This was likely because they were highly concerned with what they believed was an erroneous connection between the two. They found quite offensive, in fact, the perception that those who do not believe in God also do not have a moral code. They did not believe that having God as an ultimate judge of their actions was the best possible motivation for just behavior.

The atheist and agnostic students also differed distinctly from the religious students when it came to defining spiritual. Although the Christian, Jewish, and Muslim students heavily defined spirituality as a connection to something greater, this idea only came up twice over all the conversations with atheist/agnostic students. Instead, they tended to view spirituality as more of a grounded event having to do with one's mindset or way of life. They described spirituality as being self-reflective, as noticing or being aware, and as being outside the everyday.

The ways that atheist/agnostic students generally understand religion and spirituality have implications for the moral and equitable application of language on college campuses. Just as educators have become practiced at ensuring that their language does not contain biases around gender, race, and sexual orientation and gender identity, so too should we ensure that we do not inadvertently privilege the religious with our speech. Becoming practiced at discussing the diversity of faith, rather than the more typical notion of religious diversity, is necessary to include nonbelieving students. Inter*faith* dialogue differs from inter*religious* dialogue because the latter is limited to the religiously affiliated. Interfaith dialogue evens the ground somewhat by positing through its label that everyone shares in faith and that everyone can engage in dialogue on the basis of that faith.

Research on marginalized religious populations. The realm of higher education research also must be upgraded to become more moral and equitable around students' diversity of faith. As I have already indicated, research considering the spiritual identities of religious minorities is quite sparse, particularly when it comes to Muslim and atheist/agnostic students. This book opens avenues for exploration of these students' identities. With Muslim students, future research could study their issues with sacred/secular balance, their understandings of religious marginalization in post-September 11th America, the relationship between immigrant status and identity, and the importance of being able to enact their ritual practices on college campuses. With atheist/agnostic students, future research could study their feelings on being minorities in a religious society, their spiritual explorations outside traditional religious institutions, and the various influences (such as science and humanism) that inform their faith framework.

In addition, questions remain about the many faiths not included in my current work. Future researchers exploring the topic of faith and spiritual identity development should also strive to include members of religious groups that were not included in this work, such as Hinduism, Buddhism, Jainism, and Sikhism. In particular, polytheistic believers may have quite different frames for understanding the world than do followers of the monotheistic religions.

Finally, I believe large-scale quantitative studies must be conducted alongside the more personal, nuanced qualitative studies like the one informing this book. In fact, additional quantitative research that I have conducted with a colleague suggests that affiliating with a marginalized religion leads to less spiritual growth in college (Bowman & Small, 2010) and reduced psychological well-being (Bowman & Small, in press), as well as greater religious skepticism (Small & Bowman, 2011).

Research on students' multiple identities. I am also left with lingering questions about the interaction between faith and other forms of students' identities and the impact of what scholars call "intersectionality," which has been developed as "analytic lens to include both multiple identities and larger social structures of power and inequality" (Torres, Jones, & Renn, 2009, p. 588). Students did not come to this study identifying singularly as religious and/or spiritual individuals. Often their races, ethnicities, sexual preferences, political viewpoints, and nationalities influenced their interactions with others. There were several clear instances of students' other identities having an impact on the dialogue. Jada and Brooke, two African-American Christian women, engaged in often contentious talk with one another, calling on value-laden family and community anecdotes to bolster their arguments. Rick, a transgender student, openly expressed how his marginalized gender identity directly influenced his breaking with Catholicism and becoming an atheist. Inaara, born in Afghanistan, held political beliefs that were complicated by her immigrant status as well as her ethnicity. These students may not have been "living comfortably with multiple identities" (Jones & McEwan, 2002, p. 168), and they were certainly experiencing the interactions of those identities in profound ways.

Due to the limitations of my research design, I was unable to deeply analyze the roles these multiple identities played in the study. In addition, having only 21 participants meant being limited in how much data could be collected on these identities. The study included only small subsets of non-White races and ethnicities (Brooke, Jada, and Misty identified as fully or partly African American; Sabur, Shashi, Suha, and Will identified as Asian/Pacific Islander; Meghan labeled herself Mexican/Chinese; and Inaara labeled herself Persian). Rick was the only student who openly discussed a minority gender identity. Finally, although several of the students (most significantly within the Muslim group) were first- or second-generation Americans, they hailed from different countries and did not often talk about the nuances in belief to which this may have led. Future research pieces should consider the other forms of identity students hold, such as race, gender, sexual preference, and nationality, and how they interact with religion and spirituality over a lifetime of identity growth. In addition, I urge researchers examining other forms of diversity and intersectionality to include religion, spirituality, and faith in their scholarship.

Summary. As I have said from the outset of this text, my work exists not only to present learning in the specific topic area of students' diverse faiths but also to promote change in higher education to make our college and university campuses more moral and equitable places for students to spend some of the formative years of their lives. Conscientious practitioners may be able to foster great change in their local environments to reduce students' feelings of marginalization or guilt over inadvertently wielding their privilege in ways that hurt others. For scholars interested in bolstering the research on this topic area, much work remains to be done, with so many avenues wide open for further exploration. Those from around the field of higher education who come together around this cause can improve the lives of so many diverse students.

CONCLUSION

Throughout the course of *Understanding College Students' Spiritual Identities*, I have demonstrated that students from different faith backgrounds have divergent ways of viewing the world and interacting within it. The four faith frames I described provide a foundation for understanding those divergences and a starting point for educators to productively work with Christian, Jewish, Muslim, and atheist/agnostic college students.

The frames come into play when working with students on a one-on-one basis and when situations arise within a faith community. Atheist, agnostic, and other heterodox students, in particular, require and deserve special attention by those practitioners attempting to work with campus faith groups, as they have their own special needs that have been consistently overlooked in student affairs.

In addition, the frames can be used to raise the level of educational success in interfaith settings. Bringing diverse students together in interfaith dialogue provides opportunity for them to develop tolerance and grow in their own self-understanding. The discourse moves that students employ in these settings can be levers for facilitators to use in persuading students to interact more constructively. They can also be tools used in other educational settings to promote healthier relationships between the diverse of faith.

Finally, all of this discussion of faith, diversity, language, and interaction can lead to the critical examination of religious privilege and marginalization and students' perceptions of these social structures. Although the problems relating to religion—and inter- and intrafaith disputes—that face American society cannot be solved solely through changes in higher education, they can begin to teach a generation of young adults how to contribute positively to dialogue and understanding—and to Patel's (2008) notion of true pluralism:

> … Religious pluralism is neither mere coexistence nor forced consensus. It is not a watered-down set of common beliefs that affirms the bland and obvious, nor a sparse tolerance that leaves in place ignorance and bias of the other. Instead, religious pluralism is "energetic

engagement" that affirms the unique identity of each particular religious tradition and community, while recognizing that the well-being
of each depends upon the health of the whole. (p. 21)

In addition to simply creating a fuller picture of faith diversity at
America's colleges and universities, this book is intended to motivate
every type of campus professional to make changes in the environments
around them, to make colleges and universities more inclusive and supportive, and to help students grow and relate with one another in positive manners. Indeed, educators have a moral imperative to improve
their campus environments in these ways so that all students, regardless
of religious affiliation, are justly treated. The relative positions of students' faith groups in American society indicate that we must be diligent
in our efforts. The practice of working with college students incorporates
the imperative to honor the unique contributions of a myriad of faith perspectives and to dismantle the continued social injustice of Christian
privilege on college campuses.

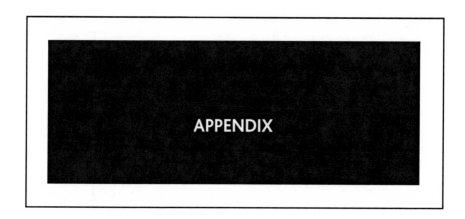

APPENDIX

In this section, I offer further information about my research methods and the strategies I used to ensure the trustworthiness and rigor of my study.

FOCUS GROUPS

Two sets of focus groups were conducted. The first set consisted of religiously homogenous participants, one each for Christians, Jews, Muslims, and atheists. These focus group conversations ranged in length from 66 to 90 minutes. One reason for conducting homogenous groups was to allow students to begin thinking about their faith identities in the relatively safe space of a group with which they religiously affiliate (or share in nonaffiliation). The intent was to ensure that "the participants in each group both have something to say about the topic and feel comfortable saying it to each other" (Morgan, 1997, p. 36). Although homogenous groups are recommended in focus groups (Krueger & Casey, 2000), this safety was considered relative in the study due to the fact that students from different subgroups (such as Orthodox and Reform Jews) may have perceived themselves as having quite dissimilar values and perspectives.

Guiding questions for the round one focus groups centered on potential similarities among participants, for example, asking about their religious backgrounds, the relationship between that religion (or nonreligion) and their spiritualities, and their perceptions of their faith group's status in society and the impact of that on their lives. As described in Chapter 1, I included a co-facilitator in three of the homogenous focus groups, Christian, Muslim, and atheist/agnostic.

An additional purpose of holding homogenous groups was to get an understanding of students' worldviews that was more nuanced than the information they could provide on the demographic information sheet. In fact, the term *homogenous* was not entirely appropriate after accounting for intragroup diversity. This aided the research in the next step, organizing the participants into heterogeneous focus groups.

The second set of focus groups consisted of the same participants as the first round, but they were intermixed by their faiths. During the second round, five smaller groups were convened, lasting a range of 48 to 63 minutes. I was the sole facilitator. Group consisted of three to five participants. Although the attempt was made to have one from each faith group, due to scheduling conflicts, this ended up not being possible. Ultimately, the organization was based on perceived personality complementarities, participant scheduling availability, and as much similarity in age and difference in faith that scheduling allowed.

Guiding questions for the second round focus groups focused on potential differences among participants—for example, asking them to react to each others' provided definitions of religious and spiritual. Although some of the questions were the same as they were in the first round of focus groups, it was anticipated that the varied faiths of the participants would have an impact on the responses they gave and the reactions they had to one another. It was explained at the outset of these groups that any repeated questions were designed so the participants were exposed to new perspectives.

Focus groups were selected for the main instrument of this study due to their unique capacity to provide participants the opportunities to react to each other, support each other, disagree with each other, and through dialogue construct new understandings. As a researcher, I was in the unique position to observe interaction around this topic (Morgan, 1997). As well, previous research on students within campus religious groups found that the "focus group interview method may reveal shared meaning" (Mankowski & Thomas, 2000, p. 520) among the students, which cannot be evidenced through individual interviews. In addition, involvement in a focus group may have actually assisted participating students in formulating their own tacitly or internally held beliefs in a way that could be expressed to others for the first time (Turner Kelly, 2003). As well, when participants speak in this public way, "the researcher witnesses the strength of the convictions held" (p. 51).

In addition to highlighting the individual similarities and differences among individuals, the focus groups also emphasized group-level distinguishers. Each of the sessions featured a unique collection of personalities, values, and opinions. Although the questions asked in each round were closely aligned, the students' reactions differed often on the basis of their conversation partners. The collective building of identity could only have been studied through the use of this type of interaction.

Although a limitation of focus group data was that group members could sway each other's opinions (Turner Kelly, 2003), leading to either conformity or polarization (Morgan, 1997), this phenomenon was worthy of analysis. Some students exhibited signs of learning to trust themselves as authority figures, whereas others demonstrated a high level of susceptibility to peer influence. In either case, the dynamic of the focus group itself created the circumstances for rich data (Merriam, 1998) to emerge. Students' relative strengths of conviction were an important fact to note.

FOLLOW-UP WRITINGS

One week after the students' participation in a second round focus group, each was emailed a questionnaire to be used to evaluate their experience in the conversations. The week delay was provided to allow for some reflection time. Students were asked to provide their responses within 2 weeks time via e-mail or in hard copy on the documents provided to them. The purpose of these documents was to provide the researcher with additional information on students' individual understandings of the research process, as well as to provide students with the opportunity for personal reflection. Reflection, well established as a pedagogical tool (Boud & Walker, 1998; Cowan, 1998), creates "situations in which learners are able to make their own meaning rather than have it imposed on them" (Boud & Walker, 1998, p. 199). Reflection happens when learners "analyse or evaluate one or more personal experiences, and attempt to generalize from that thinking ... so that, in the future, they will be more skillful or better informed or more effective, than they have been in the past" (Cowan, 1998, p. 17). Given time to look back on the conversations, students may have been able to articulate additional thoughts on what transpired and what they learned.

INTERVIEWS

Although it was not the main intention of this research to conduct individual interviews with participants, it was determined that some students' talk or writing warranted additional probing. Therefore, students were asked on their reflection documents whether they would be willing to be contacted for an additional individual interview. To flesh out the richest possible data, one male and one female from each worldview were interviewed on a one-on-one basis. These conversations lasted from 14 to 38 minutes. The 14-minute conversation was a low outlier in length; unfortunately, multiple probes did not provoke that student into elaborating on her thoughts. Questions during the interviews focused on reactions to the study thus far, understandings of one's status in society, beliefs in God, truth claims, and strength of beliefs.

QUALITATIVE CODING ANALYSIS

Analysis of the data was conducted using thematic qualitative coding as well as various discourse analysis methodologies. For the first round of analysis, thematic coding was applied to the full data corpus. This coding was conducted in a "line-by-line" (A. Strauss & Corbin, 1998, p. 199) manner. Open codes (A. L. Strauss, 1987) were created through a reading of the texts themselves and not based on using "preestablished" categories of analysis (Emerson, Fretz, & Shaw, 1995, p. 152). This helped to ensure that the coding was based on what was actually said by the participants and not by the researcher's inherent biases.

After the initial coding process was completed, levels of broader or interrelated codes were created. These series of axial (A. L. Strauss, 1987) or focused (Emerson, Fretz, & Shaw, 1995) codes were used to categorize the open codes around important themes and relationships. When these two levels of coding were complete, several types of analysis were conducted to ascribe yet more meaning to students' spoken and written words. The Atlas/ti software used for the analysis provided the capabilities to examine the most important codes based on groundedness, the "number of text passages of a code or memo," and density, the "number of other codes connected with a code" (A. Strauss & Corbin, 1998, p. 277). Codes were also used to compare between what a student said in two different focus groups. A code that made an appearance in one place and not the other for the same student received extra scrutiny to determine the reasons for this. All of these analytic techniques enabled the development of a final layer of this analysis, examinations of the most important codes for each group and those that held significant variations among the groups.

DISCOURSE ANALYSIS

The discourse analysis techniques that were used in this study provided a window into the ways that students use language to define their faith identities. I previously used these techniques in a study that employed discourse analysis to understand student spirituality (Small, 2007). I selected three transcript elements per faith group. At least one was drawn from the corresponding homogenous focus group. At least one was drawn from a heterogeneous focus group featuring a student or multiple students from that faith actively demonstrating an important discourse move. The third segment was drawn either from the same homogenous group or from a different heterogeneous group depending on which better illustrated the story being told by the students. I also endeavored to keep some balance among the students, providing somewhat equal presentations of the experiences of each one. These main episodes were used to examine the ways the students framed their faith identities in conversation and how those descriptions changed depending on who they were talking to. The episodes were examined through discourse analysis.

To conduct the data selection, I first selected qualitative codes that corresponded with the discourse analysis techniques being considered for the study and examined quotations from the focus groups to determine when the types of discourse had taken place. For example, to locate examples of norming, I examined codes that represented instances of students working discursively to establish norms or of existing norms being acknowledged. As a second means for pointing to potential segments, I reviewed the students' questionnaires and interview transcripts to determine the focus group conversations that they found concerning, enlightening, or stressful. I looked for discursive segments that represented a significant interaction between participants within a focus group, had an emotional resonance, and related to theories-in-use. I also looked for the richest data elements (Merriam, 1998), those in which the students' language gave the most descriptive picture of their own ideas.

To read more about these types of discourse moves, I suggest the following texts: Davies and Harre (2001), Erickson (2004), Garfinkel (1967), Goffman (1967), and Johnstone (2002).

ROLE OF THE RESEARCHER

According to Merriam (1998), there are several stances a researcher can take toward the subject of his or her research. In this study, I conducted the research utilizing the stance of "participant as observer" (p. 101), convening the group with the advance understanding of the researcher role, a role that took precedence during the research proceedings. That being said, spirituality may be a sensitive topic for some students, and therefore I took the following precautions during my work with them:

1. I reviewed the informed consent paperwork at the beginning of all focus groups and informed them that their spoken and written words would be marked with pseudonyms, not their real names.
2. I informed students, particularly during the heterogeneous focus groups, that bringing together students from varied perspectives was being done with the intention of facilitating learning. It was not being done to test anyone or create conflict.
3. Although I encouraged students to comment on and question each others' statements during the focus groups, I planned to intervene if any interaction seemed to be emotionally disturbing to a participant. Fortunately, this did not end up being necessary.

Overall during the course of this study, I attempted to exemplify the Social Constructivism paradigm, which defines meanings as being jointly created and contextual (Creswell, 2003). In this paradigm, knowledge is viewed as "individual reconstructions coalescing around consensus" (Lincoln & Guba, 2000, p. 170) and the researcher acts as a "'passionate participant' as facilitator of multivoice reconstruction" (p. 171). This paradigm is manifested in research in the following manner:

> Individuals seek understanding of the world in which they live and work. They develop subjective meanings of their experiences— meanings directed toward certain objects or things. These meanings are varied and multiple, leading the researcher to look for the complexity of views rather than narrowing meanings into a few categories or ideas. The goal of the research, then, is to rely as much as possible on the participants' views of the situation being studied. (Creswell, 2003, p. 8)

Several protocols were observed to honor this understanding of knowledge. During my facilitation of the focus groups, I asked questions that did not attempt to lead students to a predetermined response. For example, instead of asking students whether they agree that Christians, Jews, Muslims, and atheists conceive of spirituality differently, I asked them how their personal spirituality interrelates with their religious life. It was up to the students to determine whether they would frame their responses to the latter question in terms of their faiths. I also encouraged the students to react to each other either in question or comment form, rather than solely reacting to me or only expecting me to offer reactions. This way, they could take the conversations in directions they felt were interesting or important; certainly, many topics were raised through this avenue that would not have otherwise been discussed.

During the analysis phase of the study, my interpretations were guided by the students' spoken and written words. True to the Social Constructivism framework, I began with their understandings of religion and spirituality as co-constructed through the focus groups. Particularly during the qualitative coding process, I let my developing theory "emerge from the data" (A. Strauss & Corbin, 1998, p. 12). This meant that I first listened to how the students defined terms for and with each other, and I used that as my starting point. This type of inquiry was possible because I was not attempting to empirically prove a theoretical construction; rather, I was trying to better understand it.

TRUSTWORTHINESS

The value of qualitative research cannot be conceived of in the same way as the value of quantitative research methods (Krefting, 1991). Because of the assumption of more than one reality existing for the multiple research participants, qualitative research must represent "those multiple realities revealed by informants as adequately as possible" (p. 215). There are numerous strategies to ensure trustworthiness and credibility in qualitative research, and I utilized several.

I engaged in triangulation of data sources to examine data that were convergent, inconsistent, or contradictory (Krefting, 1991; Mathison, 1988). I conducted triangulation of data methods by utilizing more than one data analysis technique to better understand the phenomena (Krefting, 1991). I engaged in triangulation of theory by referring to more than one theory to explain the research results (Johnson, 1997). I utilized rich description by seeking data elements in which participants' language gave the most descriptive picture of their own ideas (Merriam, 1998). I engaged in reflexivity through being critical of potential biases of myself as the researcher (Johnson, 1997; Krefting, 1991).

Finally, I conducted peer review, which means "discussing your explanation with your colleagues so that they can search for problems with it" (Johnson, 1997, p. 287). The peer review process for this study entailed engaging in post-focus group reflection with the Christian, Muslim, and atheist researchers who co-facilitated the homogenous focus groups. After recording their sessions and transcribing the key themes and explanatory points they made, I utilized this information to help guide data selection and analysis in the study. I made the decision not to employ a co-facilitator for the Jewish homogenous session because I felt that I would not need assistance interpreting the comments of those participants.

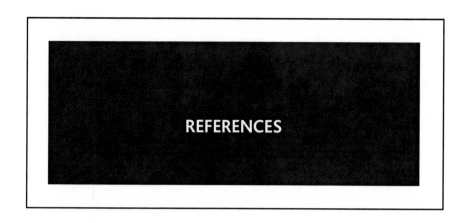

REFERENCES

Achermann, M. (1981). *Kognitive argumentationsfiguren des religiösen urteils bei atheisten.* Unpublished Lizentiatsarbeit, Pädagogisches Institut, University of Fribourg.

American College Personnel Association. (2006). *ACPA conference on religious and spirituality differences.* Retrieved September 28, 2006, from http://www.myacpa.org/pd/spirituality/.

American Council on Education. (2004a). The student personnel point of view. In E. J. Whitt (Ed.), *ASHE reader on college student affairs administration* (pp. 5–12). Boston: Pearson. (Reprinted from *Points of View*, 1937, Washington, DC: National Association of Study Personnel Administrators.)

American Council on Education. (2004b). The student personnel point of view. In E. J. Whitt (Ed.), *ASHE reader on college student affairs administration* (pp. 13–22). Boston: Pearson. (Reprinted from *Points of View*, 1949, Washington, DC: National Association of Study Personnel Administrators.)

Amyot, R. P. (1996). Jews without Judaism? Assimilation and Jewish identity in the United States. *Social Science Quarterly, 77*(1), 177–189.

Avery, W. O. (1990). A Lutheran examines James W. Fowler. *Religious Education, 85*(1), 69–83.

BBC. (2010). *Reform Judaism movement's prayer book "could upset."* Retrieved April 7, 2010, from http://news.bbc.co.uk/2/hi/uk_news/8566370.stm.

Beaman, L. G. (2003). The myth of pluralism, diversity, and vigor: The constitutional privilege of Protestantism in the United States and Canada. *Journal for the Scientific Study of Religion, 43*(3), 311–325.

Billington, R. (2002). *Religion without God.* London: Routledge.

Boud, D., & Walker, D. (1998). Promoting reflection in professional courses: The challenge of context. *Studies in Higher Education, 23*(2), 191–206.\Bowman, N. A., & Small, J. L. (2009). *Exploring a hidden form of minority status: College students' religious affiliation and well-being.* Manuscript submitted for publication.

Bowman, N. A., & Small, J. L. (2010). Do college students who identify with a privileged religion experience greater spiritual development? Exploring individual and institutional dynamics. *Research in Higher Education, 51*(7), 595-614.

Bowman, N. A., & Small, J. L. (in press). Exploring a hidden form of minority status: College students' religious affiliation and well-being. *Journal of College Student Development.*

Braskamp, L. A. (2007). Fostering religious and spiritual development of students during college [Electronic Version]. *Essay Forum on the Religious Engagements of American Undergraduates*, 1-10. Retrieved July 18, 2007, from http://religion.ssrc.org/reforum/.

Bryant, A. N. (2005). Evangelicals on campus: An exploration of culture, faith, and college life. *Religion & Education, 32*(2), 1–30.

Bryant, A. N. (2006). Exploring religious pluralism in higher education: Nonmajority religious perspectives among entering first-year college students. *Religion & Education, 33*(1), 1–25.

Bryant, A. N., & Astin, H. S. (2008). The correlates of spiritual struggle during the college years. *Journal of Higher Education, 79*(1), 1–28.

Bussema, K. E. (1999). Who am I? Whose am I? Identity and faith in the college years. *Research on Christian Higher Education, 6*, 1–33.

Campbell, C. (1998). Atheism [Electronic Version]. *Encyclopedia of Religion and Society.* Retrieved January 19, 2006, from http://hirr.hartsem.edu/ency/Atheism.htm.

Campus Information Centers. (2006). [The University] fact sheet. Retrieved June 22, 2006, from [the University's website].

Cawthon, T. W., & Jones, C. (2004). A description of traditional and contemporary campus ministries. *College Student Affairs Journal, 23*(2), 158–172.

Cherry, C., DeBerg, B. A., & Porterfield, A. (2001). *Religion on campus.* Chapel Hill: University of North Carolina Press.

Chickering, A. W., Dalton, J. C., & Stamm, L. (2005). *Encouraging authenticity & spirituality in higher education.* San Francisco: Jossey-Bass.

Claerbaut, D. (2004). *Faith and learning on the edge: A bold new look at religion in higher education.* Grand Rapids, MI: Zondervan.

Clark, C. (2003). Diversity initiatives in higher education: A case study of multicultural organizational development through the lens of religion, spirituality, faith, and secular inclusion. *Multicultural Education, 10*(3), 48–54.

Clydesdale, T. (2007). Abandoned, pursued, or safely stowed? [Electronic Version]. *Essay Forum on the Religious Engagements of American Undergraduates*, 1–8. Retrieved July 18, 2007, from http://religion.ssrc.org/reforum/.

Cohen, S. M. (1988). *American assimilation or Jewish revival?* Bloomington: Indiana University Press.

Cole, D., & Ahmadi, S. (2003). Perspectives and experiences of Muslim women who veil on college campuses. *Journal of College Student Development, 44*(1), 47–66.

Cornille, C. (2008). *The im-possibility of interreligious dialogue.* New York: Crossroad Publishing.

Council of Centers on Jewish-Christian Relations. (2009). *Regular members.* Retrieved April 5, 2010, from http://www.ccjr.us/.

Cowan, J. (1998). *On becoming an innovative university teacher.* Buckingham, England: SRHE and Open University Press.

Creswell, J. W. (2003). *Research design: Qualitative, quantitative, and mixed methods approaches* (2nd ed.). Thousand Oaks, CA: Sage.

Cross, W. E., Jr. (1995). The psychology of Nigrescence: Revising the Cross model. In J. G. Ponterotto, J. M. Casas, L. A. Suzuki, & C. M. Alexander (Eds.), *Handbook of multicultural counseling* (pp. 93–122). Thousand Oaks, CA: Sage.

Dalton, J. C., Eberhardt, D., Bracken, J., & Echols, K. (2006). Inward journeys: Forms and patterns of college student spirituality [Electronic Version]. *Journal of College and Character, 7*(8), 1–21.

Davies, B., & Harre, R. (2001). Positioning: The discursive production of selves. In M. Wetherell, S. Taylor, & S. J. Yates (Eds.), *Discourse theory and practice: A reader* (pp. 261–271). Thousand Oaks, CA: Sage.

Downs, P. G. (1995). The power of Fowler. In J. C. Wilhoit & J. M. Dettoni (Eds.), *Nurture that is Christian: Developmental perspectives on Christian education* (pp. 75–90). Grand Rapids, MI: Baker Books.

Eck, D. L. (2001). *A new religious America: How a "Christian country" has now become the world's most religiously diverse nation.* San Francisco: HarperCollins.

Emerson, R. M., Fretz, R. I., & Shaw, L. L. (1995). *Writing ethnographic fieldnotes.* Chicago: University of Chicago Press.

Epstein, G. M. (2009). *Good without God: What a billion nonreligious people do believe.* New York: HarperCollins.

Erickson, F. (2004). *Talk and social theory.* Cambridge, England: Polity Press.

Evans, N. J., Forney, D. S., & Guido-DiBrito, F. (1998). *Student development in college: Theory, research, and practice.* San Francisco: Jossey-Bass.

Fairchild, E. E. (2009). Christian privilege, history and trends in U.S. religion. In S. K. Watt, E. E. Fairchild, & K. M. Goodman (Eds.), *Intersections of religious privilege: Difficult dialogues and student affairs practice* (pp. 5–11). San Francisco: Wiley.

Fernhout, J. H. (1986). Where is faith? Searching for the core of the cube. In C. Dykstra & S. Parks (Eds.), *Faith development and Fowler* (pp. 65–89). Birmingham, AL: Religious Education Press.

Flynn, T. (2002). A secular humanist definition: Setting the record straight. *Free Inquiry, 22*(4), 35–43.

Fowler, J. W. (1981). *Stages of faith: The psychology of human development and the quest for meaning.* San Francisco: HarperCollins.

Fowler, J. W. (2004). Faith development at 30: Naming the challenges of faith in a new millennium. *Religious Education, 99*(4), 405–421.

Fried, J. (2007). Thinking skillfully and respecting difference: Understanding religious privilege on campus. *Journal of College and Character, 9*(1), 1–6.

Garfinkel, H. (1967). *Studies in ethnomethodology*. Englewood Cliffs, NJ: Prentice-Hall.

Gilgoff, D. (2010). *Episcopal Church confirms first openly lesbian bishop*. Retrieved April 7, 2010, from http://news.blogs.cnn.com/2010/03/17/episcopal-church-confirms-first-openly-lesbian-bishop/.

Goffman, E. (1967). *Interaction ritual: Essays in face-to-face behavior*. Garden City, NY: Anchor.

Gunnoe, M. L., & Moore, K. A. (2002). Predictors of religiosity among youth aged 17-22: A longitudinal study of the National Survey of Children. *Journal for the Scientific Study of Religion, 41*(4), 613–622.

Hammersla, J. F., Andrews-Qualls, L. C., & Frease, L. G. (1986). God concepts and religious commitment among Christian university students. *Journal for the Scientific Study of Religion, 25*(4), 424–435.

Hartley, H. V. (2004). How college affects students' religious faith and practice: A review of research. *College Student Affairs Journal, 23*(2), 111–129.

Heft, J. L. (2004). Introduction: Religious sources for social transformation in Judaism, Christianity, and Islam. In J. L. Heft (Ed.), *Beyond violence: Religious sources of social transformation in Judaism, Christianity, and Islam* (pp. 1–14). New York: Fordham University Press.

Helms, J. E. (Ed.). (1993). *Black and white racial identity: Theory, research and practice*. Westport, CT: Praeger.

Higher Education Research Institution. (2003). *College students' beliefs and values pilot survey methodology*. Los Angeles, CA: Author.

Higher Education Research Institution. (2005). *The spiritual life of college students: A national study of college students' search for meaning and purpose*. Los Angeles: Author.

Higher Education Research Institution. (n.d.). *Spirituality in higher education: A national study of college students' search for meaning and purpose*. Retrieved December 11, 2009, from http://www.spirituality.ucla.edu/index.html.

Hill, P. C., Pargament, K. I., Hood, R. W., McCullough, M. E., Swyers, J. P., Larson, D. B., & Zinnbaur, B. J. (2000). Conceptualizing religion and spirituality: Points of commonality, points of departure. *Journal for the Theory of Social Behaviour, 30*(1), 51–77.

Hodges, S. (1999). Making room for religious diversity on campus: The Spiritual Pathways Series at the University of Minnesota-Morris. *About Campus, 4*(1), 25–27.

Hoehn, R. A. (1983). Book review—Stages of faith: The psychology of human development and the quest for meaning. *Review of Religious Research, 25*(1), 77–79.

Holmes, S. L., Roedder, B. S., & Flowers, L. A. (2004). Applying student development theory to college students' spiritual beliefs. *College Student Affairs Journal, 23*(2), 130–145.

Hoppe, S. L., & Speck, B. W. (2005). Editors' notes. *New Directions for Teaching and Learning, 2005*(104), 1–2.

Hunsberger, B., Alisat, S., Pancer, S. M., & Pratt, M. (1996). Religious fundamentalism and religious doubts: Content, connections, and complexity of thinking. *The International Journal for the Psychology of Religion, 6*(3), 201–220.

Interfaith Youth Core. (n.d.). *About the core*. Retrieved April 9, 2010, from http://www.ifyc.org/about_core.

Jablonski, M. A. (Ed.). (2001). *The implications of student spirituality for student affairs practice*. New York: Jossey-Bass.

Jewish Reconstructionist Federation. (2007). *Is Reconstructionist Judaism for you?* Retrieved April 1, 2010, from http://jrf.org/showres&rid=141.

Johnson, R. B. (1997). Examining the validity structure of qualitative research. *Education, 118*(2), 282–292.

Johnstone, B. (2002). *Discourse analysis*. Malden, MA: Blackwell.

Jones, S. R., & McEwan, M. K. (2002). A conceptual model of multiple dimensions of identity. In S. B. Merriam (Ed.), *Qualitative research in practice: Examples for discussion and analysis* (pp. 163–174). San Francisco: Jossey-Bass.

Kazanjian, V. H., & Lawrence, P. L. (Eds.). (2000). *Education as transformation: Religious pluralism, spirituality and a new vision for higher education in America*. New York: Peter Lang Publishing.

Kohlberg, L. (1984). *The psychology of moral development: The nature and validity of moral stages* (Essays on moral development, volume 2). San Francisco: Harper & Row.

Kolowich, S. (2009). Humanist chaplains [Electronic Version]. Retrieved December 22, 2009, from http://www.insidehighered.com/news/2009/11/12/chaplain.

Krefting, L. (1991). Rigor in qualitative research: The assessment of trustworthiness. *The American Journal of Occupational Therapy, 45*(3), 214–222.

Krueger, R. A., & Casey, M. A. (2000). *Focus groups: A practical guide for applied research* (3rd ed.). Thousand Oaks, CA: Sage.

Kuh, G. D., Whitt, E. J., & Shedd, J. D. (1987). *Student affairs work, 2001: A paradigmatic odyssey*. Alexandria, VA: American College Personnel Association.

Kuhmerker, L. (1978). James Fowler talks with Lisa Kuhmerker about faith development. *Moral Education Forum, 3*, 1–8.

Lee, J. (2000). *Changing religious beliefs among college students*. Paper presented at the annual meeting of the American Educational Research Association, New Orleans, LA. (ERIC Document Reproduction Service No. ED442437)

Lee, J. J. (2002). Religion and college attendance: Change among students. *The Review of Higher Education, 25*(4), 369–384.

Leonard, K. I. (2003). *Muslims in the United States: The state of research*. New York: Russell Sage Foundation.

Lincoln, Y. S., & Guba, E. G. (2000). Paradigmatic controversies, contradictions, and emerging confluences. In N. K. Denzin & Y. S. Lincoln (Eds.), *Handbook of qualitative research* (2nd ed., pp. 163–188). Thousand Oaks, CA: Sage.

Love, P. (2002). Comparing spiritual development and cognitive development. *Journal of College Student Development, 42*(3), 357–373.

Love, P., & Talbot, D. (1999). Defining spiritual development: A missing consideration for student affairs [Electronic Version]. *NASPA Journal, 37*, 1–10.

Ma, S. Y. (2003). The Christian college experience and the development of spirituality among students. *Christian Higher Education, 2*(4), 321–339.

Mankowski, E. S., & Thomas, E. (2000). The relationship between personal and collective identity: A narrative analysis of a campus ministry community. *Journal of Community Psychology, 28*(5), 517–528.

Markstrom-Adams, C., Hofstra, G., & Dougher, K. (1994). The ego-virtue of fidelity: A case for the study of religion and identity formation in adolescence.
Journal of Youth and Adolescence, 23(4), 453–469.

Mathison, S. (1988). Why triangulate? *Educational Researcher, 17*(2), 13–17.

Mayhew, M. J. (2004). Exploring the essence of spirituality: A phenomenological
study of eight students with eight different worldviews. *NASPA Journal,
41*(3), 647–674.

Mayrl, D. (2007). Introduction [Electronic Version]. *Essay Forum on the Religious
Engagements of American Undergraduates, 1–19.* Retrieved July 18, 2007, from
http://religion.ssrc.org/reform/.

Mayrl, D., & Oeur, F. (2009). Religion and higher education: Current knowledge
and directions for future research. *Journal for the Scientific Study of Religion,
48*(2), 260–275.

McCullough, M. E., Weaver, A. J., Larson, D. B., & Aay, K. R. (2000).
Psychotherapy with mainline Protestants: Lutheran, Presbyterian,
Episcopal/Anglican, and Methodist. In P. S. Richards & A. E. Bergin (Eds.),
Handbook of psychotherapy and religious diversity (pp. 105–129). Washington,
DC: American Psychological Association.

Merriam, S. B. (1998). *Qualitative research and case study applications in education.*
San Francisco: Jossey-Bass.

Miller, V. W., & Ryan, M. M. (Eds.). (2001). *Transforming campus life: Reflections on
spirituality & religious pluralism.* New York: Peter Lang.

Moran, C. D. (2007). The public identity work of Evangelical Christian students.
Journal of College Student Development, 48(4), 418–434.

Moran, C. D., Lang, D. J., & Oliver, J. (2007). Cultural incongruity and social status ambiguity: The experiences of evangelical Christian student leaders at
two Midwestern public universities. *Journal of College Student Development,
48*(1), 23–38.

Morgan, D. L. (1997). *Focus groups as qualitative research* (2nd ed.). Thousand Oaks,
CA: Sage.

Mubarak, H. (2007). How Muslim students negotiate their religious identity and
practices in an undergraduate setting [Electronic Version]. *Essay Forum on the
Religious Engagements of American Undergraduates, 1–12.* Retrieved July 18,
2007, from http://religion.ssrc.org/reform/.

Nash, R. J. (2001). *Religious pluralism in the academy: Opening the dialogue.* New
York: Peter Lang Publishing.

Nash, R. J. (2003). Inviting atheists to the table: A modest proposal for higher education. *Religion and Education, 30*(1), 1–23.

Nash, R. J. (2007). Understanding and promoting religious pluralism on college
campuses [Electronic Version]. *Spirituality and Higher Education Newsletter,
3*(4), 1–9.

Nash, R. J., Bradley, D. L., & Chickering, A. W. (Eds.). (2008). *How to talk about hot
topics on campus: From polarization to moral conversation.* San Francisco: Wiley.

Nasir, N. S., & Al-Amin, J. (2006). Creating identity-safe spaces on college campuses for Muslim students. *Change, 38*(2), 22–27.

Nelson, C. E. (1982). Does faith develop? An evaluation of Fowler's position. *The
Living Light, 19*(2), 162–174.

Newman, L. L., & Smith, C. (2004). Introduction to the special issue. *College Student Affairs Journal, 23*(2), 100–101.

Oser, F. K., Reich, K. H., & Bucher, A. A. (1994). Development of belief and unbelief in childhood and adolescence. In J. Corveleyn & D. Hutsebaut (Eds.), *Belief and unbelief: Psychological perspectives* (pp. 39–62). Amsterdam: Rodopi.

Pargament, K. I. (1986). Refining fit: Conceptual and methodological challenges. *American Journal of Community Psychology, 14*(6), 677–684.

Parks, S. (1986). *The critical years: The young adult search for a faith to live by*. New York: Harper & Row.

Parks, S. D. (2000). *Big questions, worthy dreams: Mentoring young adults in their search for meaning, purpose and faith*. San Francisco: Jossey-Bass.

Parks, S. L. (1980). *Faith development and imagination in the context of higher education*. Unpublished doctoral dissertation, Harvard University, Cambridge, MA.

Pascarella, E. T. (2006). How college affects students: Ten directions for future research. *Journal of College Student Development, 47*(5), 508–520.

Pascarella, E. T., & Terenzini, P. T. (Eds.). (2005). *How college affects students: Volume 2. A third decade of research*. San Francisco: Jossey-Bass.

Patel, E. (2008). Religious pluralism in the public square. In S. Steenland (Ed.), *Debating the divine: Religion in 21st century American democracy* (pp. 16–25). Washington, DC: Center for American Progress.

Peek, L. (2005). Becoming Muslim: The development of a religious identity. *Sociology of Religion, 66*(3), 215–242.

Pew Forum on Religion & Public Life. (2009). *Faith in flux: Changes in religious affiliation in the U.S.* Washington, DC: Author.

Prothero, S. (2010, April 25). Separate truths: It is misleading—and dangerous—to think that religions are different paths to the same wisdom. *Boston Globe*, pp. D1–D2.

Regnerus, M. D., & Uecker, J. E. (2007). How corrosive is college to religious faith and practice? [Electronic Version]. *Essay Forum on the Religious Engagements of American Undergraduates*, 1–6. Retrieved July 18, 2007, from http:// religion.ssrc.org/reforum/.

Riley, N. S. (2005, July 8). Happy—and chaste—on the college campus. *The Chronicle of Higher Education*, p. B12.

Rodgers, R. F. (1990). Recent theories and research underlying student development. In D. G. Creamer (Ed.), *College student development: Theory and practice for the 1990s* (pp. 27–79). Lanham, MD: University Press of America.

Rogers, J. L., & Love, P. (2007). Exploring the role of spirituality in the preparation of student affairs professionals: Faculty constructions. *Journal of College Student Development, 48*(1), 90–104.

Roof, W. C., & McKinney, W. (1987). *American mainline religion: Its changing shape and future*. New Brunswick, NJ: Rutgers University Press.

Sales, A. L., & Saxe, L. (2006). *Particularism in the university: Realities and opportunities for Jewish life on campus*. Waltham, MA: Brandeis University.

Sax, L. (2002). *America's Jewish freshmen: Current characteristics and recent trends among students entering college*. Los Angeles: University of California, Higher Education Research Institution.

Schlosser, L. Z. (2003, January). Christian privilege: Breaking a sacred taboo. *Journal of Multicultural Counseling and Development, 31,* 44–51.

Schmalzbauer, J. (2007). Campus ministry: A statistical portrait [Electronic Version]. *Essay Forum on the Religious Engagements of American Undergraduates,* 1–14. Retrieved July 18, 2007, from http://religion.ssrc.org/reforum/.

Scobie, G. E. W. (1994). Belief, unbelief and conversion experience. In J. Corveleyn & D. Hutsebaut (Eds.), *Belief and unbelief: Psychological perspectives* (pp. 87–98). Amsterdam: Rodopi.

Secular Student Alliance. (2006). *A brief history of the Secular Student Alliance.* Retrieved April 7, 2010, from http://www.secularstudents.org/node/154.

Seifert, T. (2007). Understanding Christian privilege: Managing the tensions of spiritual plurality. *About Campus, 12*(2), 10–18.

Seifert, T. (2008, January). *Recognizing Christian privilege on campus: Suggestions for creating an inclusive environment for inner development.* Paper presented at the annual meeting of the Association of American Colleges and Universities, Washington, DC.

Shire, M. J. (1987, July). Faith development and Jewish education: A critical look. *Compass Magazine,* pp. 17–18, 24–25.

Shire, M. J. (1997). Jewish spiritual development and curriculum theory. *International Journal of Children's Spirituality, 2*(2), 53–59.

Sinclair, J., & Milner, D. (2005). On being Jewish—A qualitative study of identity among British Jews in emerging adulthood. *Journal of Adolescent Research, 20*(1), 91–117.

Small, J. L. (2007). "Do you buy into the whole idea of 'God the Father'?" How college students talk about spiritual transformation. *Religion & Education, 34*(1), 1–27.

Small J.L., & Bowman, N.A. (2011). Religious commitment, skepticism, and struggle among college students: The impact of majority/minority religious affiliation and institutional type. *Journal for the Scientific Study of Religion, 50*(1), 154-174.

Smith, C., with Denton, M. L. (2005). *Soul searching: The religious and spiritual lives of American teenagers.* New York: Oxford University Press.

Smith, C., with Snell, P. (2009). *Souls in transition: The religious & spiritual lives of emerging young adults.* New York: Oxford University Press.

Smith, G. H. (1979). *Atheism: The case against God.* Buffalo, NY: Prometheus.

Smith, T. W. (2002). Religious diversity in America: The emergence of Muslims, Buddhists, Hindus and others. *Journal for the Scientific Study of Religion, 41*(3), 577–585.

Social Science Research Council. (n.d.). *SSRC guide: Religious engagement among American undergraduates.* Retrieved July 18, 2007, from http://religion.ssrc.org/reguide/.

Stamm, L. (2005). The influence of religion and spirituality in shaping American higher education. In A. W. Chickering, J. C. Dalton, & L. Stamm (Eds.), *Encouraging authenticity & spirituality in higher education* (pp. 66–91). San Francisco: Jossey-Bass.

Stamm, L. (2006). The dynamics of spirituality and the religious experience. *Religion & Education, 33*(2), 91–113.

Steele, L. L. (1990). *On the way: A practical theology of Christian formation.* Grand Rapids, MI: Baker Book House.

Stein, G. (Ed.). (1985). *The encyclopedia of unbelief* (Vols. I and II). Buffalo, NY: Prometheus.

Strauss, A., & Corbin, J. (1998). *Basics of qualitative research* (2nd ed.). Thousand Oaks, CA: Sage Publications.

Strauss, A. L. (1987). *Qualitative analysis for social scientists.* New York: Cambridge University Press.

Streib, H. (2003). Faith development research at twenty years. In R. R. Osmer & F. L. Schweitzer (Eds.), *Developing a public faith: New directions in practical theology* (pp. 15–42). St. Louis, MO: Chalice Press.

Swanbrow, D. (2004). *U-M World Values Study explores why religion endures.* Ann Arbor: University of Michigan News Service.

Synnott, M. G. (1979). The admission and assimilation of minority students at Harvard, Yale, and Princeton, 1900–1970. *History of Education Quarterly, 19*(3), 285–304.

Takim, L. (2004). From conversion to conversation: Interfaith dialogue in post 9-11 America. *The Muslim World, 94*(3), 343–355.

The program on intergroup relations. (2009). Retrieved April 5, 2010, from http://www.igr.umich.edu/.

This year's freshmen at 4-year colleges: A statistical profile. (2006). *The Chronicle of Higher Education, 52*(22), A41.

This year's freshmen at 4-year colleges: Highlights of a survey. (2010). Retrieved April 9, 2010, from http://chronicle.com/article/This-Years-Freshmen-at-4-Y/63672/.

Tisdell, E. J. (2003). *Exploring spirituality and culture in adult and higher education.* San Francisco: Jossey-Bass.

Torres, V., Jones, S. R., & Renn, K. A. (2009). Identity development theories in student affairs: Origins, current status, and new approaches. *Journal of College Student Development, 50*(6), 577–596.

Turner Kelly, B. (2003). Focus group interviews. In F. K. Stage & K. Manning (Eds.), *Research in the college context: Approaches and methods* (pp. 49–62). New York: Brunnier-Routledge.

Uecker, J. E., Regnerus, M. D., & Vaaler, M. L. (2007). Losing my religion: The social sources of religious decline in early adulthood. *Social Forces, 85*(4), 1667–1692.

Unitarian Universalist Association of Congregations. (2010). *Welcome to Unitarian Universalism!* Retrieved April 1, 2010, from http://www.uua.org/visitors/index.shtml.

United Jewish Communities. (2003). *The national Jewish population survey 2000-01: Strength, challenge and diversity in the American Jewish population.* New York, NY. Retrieved August 8, 2009, from http://www.ujc.org/local_includes/downloads/4606.pdf.

Wakin, D. J. (2010, April 5). Easter support for pope, and some apologies. *New York Times,* p. A1.

Watt, S. K. (2009). Facilitating difficult dialogues at the intersections of religious privilege. In S. K. Watt, E. E. Fairchild, & K. M. Goodman (Eds.), *Intersections of religious privilege: Difficult dialogues and student affairs practice* (pp. 65–73). San Francisco: Wiley.

Watt, S. K., Fairchild, E. E., & Goodman, K. M. (Eds.). (2009). *Intersections of religious privilege: Difficult dialogues and student affairs practice.* San Francisco: Wiley.

Winkle-Wagner, R. (2007, November). *Self, college experiences, and society: Rethinking student development theory from a sociological perspective.* Paper presented at the Association for the Study of Higher Education, Louisville, KY.

Wuthnow, R. (2007). Can faith be more than a side show in the contemporary academy? [Electronic Version]. *Essay Forum on the Religious Engagements of American Undergraduates,* 1–11. Retrieved July 18, 2007, from http://religion.ssrc.org/reforum/.

Zabriskie, M. (2005). *College student definitions of religiosity and spirituality.* Unpublished doctoral dissertation, University of Michigan, Ann Arbor, MI.

AUTHOR INDEX

Aay, K.R., 16, *174*
Achermann, M., 22, 58, *169*
Ahmadi, S., 49, *171*
Al-Amin, J., 49, *174*
Alisat, S., 58, *172*
American College Personnel
  Association, 5, *169*
American Council on Education, 13
  13(n8), *169*
Amyot, R.P., 47, *169*
Andrews-Qualls, L.C., 29, *172*
Astin, H.S., 129(n21), *170*
Avery, W.O., 29, *169*

BBC, xvi, *169*
Beaman, L.G., xv, *169*
Billington, R., 11, *170*
Boud, D., 163, *170*
Bowman, N.A., 16(n10), 20, 157, *170*,
  176
Bracken, J., 11, 15(n9), 16(n10), *171*
Bradley, D.L., 15(n9), 74(n17), *174*
Braskamp, L.A., 12, *170*

Bryant, A.N., 16, 30, 40, 48, 49,
  129(n21), *170*
Bucher, A.E., 11, 22, *175*
Bussema, K.E., 30, *170*

Campbell, C., 11, *170*
Campus Information Centers, 6(n3),
  170
Casey, M.A., 161, *173*
Cawthon, T.W., 15(n9), *170*
Cherry, C., 15(n9), 16(n10), *170*
Chickering, A.W., 15(n9), 74(n17), *170*,
  174
Claerbaut, D., 15(n9), *170*
Clark, C., 155, *170*
Clydesdale, T., 16(n10), *170*
Cohen, S.M., 47, *170*
Cole, D., 49, *171*
Corbin, J., 164, 167, *177*
Cornille, C., xvi, 149, *171*
Council of Centers on Jewish-Christian
  Relations, xvi, *171*
Cowan, J., 163, *171*

Creswell, J.W., 166, 171
Cross, W.E., 128(n20), 171

Dalton, J.C., 11, 15(n9), 16(n10), 170, 171

Davies, B., 165, 171
DeBerg, B.A., 15(n9), 16(n10), 170
Denton, M.L., 16, 176
Dougher, K., 111, 174
Downs, P.G., 29, 171

Eberhardt, D., 11, 15(n9), 16(n10), 171
Echols, K., 11, 15(n9), 16(n10), 171
Eck, D.L., xv, 171
Emerson, R.M., 164, 171
Epstein, G.M., xvi, 171
Erickson, F., 165, 171
Evans, N.J., 17, 27(n12), 128(n20), 171

Fairchild, E.E., 12, 17, 171, 178
Fernhout, J.H., 29, 171
Flowers, L.A., 16(n10), 172
Flynn, T., 11, 171
Forney, D.S., 17, 27(n12), 128(n20), 171
Fowler, J.W., 13, 14, 29, 58, 67, 171
Frease, L.G., 29, 172
Fretz, R.I., 164, 171
Fried, J., 18, 171

Garfinkel, H., 165, 172
Gilgoff, D., xv, 172
Goffman, E., 165, 172
Goodman, K.M., 12, 178
Guba, E.G., 166, 173
Guido-DiBrito, F., 17, 27(n12), 128(n20), 171
Gunnoe, M.L., 16(n10), 172

Hammersla, J.F., 29, 172
Harre, R., 165, 171
Hartley, H.V., 14, 16, 16(n10), 172
Heft, J.L., 105, 172
Helms, J.E., 128(n20), 172
Higher Education Research Institution, 15, 15(n9), 16(n10), 30, 40, 58, 172
Hill, P.C., 10, 172
Hodges, S., 16(n10), 172
Hoehn, R.A., 14, 172
Hofstra, G., 111, 174
Holmes, S.L., 16(n10), 172

Hood, R.W., 10, 172
Hoppe, S.L., 15(n9), 172
Hunsberger, N., 58, 172

Interfaith Youth Core, 2, 154, 173

Jablonski, M.A., 15(n9), 173
Jewish Reconstructionist Federation, 3(n2), 173
Johnson, R.B., 167, 173
Johnstone, B., 74, 165, 173
Jones, C., 15(n9), 170
Jones, S.R., 158, 173, 177

Kazanjian, V.H., 15(n9), 173
Kohlberg, L., 21, 173
Kolowich, S., 1, 173
Krefting, L., 167, 173
Krueger, R.A., 161, 173
Kuh, G.D., 27(n12), 173
Kuhmerker, L., 57, 173

Lang, D.J., 114, 174
Larson, D.B., 10, 16, 172, 174
Lawrence, P.L., 15(n9), 173
Lee, J.J., 16(n10), 173
Leonard, K.I., 48, 173
Lincoln, Y.S., 166, 173
Love, P., 15(n9), 173, 175

Ma, S.Y., 29, 173
Mankowski, E.S., 162, 173
Markstrom-Adams, C., 111, 174
Mathison, S., 167, 174
Mayhew, M.J., 40, 49, 58, 174
Mayrl, D., 15(n9), 174
McCullough, M.E., 10, 16, 172, 174
McEwan, M.K., 158, 173
McKinney, W., 76, 175
Merriam, S.B., 163, 165, 167, 174
Miller, V.W., 15(n9), 174
Milner, D., 39, 176
Moore, K.A., 16(n10), 172
Moran, C.D., 30, 114, 174
Morgan, D.L., 161, 162, 163, 174
Mubarak, H., 49, 174

Nash, R.J., 11, 12, 15(n9), 16, 57, 74(n17), 174
Nasir, N.S., 49, 174

Nelson, C.E., 14, *174*
Newman, L.L., 15(n9), *175*

Oeur, F., 15(n9), *174*
Oliver, J., 114, *174*
Oser, F.K., 11, 22, *175*

Pancer, S.M., 58, *172*
Pargament, K.I., 10, 129, *172, 175*
Parks, S.D., 13, 14, 15, *175*
Parks, S.L., 14, *175*
Pascarella, E.T., 16, 16(n10), *175*
Patel, E., xvi, 159, *175*
Peek, L., 21, 48, *175*
Pew Forum on Religion and Public
    Life, xv, *175*
Porterfield, A., 15(n9), 16(n10), *170*
Pratt, M., 58, *172*
Prothero, S., xv, *175*

Regnerus, M.D., 16(n10), *175, 177*
Reich, K.H., 11, 22, *175*
Renn, K.A., 158, *177*
Riley, N.S., 15(n9), *175*
Rodgers, R.F., 12, *175*
Roedder, B.S., 16(n10), *172*
Rogers, J.L., 15(n9), *175*
Roof, W.C., 76, *175*
Ryan, M.M., 15(n9), *174*

Sales, A.L., 68, *175*
Sax, L., 39, *175*
Saxe, L., 68, *175*
Schlosser, L.Z., 12, 12(n7), *176*
Schmalzbauer, J., 16(n11), *176*
Scobie, G.E.W., 11, 58, *176*
Secular Student Alliance, 2, *176*
Seifert, T., 12, 15(n9), 128, *176*
Shaw, L.L., 164, *171*
Shedd, J.R., 27(n12), *173*
Shire, M.J., 21, 39, *176*
Sinclair, J., 39, *176*
Small, J.L., 16(n10), 20, 157, 165, *170,
    176*

Smith, C., 11, 12(n7), 15(n9), 16, *175,
    176*
Smith, G.H., 11, *176*
Smith, T.W., xv, *176*
Snell, P., 11, 12(n7), 16, *176*
Social Science Research Council,
    15(n9), *176*
Speck, B.W., 15(n9), *172*
Stamm, L., 15(n9), 16, 27(n12), *170, 176,
    177*
Steele, L.L., 29, *177*
Stein, G., 12, *177*
Strauss, A.L., 164, 167, *177*
Streib, H., 14, *177*
Swanbrow, D., xv, *177*
Swyers, J.P., 10, *172*
Synnott, M.G., 119, *177*

Takim, L., xvi, *177*
Talbot, D., 10, 15(n9), *173*
Terenzini, P.T., 16(n10), *175*
Thomas, E., 162, *173*
Tisdell, E.J., 15(n9), *177*
Torres, V., 158, *177*
Turner Kelly, B., 162, 163, *177*

Uecker, J.E., 16(n10), *175, 177*
Unitarian Universalist Association of
    Congregations, 8(n5), *177*
United Jewish Communities, 42(n13),
    177

Vaaler, M.L., 16(n10), *177*

Wakin, D.J., xv, *177*
Walker, D., 163, *170*
Watt, S.K., 12, 74(n17), *178*
Weaver, A.J., 16, *174*
Whitt, E.J., 27(n12), *173*
Winkle-Wagner, R., 27(n12), *178*
Wuthnow, R., 16(n10), *178*

Zabriskie, M., 40, *178*
Zinnbaur, B.J., 10, *172*

SUBJECT INDEX

Academic courses, ix, 19, 29, 54, 117, 129, 133-137, 141, 143, 145-146, 152-153, 155-156

Achermann, Markus, 22, 58

Agnosticism (*see* atheism/agnosticism)

Allah, 91-92

American College Personnel Association, 5

American Council on Education, 12-13

Arabic, 54, 69, 91

Atheism/agnosticism
  definition of, 10-12, 65-66, 129
  secular humanist, xvi, 1-2, 11, 57, 60-61, 157
  various types, 11-12, 22

Avoidance/engagement of religious differences, xvi, 19, 60, 63-65, 67, 72-73, 106, 115-117, 119, 128, 130, 132-133, 136-138, 140-141, 143, 148, 151-154, 157, 159-160

Behavior (standards for), 24-25, 27, 39, 42, 44-49, 51-56, 62, 64, 67-69, 81, 83, 85-87, 89-90, 99, 114, 122-125, 148, 156

Bible, 25, 29, 32, 34, 37, 76, 95, 97, 112, 148

Breach
  definition of, 82
  examples of, 82-83, 93, 100, 105, 121, 141, 153

Buddhism, 1, 6, 134, 157

Campus Crusade for Christ (Cru), 112-113, 137, 147

Campus Information Centers, 6

Christian denominations
  Baptist, 6, 29-30, 58, 75
  Disciples of Christ, 29
  Eastern Orthodox, 6
  Episcopalian/Episcopal Church, xv, 6, 29-30, 32, 35, 75, 77-78, 118, 136
  Lutheran, 6, 28-29, 31, 34, 72, 75, 116, 134
  Methodist, 2, 6, 25, 28-29, 31, 33, 102, 110, 133, 140, 150

nondenominational, 31-34, 37, 79,
    116, 136
Presbyterian, 6, 30
Roman Catholic/Roman Catholic
    Church, ix, xv, 1, 6, 13-14, 40, 57,
    59-60, 94-97, 99, 146, 158
United Church of Christ, 6, 30
Christmas, 95, 97, 156
Church, xv, 25, 28, 31-33, 35-37, 63, 75,
    95-97, 117, 136-137, 139-140
Coding, qualitative data, 26, 164, 167
Co-facilitators of focus groups, 9, 75,
    77, 90, 94-95, 150, 162, 167-168
College/campus environment, ix-xi, 1-
    2, 4-5, 12, 16-20, 23, 29-30, 40, 46, 48-
    49, 57, 59, 63, 69-70, 72, 103, 105-106,
    109, 111-112, 115, 120, 128-160
Community service/volunteerism, 17,
    24, 40, 154
Competition/judgment between
    students, 3, 34-36, 41-42, 45, 72, 75-
    76, 80, 86-87, 92-93, 99-105, 115-116,
    132, 147, 155
Confirmation, 94-97
Conversion/denominational change,
    35, 61, 65, 75-77, 95-96, 118, 122, 137-
    138, 150, 156
Cooperative Institutional Research
    Program, 7
Council of Centers on Jewish-Christian
    Relations, xvi

Dietary restrictions, 38, 44, 51, 53, 87
Differentiation from faith group, 134-
    136
Discourse analysis (as a method) and
    general techniques, 5, 9, 18-19, 26,
    37, 72-74, 76, 105-107, 143-144, 149-
    150, 159, 164-165
Discourse communities, 74, 93, 105
Discrimination/stereotypes, 49, 53, 55,
    59, 92-93, 106, 110, 119-121, 125, 134

Easter, xv
Ecumenism, 30, 37, 40, 80, 127-128
Face saving
    definition of, 83
    examples of, 19, 79, 83, 85, 92, 101-
        102, 106, 115, 141, 149, 151

post-hoc, 100, 104, 107
Faith, definition of, 9-10, 13, 156-157
Faith development theory, 12-17, 19-22,
    29, 39, 48, 57, 128-129
Faith frames
    Atheist/agnostic, 56-68, 94-100, 104,
        106, 115, 124-126, 157
    Christian, 28-38, 46, 67, 74-81, 101,
        106, 115-119, 136, 148
    general concept of (and faith
        identities), 4-6, 9, 11, 17-20, 23-27,
        67-70, 73-74, 100, 104-111, 115-116,
        128-131, 142-155, 157, 159, 161,
        165
    Jewish, 38-47, 67, 81-87, 102, 106,
        115, 119-121, 148;
    Muslim, 47-56, 68, 87-94, 103, 106,
        115, 121-123, 139, 157
Familiar communities, 69-70, 74, 84, 91,
    105, 148
Family, 15-16, 25, 28, 31, 40, 44, 46, 49-
    51, 56, 63, 66, 75, 80, 90, 94-97, 99,
    104, 110-111, 120, 122, 124, 135, 138-
    140, 158
Focus (also: discussion) groups (as a
    method), x, 7, 9, 20, 25-26, 41, 73,
    139, 141, 161-168
Focus group transcripts, 75-76, 79, 81-
    82, 85-88, 92-95, 99, 112, 165
Footing
    definition of, 78, 90
    examples of, 77-78, 83
Fowler, James W., ix, 13-15, 20-21, 29,
    39, 57-58, 66-67
Fraternities/sororities, 42, 46, 119, 140,
    147
Freethought Society, 1
Future research, 4-6, 126, 128, 157-158

Gender, 23, 29, 59, 99, 118, 136, 145-146,
    155, 157-158
God, x, 3-5, 11-15, 18, 21-22, 24-25, 29-
    31, 33-34, 36-37, 40, 42-44, 46-53, 55-
    59, 61-64, 66-68, 70, 72, 78, 84, 87-89,
    92, 94, 99-100, 102, 110-113, 115-116,
    118, 124-125, 135, 140, 145-146, 154,
    156, 164
God consciousness, 24, 50, 52, 87-89

Heaven, 34, 36, 72, 75
Hebrew, 25, 44, 64, 69, 82-83
Hedges/hedging
    definition of, 86-67
    examples of, 77, 86, 89-90, 141, 144
Hell, 63, 112-113
Heterodoxy, 12, 23
Higher Education Research Institution,
    15-16, 30, 39-40, 58
Hijab, 50, 90
Hillel: The Foundation for Jewish
    Campus Life, 16, 39, 42, 44, 46, 66, 84
Hinduism, x, 6, 132, 134, 157
Holidays, 44, 156
Holocaust, 38, 120

Identities/presentations of self
    definition of, 88
    examples of, 89-90, 95-97, 123, 144
Immigration/immigrant status, xv, 53,
    120, 122-123, 157-158
Interfaith (also: mixed, heterogeneous)
    dialogues, x, xvi, 2-3, 7, 9, 18-21, 34-
    37, 44, 53-55, 64, 66-69, 71-74, 77, 79-
    80, 84-86, 91-95, 98-106, 112-113, 115,
    123, 126-127, 130, 141, 149-154, 157,
    159-160, 162, 165-166
Interfaith Youth Core, 2, 154
Interviews (as a method), 9, 25-26, 44,
    71, 73, 78, 88, 90, 101, 118, 162-165
Intrafaith (also: homogenous)
    dialogues, x, 9, 18-19, 35, 44, 46, 54,
    56, 64-68, 70-78, 81-84, 87-91, 93-100,
    103-106, 118, 126-127, 130, 135, 141,
    144, 147-148, 154, 159, 161-162, 165,
    167-168
Iraq, 50
Israel, 38, 45-46, 70, 81-84, 102, 120, 135,
    147-148, 151, 153

Jainism, 132, 157
Jesus Christ, 3, 25, 34-37, 64, 72, 75-76,
    79-80, 94-95, 97, 113, 118
Jewish denominations—
    Conservative, 3, 38, 41-43, 45, 103,
        112, 120, 138, 140, 147-148
    Orthodox, 39, 161
    Reconstructionist, 3, 41-42, 44-45,
        72, 135, 153

Reform, xvi, 19-21, 41, 84, 161
Kohlberg, Lawrence, 21
Koran, xv, 24, 88, 134
Kosher (see dietary restrictions)

Language, 2, 5, 10, 15, 18, 35-36, 54-55,
    64, 68-75, 80-81, 87-88, 91-92, 94, 100,
    103, 106-107, 123, 127, 130, 151, 154,
    156-157, 159, 165, 167
Limitations of research design, 158, 163

Majority status, 115-116, 118, 126-127,
    129
Marginalization
    awareness of/opposition to, 5, 12,
        19, 27, 50-51, 59, 109-111, 114-126,
        128-130, 155-156
    religious, xv, 2, 4, 6, 9, 17, 38, 47, 49,
        55, 67-68, 84, 157-158
Religious Marginalization
    Awareness Scale, 126-128, 130
Meditation, 40, 64
Minority/non-majority status, 1, 4, 12-
    13, 16, 20, 24, 39, 46-50, 55, 59, 63-66,
    85-86, 94, 104, 106, 110-111, 113-119,
    121, 123-124, 126-130, 146, 152, 155-
    158
Missionaries, 28, 35, 63, 86, 118, 138,
    141, 156
Mohammed, 24, 47, 51, 88-90
Mormonism, 6, 58
Mosque, 64, 134
Multiple identities, 23, 27, 88, 157-158
Muslim denominations
    Sunni, 24, 50-52, 123, 134, 145
Muslim Students Association (MSA),
    54, 90-91, 103-104, 135, 138-139, 147,
    151

Nash, Robert J., 11-12, 15-16, 57, 74
Nature, 3, 11, 15, 43, 146-147
Norm (discourse move)
    definition of, 76
    examples of, 37, 55, 70, 76-77, 81-83,
        85, 87, 90, 92-93, 97-98, 100, 121,
        126, 141, 144
    identifying, 165

Parks, Sharon Daloz, 13-15, 20-21, 29
Peek, Lori, 21, 48
Pew Forum on Religion & Public Life, xv
Politics, 38-40, 45, 48, 50-51, 53, 55, 58, 70, 84, 117, 120, 122-124, 127, 135, 138, 145-146, 152-153, 156, 158
Positioning
    definition of, 77
    examples of, 19, 76-80, 83, 85, 90, 92, 106-107, 141, 152
    post-hoc, 100-104
Prayer, xvi, 21, 24, 37, 40, 42, 44, 49, 52-53, 55, 58, 81, 83, 87-89, 111, 113, 132, 137, 147, 151
Presentations of self (see identities/presentations of self)
Privilege
    awareness of/opposition to, 10, 12, 19, 31-32, 40-42, 49-51, 59-60, 109-111, 114, 116-119, 122-130, 155-157
    Christian, 12, 14, 16-17, 37-38, 46, 67, 69-70, 74, 102, 106, 114, 121, 126-128, 145, 160
    religious, 2, 4, 6, 17, 47, 55, 116, 119, 159; other forms of, 127
    three-tiered structure of religious, 19, 112-116
Program on Intergroup Relations, 2

Quakers, 6, 66
Questionnaires, 9, 26, 71, 73, 77-78, 84, 146-147, 152, 163-165

Race, xvi, 8, 16, 20, 23, 31, 40, 50, 53, 60, 95, 97, 127-128, 130, 146, 153, 155, 157-158
Ramadan, 88
Religion, definition of, 3, 9-10, 32-33, 37, 42-43, 46, 51-52, 55, 61, 66, 75, 81, 87-90, 92, 149, 156, 162
Religious/faith diversity, xv-xvi, 1, 4-5, 10, 16-20, 27, 31-32, 36, 48, 54, 64-65, 70, 73, 77, 79, 85, 92, 100-101, 105-106, 109, 113, 115-119, 123-124, 128-133, 137-144, 149-152, 154-160, 162
Religious pluralism, xv-xvi, 11, 16, 50, 57, 132, 141, 151, 159-160

Representing one's faith group, 35, 46, 48, 53-56, 59, 64, 68, 92, 98, 110, 119-123, 151
Roommates, 120, 137, 151-152
Rosh Hashanah, 148
Secular Student Alliance, 1-2

September 11, 2001, xvi, 48-49, 53-54, 121-122, 157
Sexual orientation, xv, 23, 118, 127, 136-138, 157-158
Shabbat/Shabbos, 81, 138
Shire, Michael J., 21, 39
Sikhism, 157
Small, Jenny L., 16, 20, 157, 165
Social Constructivism, 166-167
Social justice/equity/morality, 2, 4-5, 11, 14, 18-21, 39, 47, 51, 55-57, 59, 61, 68, 70, 99, 109, 111, 115, 117-118, 124, 127, 130, 145-146, 154-158, 160
Social status ambiguity, 114
Solidarity/situational co-membership
    definition of, 78, 96
    examples of, 77-78, 96-100, 112-113, 141
Sororities (see fraternities/sororities)
Spirituality, definition of, 3, 10, 24-25, 32-33, 37, 42-43, 46, 51-52, 55, 61, 66, 87-90, 92-93, 98, 149-150, 156, 162
Spirituality in Higher Education Project, 15, 20
Statistics, xv, 1, 6, 13, 16-17, 39-40, 42, 58, 68
Student religious organization/club, 1-2, 39, 42, 44, 46, 54, 57, 62, 66, 69, 84, 90-91, 98, 103-104, 112-114, 136-141, 147-148, 151, 153, 159, 162
Students
    Brooke, 8, 28, 31-32, 35-37, 68, 70, 101, 117-118, 137-139, 158
    Carl, 8, 56, 60-63, 85, 94-97, 104, 125-126, 133
    David, 8, 28, 31-32, 34, 36, 71-72, 75-78, 85, 116-118, 134
    Inaara, 8, 24, 50-52, 85, 87-90, 103-104, 123, 134, 145, 158

Jada, 8, 31-37, 79-80, 101, 116, 118, 136, 158
Jasmine, 2-3, 8, 41-45, 70, 72, 81-84, 92-93, 102, 115, 120, 135, 153
Jesse, 8, 25, 39, 41-43, 79-84, 102, 113, 119-120, 133, 140-141
Joanna, 8, 20-21, 33, 38, 41-44, 46, 68, 70, 81-84, 102, 110-111, 120-121, 137, 148
Judy, 8, 38, 41-42, 81-86, 102-103, 119, 140, 146-147
Karen, 8, 25, 31-33, 35, 101-102, 110-111, 117-118, 133, 150
Kristin, 2-3, 8, 28, 31-32, 35, 79, 116-118, 139-140
Meghan, 2-3, 8, 60-61, 65, 72, 79, 96, 104, 113, 124, 126, 134, 141, 158
Melanie, 8, 59-60, 62, 68-69, 94-97, 104, 112-114, 125, 133-134, 138, 141, 152
Misty, 8, 24, 56, 60-63, 92-93, 95-98, 104, 124, 133, 151, 158;
Rick, 8, 57, 59-60, 64-66, 95-97, 99-100, 111, 124-125, 138, 141, 158;
Sabur, 8, 47-48, 50-52, 54, 87-91, 103, 122, 132-133, 135, 139, 151, 158
Sam, 2-3, 8, 41-43, 45, 68, 81-82, 84, 112-113, 120, 138, 141
Shashi, 8, 48, 50, 52-53, 88-93, 103-104, 122, 135, 138-139, 158

Suha, 8, 50-52, 54-55, 66, 71, 88, 90-91, 99, 103, 122, 133-135, 146, 158
Will, 8, 32, 35, 75-78, 101, 117-118, 136, 158
Yusuf, 2-4, 8, 47, 50, 53, 68, 88-90, 110-113, 122-123, 138
Synagogue, 20-21, 42, 44, 81, 135

Taoism, 134
Theology, 29-30, 34-35, 52-53, 70, 117-118, 135-137, 146
Torah, 44-45, 82-83
Trustworthiness, in research, 9, 161, 167-168

Union for Reform Judaism, 20
Unitarian Universalism, 6, 8, 16, 57, 59-60, 62, 66, 68, 95-96, 104, 112, 114, 129, 134, 138, 152

Vocation/employment, 18, 24, 26, 124, 145

War, 38, 53, 123
Worship services, 22-23, 29, 40, 43, 49, 57, 69, 82-83, 97, 113-114, 139, 148, 154, 156

Zionism, 45, 135, 147

CPSIA information can be obtained
at www.ICGtesting.com
Printed in the USA
FFOW03n1539110515
13222FF